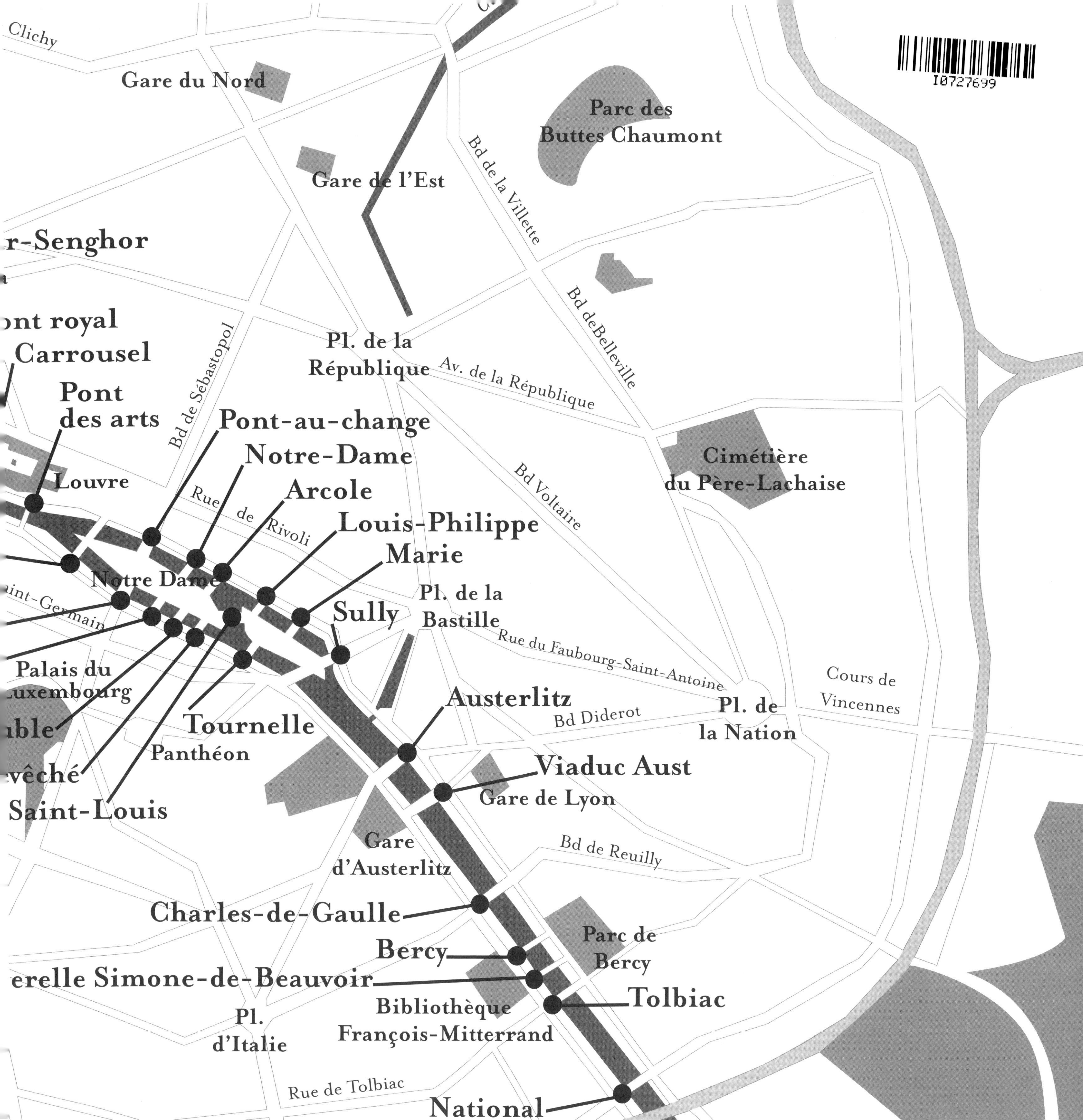

Clichy
Gare du Nord
Parc des Buttes Chaumont
Gare de l'Est
Bd de la Villette
Bd deBelleville
r-Senghor
ont royal
Carrousel
Pont des arts
Bd de Sébastopol
Pl. de la République
Av. de la République
Pont-au-change
Notre-Dame
Louvre
Rue de Rivoli
Arcole
Louis-Philippe
Marie
Bd Voltaire
Cimétière du Père-Lachaise
Notre Dame
aint-Germain
Sully
Pl. de la Bastille
Rue du Faubourg-Saint-Antoine
Palais du uxembourg
Austerlitz
Cours de Vincennes
ble
Tournelle
Pl. de la Nation
Bd Diderot
vêché
Panthéon
Saint-Louis
Viaduc Aust
Gare de Lyon
Gare d'Austerlitz
Bd de Reuilly
Charles-de-Gaulle
Parc de Bercy
Bercy
erelle Simone-de-Beauvoir
Bibliothèque François-Mitterrand
Tolbiac
Pl. d'Italie
Rue de Tolbiac
National

THE GLOW OF PARIS

THE BRIDGES OF PARIS AT NIGHT

GARY ZUERCHER

Published by Marcorp Editions
P.O. Box 53231
Washington, DC 20009

www.marcorp-editions.com

ISBN: 978-0-9906309-0-6

Library of Congress Control Number: 2014913853

For further information about Gary Zuercher's photographs visit www.glz.com.

Printed in Canada.

Table of Contents

FOREWORD

In 1957, the important French publishing house Editions des Deux-Mondes added to its series of books on the treasures of European art and architecture *Paris Bridges Throughout the Centuries* [*Ponts de Paris, A travers les Siècles*]. This fascinating publication documents the history of the thirty-two bridges that at the time spanned the Seine from the Pont National upstream to the Viaduc d'Auteuil downstream.

Written by the novelist/historian Henry-Louis Dubly (1901–1985), with a preface by the writer/poet Francis Carco (1886–1958), the book is profusely illustrated in black and white by three photographers: Marcel Bovis, Gilbert Houel, and René-Jacques. Although Houel (1919–2007) did not make a career in photography but rather was a musician for the National Orchestra of France, Bovis (1904–1997) and René-Jacques (1908–2003) were important twentieth-century photographers who, along with Robert Doisneau and Willy Ronis, in 1946 founded the photographers' collective *Le Group des XV*. Carco describes in his preface how as a young man he left the bohemian life of Montmartre and ventured down to live near the river where "during the great part of my life, I had under my eyes almost all the bridges of Paris." While Carco often wrote of Paris and the Seine, he summed up his affection for the bridges of Paris with this verse taken from the popular 1914 Rodor and Scotto song "Sous les ponts de Paris":

> *Sous les ponts de Paris, lorsque descend la nuit . . . Un couple heureux vient s'aimer en cachette.*
> *Under the bridges of Paris, when the night falls . . . Lovers come for secret romance.*

Gary Zuercher's romance with Paris and its bridges also begins only "when the night falls." There have been numerous photographers over the past 150 years who have used Paris as their subject, but Zuercher's approach of depicting Paris bridges at night is a truly unique aesthetic vision of the city. His manipulation of the camera, playing with shadow and light effects, isolates and elevates these important architectural symbols of Paris far beyond their daily, prosaic function. As with mid-nineteenth-century photography, in which the exposure time is by necessity long, Zuercher's "City of Lights" becomes people-less—still, quiet, frozen in time.

This powerful collection of views of Paris bridges presents bold, dynamic images with sweeping perspectives and dramatic rays of artificial light, creating a vision of Paris at night unobtainable by the naked eye. Sculptural elements normally overlooked, such as those by Dalou found on the Pont Alexandre III, regain their rightful status as major artistic statements of their era.

Often, as seen in the photograph of the Pont Royal, the surfaces of sky and water play important roles. In this view the bridge, the Musée d'Orsay, and the Eiffel Tower are sandwiched between a cloud-ridden sky and an icy river on which the lights of the three structures reverberate, producing opposing textures that elicit turmoil on the one hand and calm on the other.

Some of Zuercher's images also play with history. One example is his depiction of the Pont des Arts. In one photo the diagonal plunge of the stone stairway and its decorative iron balustrade not only point our way to the footbridge in the distance, but also bring to our attention the important historical fact that the Pont des Arts is the first bridge to use iron as its structural framework. In another rendition, as a visual pun, the bridge's *benches* focus our attention on the domed structure that houses the *seats* of academic power: the Institut de France.

During the last quarter of the nineteenth century, a popular photographic view of Paris was *The Seven Bridges*. The photo was taken from atop the tower of the Saint-Gervais Cathedral, located on the right bank just to the east of the Hôtel de Ville. The view is of the great central expanse of the city, encompassing the bridges and the quais from the Pont d'Arcole to the Pont Royal. Also in view are the monuments of the Ile de la Cité, Sainte-Chapelle, the Tribunal de Commerce, and the Palais de Justice. This documentary image was one of many found in stereoscopic photo series and photographic albums of Paris produced for tourist consumption. Zuercher's night photo of a view similar to that of *The Seven Bridges* was taken from the tower of the Hôtel de Ville. It is more expansive than the nineteenth-century views and includes as its apex the glittering Eiffel Tower.

There is an important, nineteenth-century precedent to Zuercher's aesthetic manipulations that is not found in mass-produced nineteenth-century photographs. The historical images of Paris bridges that most resemble the artistic controls of those created by Gary Zuercher may be found in the limited-edition series of fourteen etchings titled. *Eaux-Fortes sur Paris,* created by the enigmatic artist Charles Meryon (1821–1868) between 1850 and 1854. Of the fourteen views, eight depict bridges.

In the second half of the nineteenth century, Paris was undergoing great physical change. The old streets, bridges, and buildings that for so long gave the city its medieval flavor and spirit were being torn down and replaced by new structures in the mode of the Second Empire. It was these gothic vestiges, threatened by demolition, that Meryon in 1850 set out to record. In reality no single views exist such as those depicted in four of Meryon's bridge prints: *Le Petit Point*, *L'Arche du Pont Notre-Dame*, *La Tour de l'Horloge*, and *Le Pont Neuf*. Each of these etchings consists of composite views in which Meryon brought together two separate and distinct views in order to create one.

Meryon's depictions of Paris are personal statements of the city he loved for its past and hated for its changes. Zuercher's bridge photographs are unique visions of a Paris that at night has a luminous life of its own. Though separated in time by more than 160 years, the printmaker and the photographer are both masters of architectural interpretation, with Paris as their chosen subject.

Phillip Dennis Cate
Curator, Special Exhibits, Musée Montmartre, Paris
Director Emeritus, Jane Voorhees Zimmerle Museum, Rutgers University, New Brunswick, NJ 

INTRODUCTION

My love for Paris began in Mexico, in the Cancun airport terminal, where I met a beautiful young French girl named Dominique. We sat together on the plane to Mexico City; I went on to business meetings in Guadalajara. That evening, after my return to Mexico City, we met for drinks. A month later we met for dinner in Paris, at the Plaza Athenée, and from there our time together blossomed. Dominique became my wife and the reason I have spent a portion of my life in Paris.

My love of photography began when I was a youth, in the makeshift darkroom I built in my parents' basement. It was there that I experienced the thrill of seeing my first black-and-white photograph emerge from its chemical bath. I was immediately captivated by the magic of photography. Over the years I have provided commercial photography for numerous advertising agencies and companies, produced more than a dozen product promotional films for industry, and at the same time built a number of successful businesses.

At the turn of the century, Dominique and I began to spend more time in Paris. I set up a darkroom in what had previously been a maid's room on the top floor of a nineteenth-century Haussmannien building. Thankfully, it had an elevator.

One night, while photographing in the city, I greatly overexposed a shot by mistake. As happens many times, a mistake can be the precursor to something positive. Such was the case with this mistake. The negative from that shot produced a breathtaking photograph. It was a photograph of the Pont Alexandre III, one of the most beautiful bridges in Paris, if not the world. That photograph inspired me to photograph all thirty-five bridges at night. The bridges are certainly alluring during the daytime, but at night they become majestic. They transform, with a luminescence that cannot be seen in the light of day. They glow.

I thought this would be a one-year project. In fact, it took more than five years to complete. And in reality it may never end because there is always another inspiring view to be found and photographed.

Some say there are thirty-seven bridges that cross the Seine in Paris. In this project I have included only the thirty-five bridges within the city: those inside the Périphérique (the beltway). The upstream and downstream bridges of the Périphérique are modern and utilitarian; they are imposing structures but they do not have the same panache as the bridges within the city. They lack the history and spirit and I therefore elected not to include them.

Soon after beginning the project, a question occurred to me: Had someone previously done the same thing? If they had, perhaps I could learn something from studying their results. With the help of a researcher, I found that numerous photographs of the individual bridges existed, and also some groupings of all the bridges, photographed in daylight. But after months of searching, I was unable to find evidence that anyone had previously photographed all thirty-five of the bridges at night, on film, and in black and white. Surprisingly, it seemed that no one had ever put together a collection like the one I was working on.

Parallel with the photography work was the research on the unique history of each of the bridges. This was an undertaking that uncovered many happy, sad, interesting, and funny moments.

Almost all the photography was shot during the winter months, primarily because Paris isn't fully dark in the summer until around 11 PM, and the lights on the bridges are turned off at midnight. In the winter dark arrives early, at 5 PM.

After an evening dinner and one glass of French wine, it can be difficult to leave the warm environment to go into the nighttime cold to take photographs. But that reluctance lasts only a short time. Once underway, the warmth and comfort of home is quickly forgotten. Winter is an enchanting time to be alone along the Seine. It is a time of serenity and emotion. It has been a moving experience to spend cold winter nights communicating with the river and the bridges.

The objective of the project has been twofold: First, to record a sampling of the more than two thousand years of history, anecdotes, and facts about the bridges; and second, to present the majesty of the Paris bridges in their most alluring setting—nighttime—when few tourists or even Parisians see them.

EPIGRAPH

"*Ils sont le prolongement des rues, le trait d'union entre les deux rives. On les traverse à pied, en voiture, en métro. On les voit sans les regarder et c'est dommage...*"

They are the extension of the streets, the hyphen between the two river banks. We cross them on foot, by car, by Metro. We see them without looking at them and that's a shame...

Author, Monique Marty, *Mini Saga des Ponts de Paris*
Publisher, Port Autonome de Paris, 1979

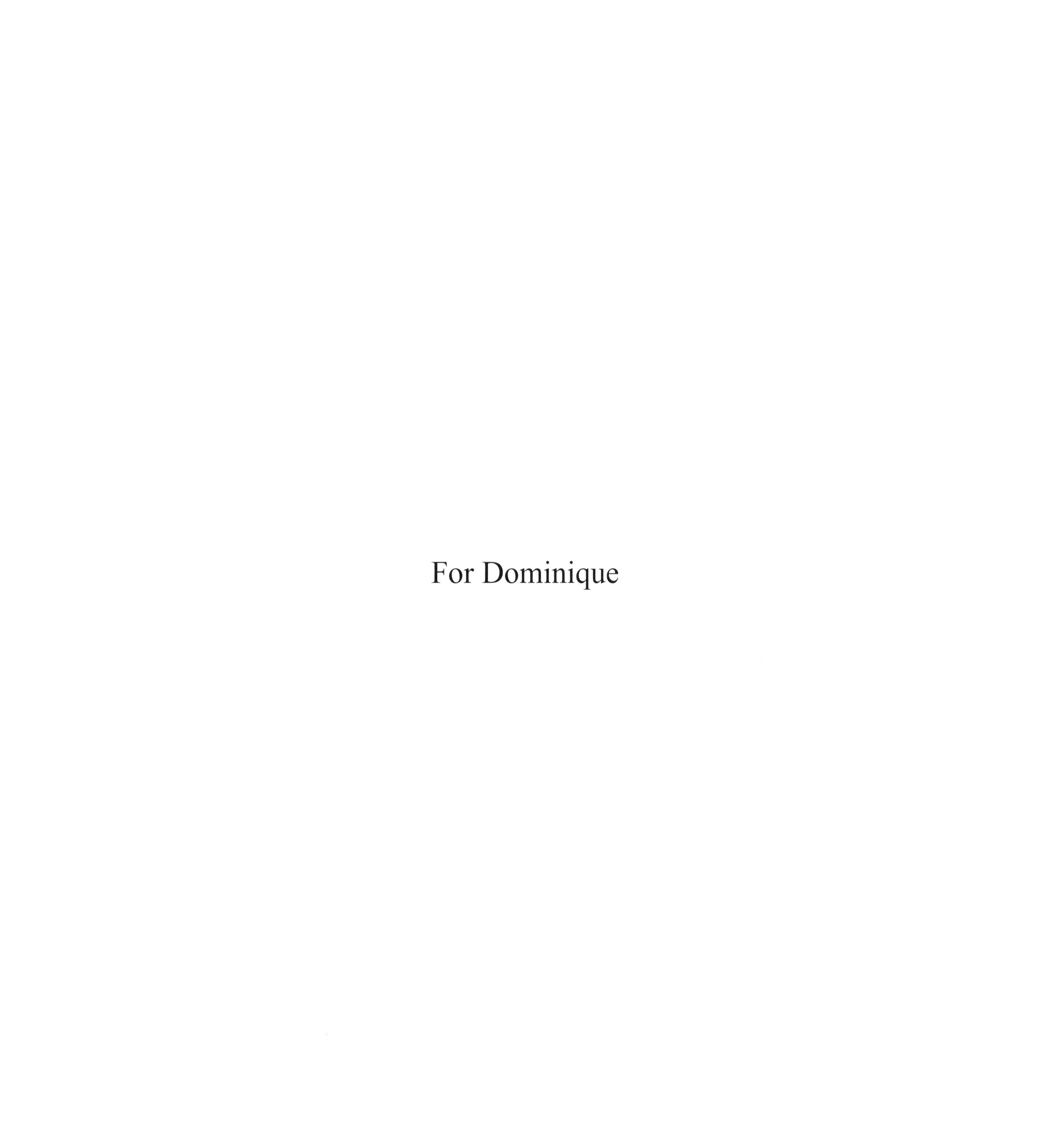

For Dominique

PROLOGUE

Murder, assault, robbery, revolution, and riot; prostitution, love, marriage, and funeral marches; all have taken place on the bridges that cross the Seine in Paris.

The history of these bridges begins before the birth of Christ. In 52 BC Julius Caesar conquered Paris; the earliest recorded mention of the bridges is found in *De Bello Gallico*, Caesar's Gallic War commentaries. Most of the later history evolves from around the time of the Middle Ages and thereafter.

In the early days of the city, the population of Paris was concentrated on the Île de la Cité, the surrounding river serving as a natural barrier against invasion by land. Consequently, the earliest Paris bridges were built to connect the island to the left and right banks of the Seine. Before the existence of any bridges, river crossings were made by ferry. Today, eight bridges link the Île de la Cité to the riverbanks and one connects to the Île Saint-Louis.

One of the eight, the Pont Neuf is the oldest standing bridge, opened by King Henri IV in 1607. It connects the tip of the Île de la Cité to both the left bank and the right bank of the Seine. The original bridge has undergone numerous works of preservation and maintenance but the design of the bridge remains as it was when first built.

The oldest bridge site, however, is where the Pont Notre-Dame now stands. Numerous bridges have existed at this site since antiquity. Time after time those bridges were destroyed and subsequently rebuilt.

The newest bridge is the Passerelle Simone de Beauvoir, which opened in 2006. For use by pedestrians and bicycles only, the footbridge is the only Paris bridge to be named in honor of a woman.

These thirty-five bridges have functioned as the arteries of Paris for millennia. 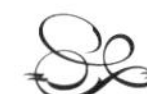

CHRONOLOGICAL SEQUENCE OF CONSTRUCTION

This list represents the dates that the bridge in use today was constructed or opened for use. Many of these bridges were preceded by bridges in the same locations—and many times with the same names—which were subsequently destroyed, or replaced by the present bridge. Some of the earliest bridges date back to antiquity.

#	Bridge	Date
1	Pont Neuf	1607
2	Pont Marie	1635
3	Pont Royal	1689
4	Pont de la Concorde	1791
5	Pont d'Iéna	1814
6	Pont de l'Archevêché	1828
7	Pont National	1853
8	Petit Pont	1853
9	Pont d'Arcole	1854
10	Pont d'Austerlitz	1854
11	Pont des Invalides	1856
12	Pont Saint-Michel	1857
13	Pont au Change	1860
14	Pont Louis-Philippe	1862
15	Pont de Bercy	1864
16	Pont Sully	1876
17	Pont de Tolbiac	1882
18	Pont au Double	1883
19	Pont Mirabeau	1893

#	Bridge	Date
20	Passerelle Debilly	1900
21	Pont Alexandre III	1900
22	Viaduc d'Austerlitz	1904
23	Pont de Bir-Hakeim	1904
24	Pont Notre-Dame	1914
25	Pont de la Tournelle	1928
26	Pont du Caroussel	1939
27	Pont de Grenelle	1968
28	Pont du Garigliano	1966
29	Pont Saint-Louis	1970
30	Pont de l'Alma	1976
31	Pont des Arts	1984
32	Pont Rouelle	1988
33	Pont Charles de Gaulle	1996
34	Passerelle Léopold-Sédar-Senghor	2000
35	Passerelle Simone de Beauvoir	2006

Sources:
1. Laboratoire Central des Ponts et Chaussées
2. Port Autonome de Paris

Toward the end of World War II the Paris bridges nearly met with catastrophe. As the Allied forces continued to advance following the Normandy landings, it became evident the Nazis would be driven from Paris. Hitler had ordered Paris defended to the last man, and demanded that the city not fall into Allied hands except as "a field of ruins." He ordered his military commander in Paris, General Dietrich von Choltitz, to plant explosives at Paris's great monuments, train stations, and bridges. On August 25, 1944, with the Allies approaching, Hitler gave the order to destroy the city. General von Choltitz refused to obey. It is said he refused because he did not want to go down in history as the man who destroyed Europe's most celebrated city.

Bridges constructed prior to the late eighteenth century normally had houses and shops built directly on them. The thinking of the time was that the weight of the buildings provided more stability; this was later proved erroneous. Floods, ice floes, fires, boat collisions, and structural failures frequently destroyed the bridges. The collapsing bridges took the houses and shops down with them, and often their occupants as well. In 1769 Louis XV finally outlawed the construction of houses on the bridges, but it took until 1808 for the last building to be removed.

For many centuries bridges were built of wood. Successive bridges were built of stone, and then came bridges constructed from metal—first in cast iron, fastened together with bolts and rivets, and later from wrought iron. The first metal bridge, the Pont des Arts, was built in 1803. Later bridges were built of concrete, followed by reinforced concrete; others were built using steel in place of iron. Most of the bridges built in the twentieth century and thereafter have been steel, reinforced concrete, or a combination of the two materials.

Today, thirty-five bridges cross the Seine between the upstream and downstream boundaries of the Boulevard Périphérique, the four-lane expressway that encircles Paris. Twenty-six bridges accommodate pedestrian and automotive traffic; four are *passerelle*s (footbridges) restricted to pedestrian and bicycle traffic; two are dedicated to rail traffic only; and three accommodate all three modes of transportation: automotive, pedestrian, and rail traffic.

The river winds 14 kilometers (8.5 miles) from the first bridge upstream, the Pont National, to the last bridge downstream, the Pont du Garigliano.

35 Bridges Cross the Seine

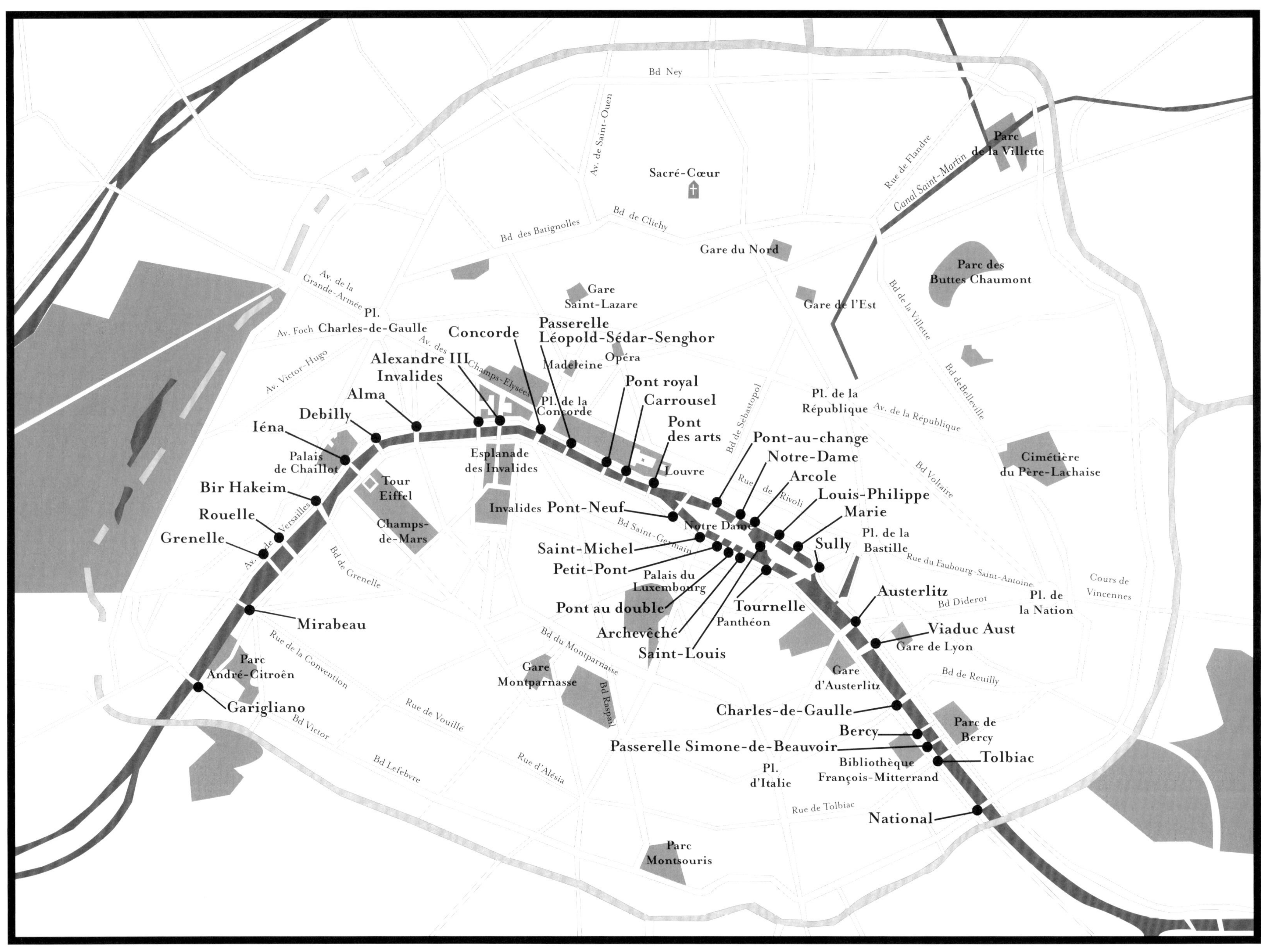

As you walk around Paris today, it is easy to fail to notice the bridges. But to do so is to miss much of the beauty of Paris. In the following pages we will take a look at them, traveling downstream from the Pont National. The bridges have been divided into four groups. In the first group are the upstream bridges; in the second are the bridges on the two islands, Île de la Cité and Île Saint-Louis; in the third group are the bridges from Pont des Arts, at the Louvre, to Pont des Invalides; and in the fourth group are the downstream bridges. The groups appear as shown in the following chart:

Bridges Upstream	
1	Pont National
2	Pont de Tolbiac
3	Passerelle Simone de Beauvoir
4	Pont de Bercy
5	Pont Charles de Gaulle
6	Viaduc d'Austerlitz
7	Pont d'Austerlitz

Louvre - Invalides	
21	Pont des Arts
22	Pont du Carrousel
23	Pont Royal
24	Passerelle Léopold-Sédar-Senghor
25	Pont de la Concorde
26	Pont Alexandre III
27	Pont des Invalides

Island Bridges	
8	Pont Sully
9	Pont de la Tournelle
10	Pont Marie
11	Pont Louis-Philippe
12	Pont Saint-Louis
13	Pont de l'Archevêché
14	Pont au Double
15	Pont d'Arcole
16	Petit Pont
17	Pont Notre-Dame
18	Pont Saint-Michel
19	Pont au Change
20	Pont Neuf

Downstream Bridges	
28	Pont de l'Alma
29	Passerelle Debilly
30	Pont d'Iéna
31	Pont de Bir-Hakeim
32	Pont Rouelle
33	Pont de Grenelle
34	Pont Mirabeau
35	Pont du Garigliano

Let's begin our tour. . .

The Seven Upstream Bridges

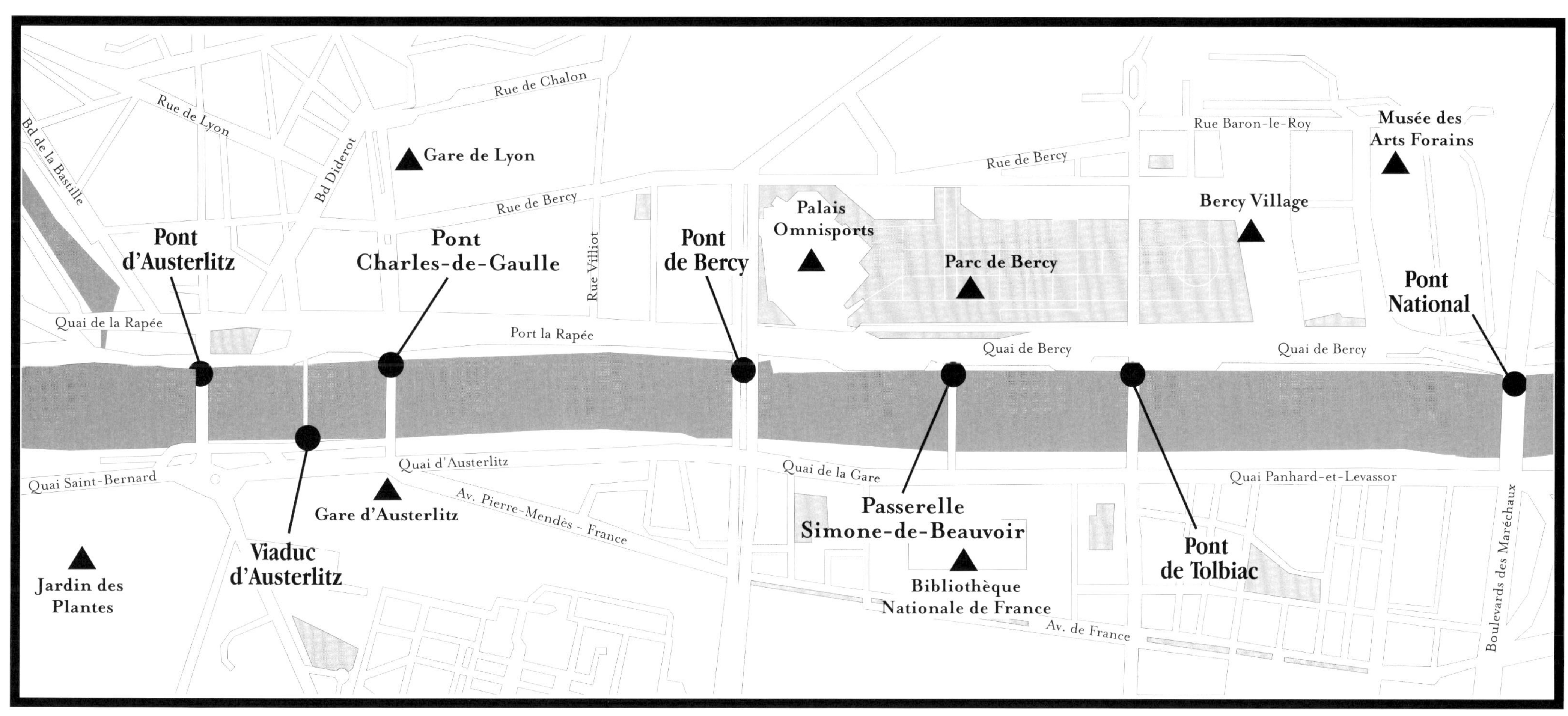

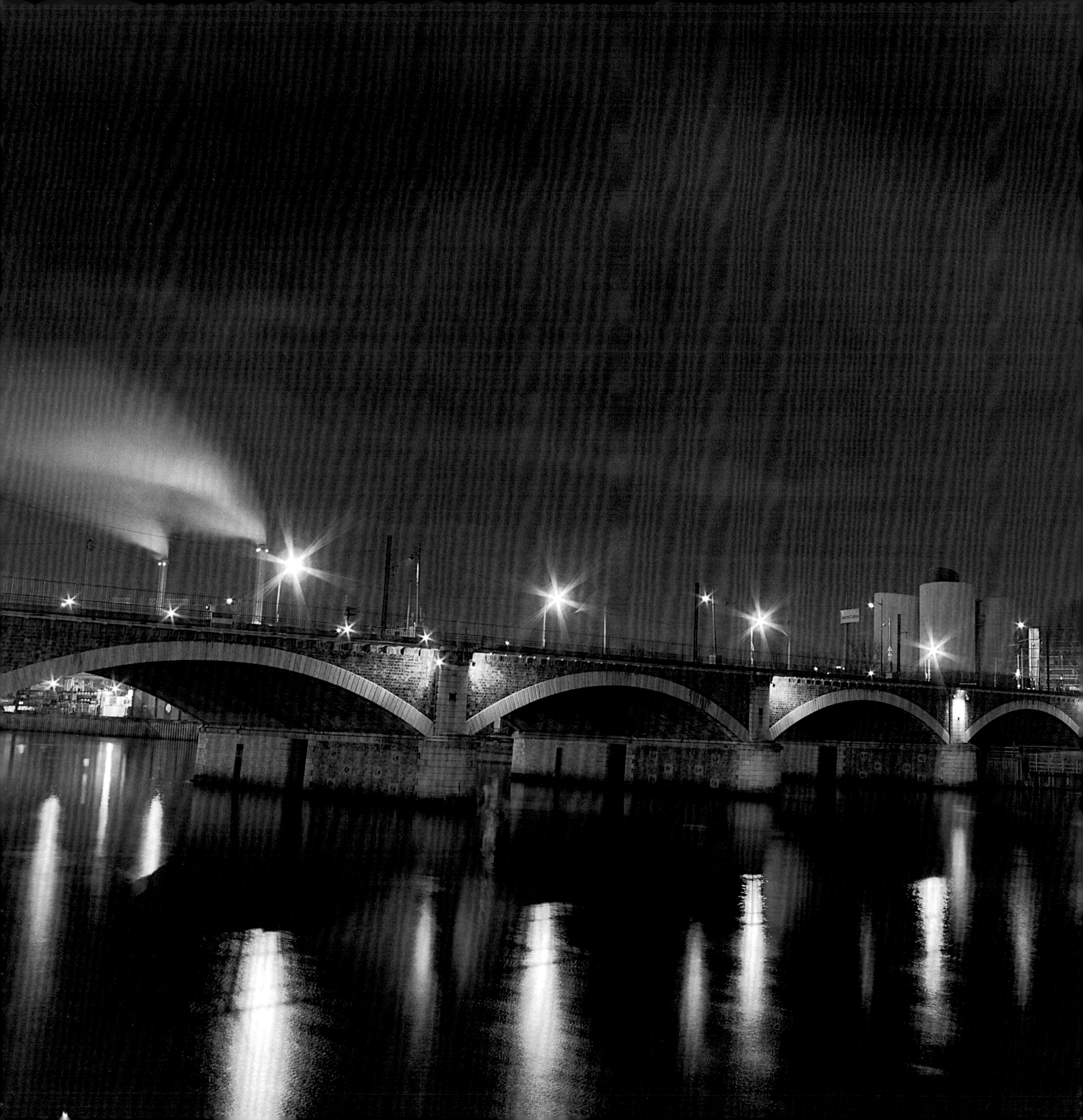

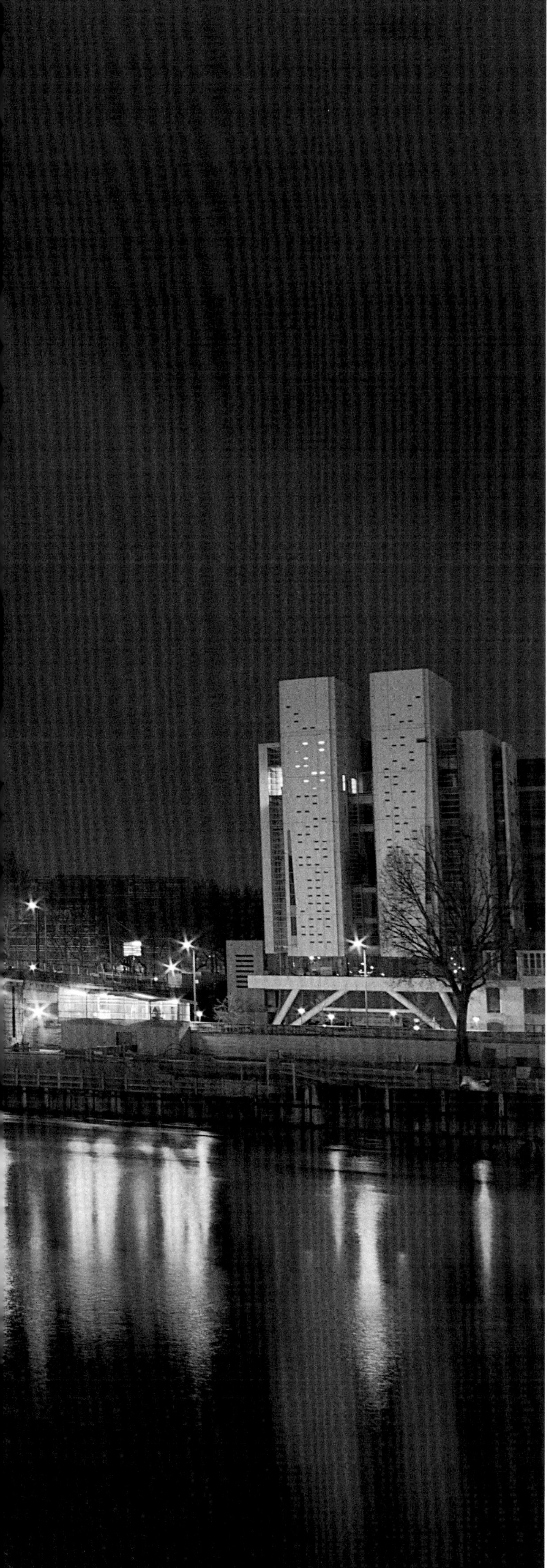

PONT NATIONAL

Traveling downstream, the Pont National is the first bridge in the chain of thirty-five that cross the Seine in the city of Paris.

Both sides of the river are heavily industrialized, with cement plants, warehouses, factories, and a large sewage treatment plant with two gigantic smokestacks belching clouds of thick smoke twenty-four hours a day. The landscape is undergoing a process of renewal and rebuilding that will eventually change its face.

Construction of the Pont National (originally named the Pont Napoleon III) started in 1852 and was completed in 1853. It was the first bridge built under the Second French Empire, when Napoleon III reigned as emperor from 1852 to 1870. During that time, Paris experienced one of the most active construction and renewal periods in the city's history, including the building of five new bridges over the Seine.

In 1870, following the defeat of France at the Battle of Sedan in the Prussian war, where Napoleon III and his entire army were captured, the bridge was renamed the Pont National.

Pont National:
View from the right bank with École
Nationale Supérieure-School of Architecture
on the left bank.

The bridge was built to link the city's military fortifications on each side of the river, and to create a crossing point for the *Petite Ceinture*, a rail line that circled the perimeter of the city. Reduced usage and the expansion of the Paris Metro system meant the rail line stopped carrying passengers in July 1934. At the time of writing, the abandoned rails at the Pont National can still be seen.

In 1936, the size of the bridge was doubled to accommodate the crossing of the *Boulevards Maréchaux*, a collection of linked boulevards encircling the city that are still in use today. The expansion was achieved by adding a second, identical structure onto the upstream side of the existing bridge. Although the work began in 1936, World War II delayed its completion until 1944.

The most recent change to the Pont National, inaugurated in December 2012, was the expansion of the T3 tramway. The Pont National is the only Paris bridge to carry the T3, a modern tramway system designed to follow the circular route of the Boulevards Maréchaux and to accommodate three hundred thousand passengers daily. To support the T3 and to avoid the need for another support leg in the Seine, a cantilevered design attached to the existing bridge was chosen. Using three 300-ton cranes, the construction of the expansion was accomplished in just one week, with all the work being done at night to avoid interruption of the river traffic.

With the T3 and new bicycle lanes, the Pont National has a fresh new face. 

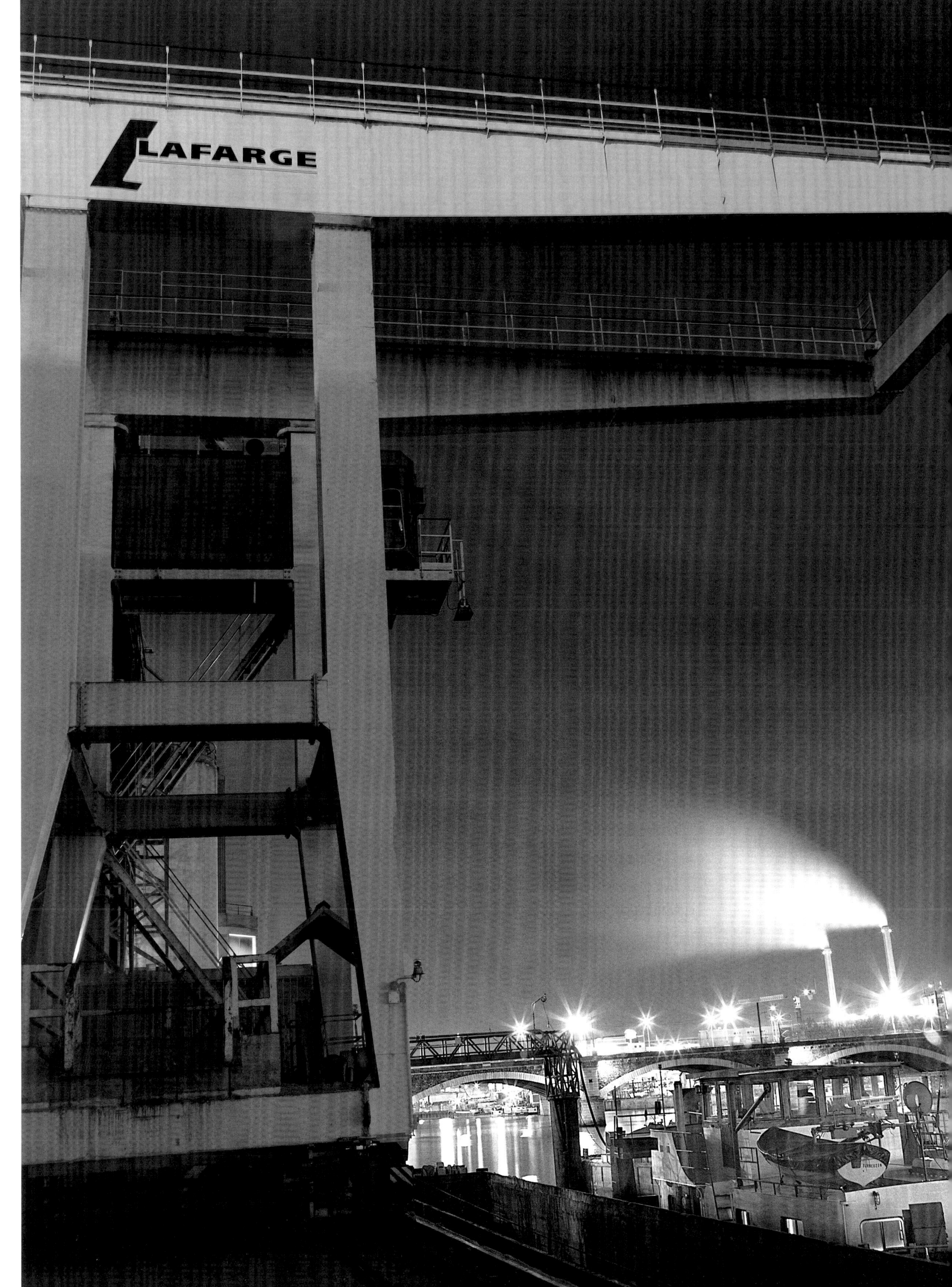

Pont National:
Right bank-industrial area.

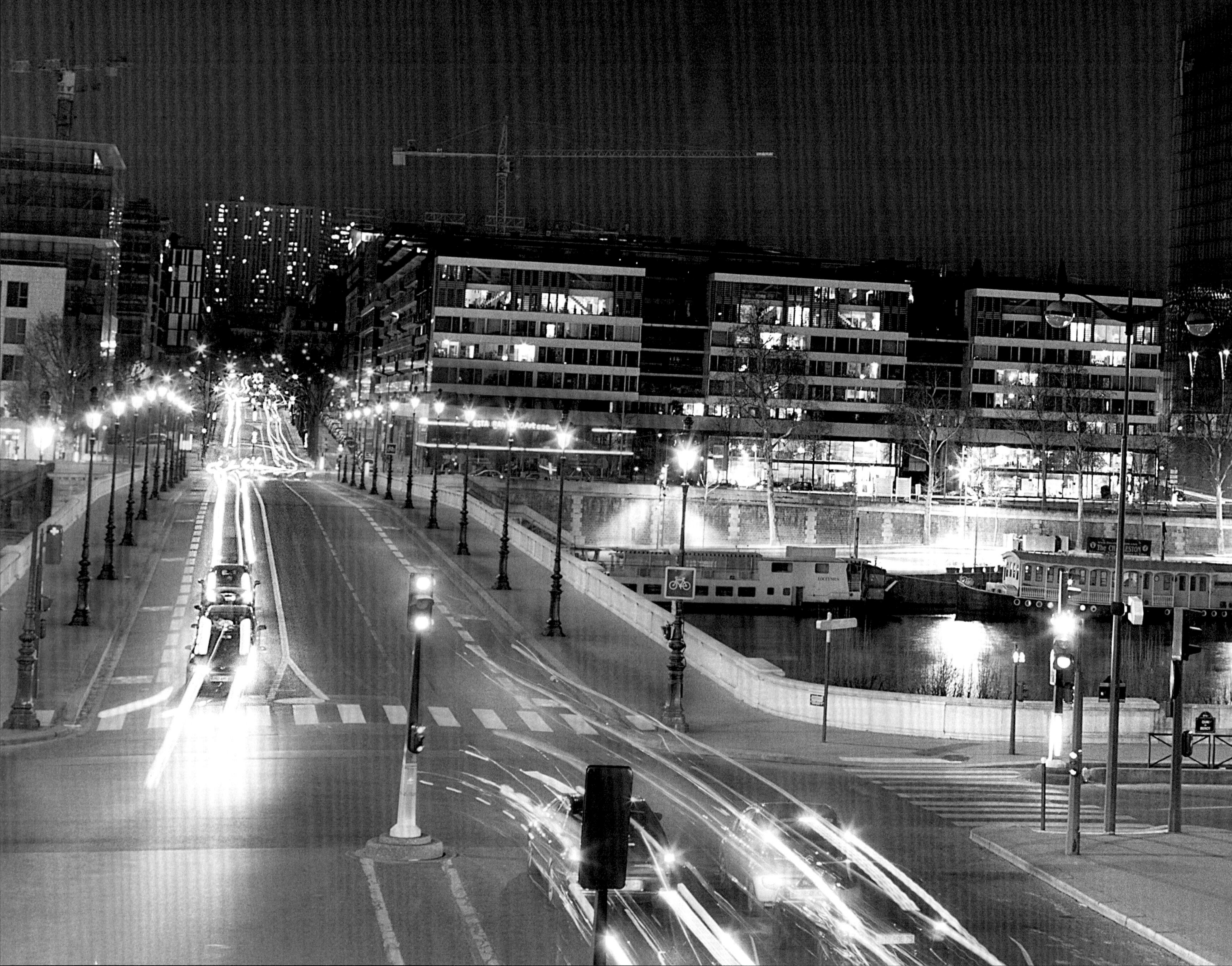

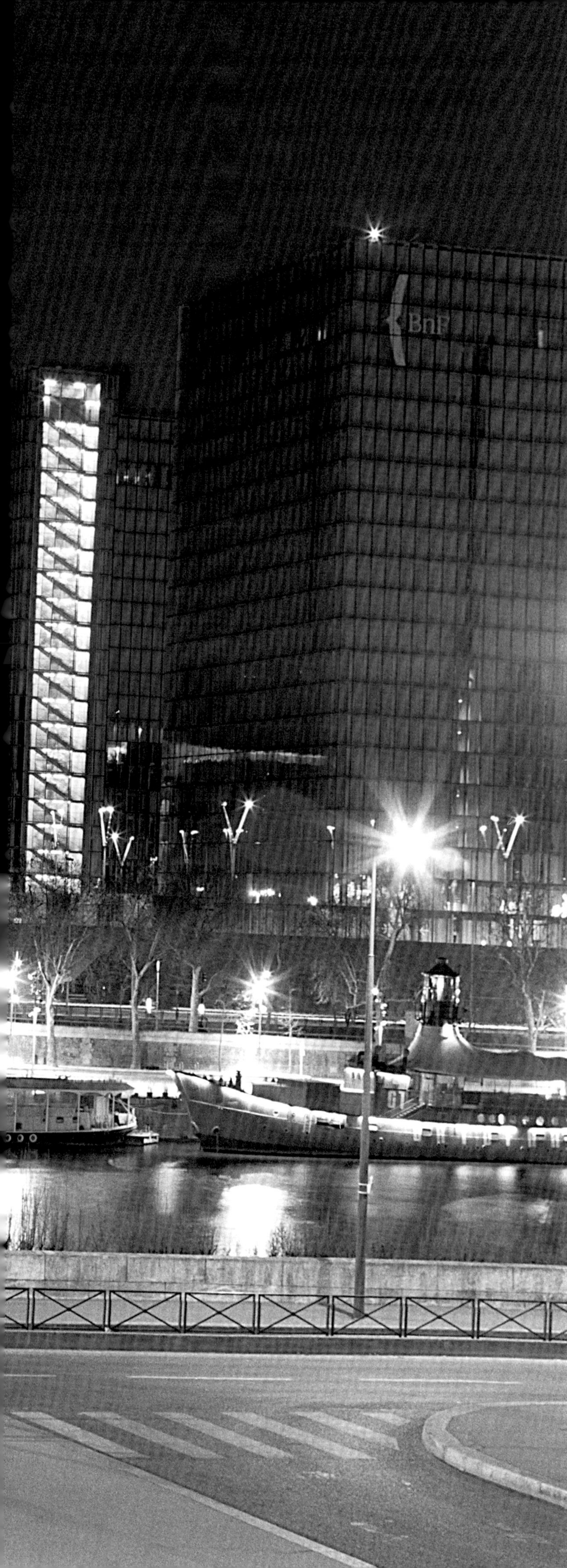

PONT DE TOLBIAC

Traveling downstream from the Pont National, the Pont de Tolbiac is the next bridge that crosses the Seine.

The name was taken from the battle of Tolbiac (496 AD) between the Franks and the Alamanni (an early Germanic tribe), which took place in what is now the German–Belgian frontier. The Franks won a decisive victory, ending Alamanni dominance in the region. The adjacent rue de Tolbiac existed before the bridge was built and the bridge took its name from that street.

A competition for the contract to design and build the bridge was held in 1874. The competition—which took place ten years before the idea of the Eiffel Tower was conceived—was between the firms of Gustave Eiffel and Bernard & Perouse Engineers. The Eiffel firm proposed an iron bridge design, considered quite radical for the time, but lost the bid to Bernard & Perouse, who designed and built the Pont de Tolbiac between 1879 and 1882.

The Pont de Tolbiac was the last Paris bridge built using stone masonry as the basis of its construction; later bridges would be of reinforced concrete, iron and steel, or a combination.

Pont de Tolbiac:
View from Parc de Bercy
on the right bank.

When the new bridge was proposed, the area on the right bank known as Bercy was a burgeoning development, then specializing in the transport and trading of wine. The objective was to connect Bercy on the right bank to the left bank and the southern part of the city.

Today the Pont de Tolbiac connects the Parc de Bercy and the Cour Saint-Émilion on the right bank to the Bibliothèque Nationale de France (the National Library of France) on the left bank. The area upstream from the Pont de Tolbiac is still heavily industrialized, with concrete mixing plants on both sides of the river and barges continuously delivering sand and gravel to those factories.

On the morning of October 3, 1943, an aircraft hit the bridge and crashed into the Seine, killing the four Frenchmen on board. The four were members of the Free French Air Force. They had flown from an airfield in England to participate in the allied bombing of a power station outside of Paris. They were flying a Douglas-Boston class aircraft and were part of the Bombardment Group "Lorraine" assigned to the British Royal Air Force. Prior to the mission, the pilots were instructed that if they had to ditch over Paris, to do so in the Seine to avoid civilian casualties. Returning from the successful mission, they encountered heavy flak from the Germans. The aircraft, piloted by twenty-seven-year-old French lieutenant Yves Lamy, was hit, and the right engine caught fire. Unable to stay aloft, he headed towards the Seine. The plane first hit the Pont de Tolbiac, then crashed into the river, killing all four: Lieutenant Lamy, Adjutant Balcaen, Sargent Roussarie, and Sargent Jouniaux.

A plaque, mounted at the center of the bridge, is a memorial to the four Frenchmen who gave their lives fighting for France.

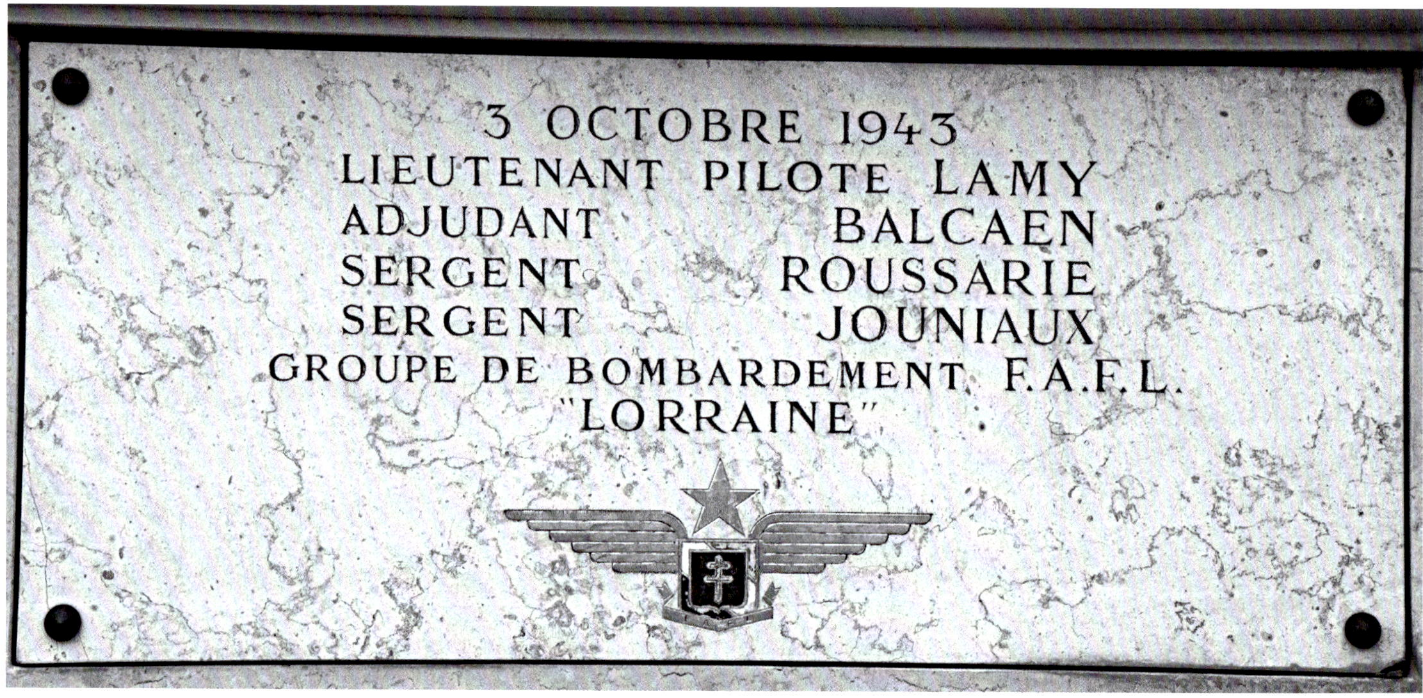

The memorial plaque mounted in the center of the Pont de Tolbiac. 

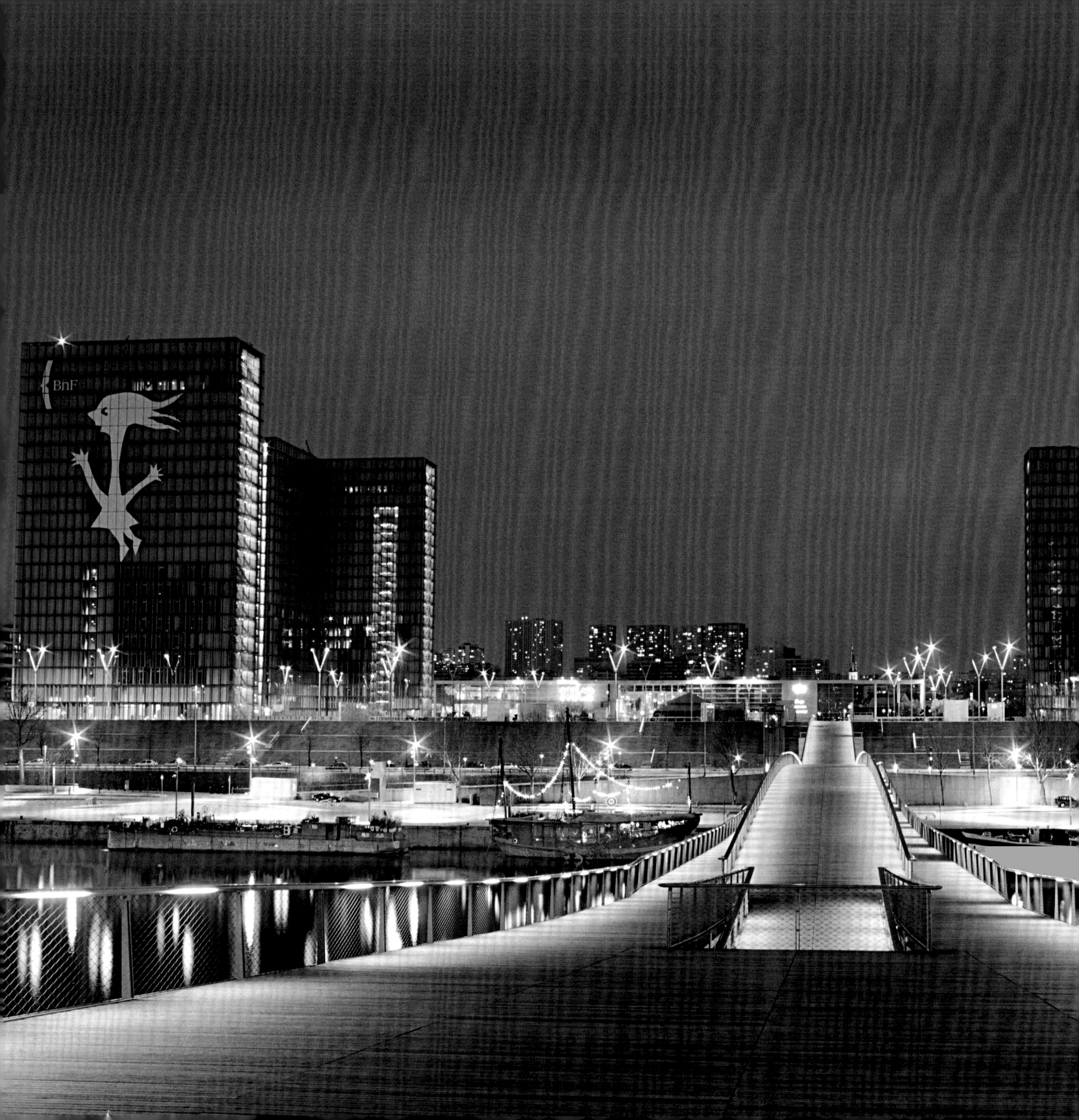

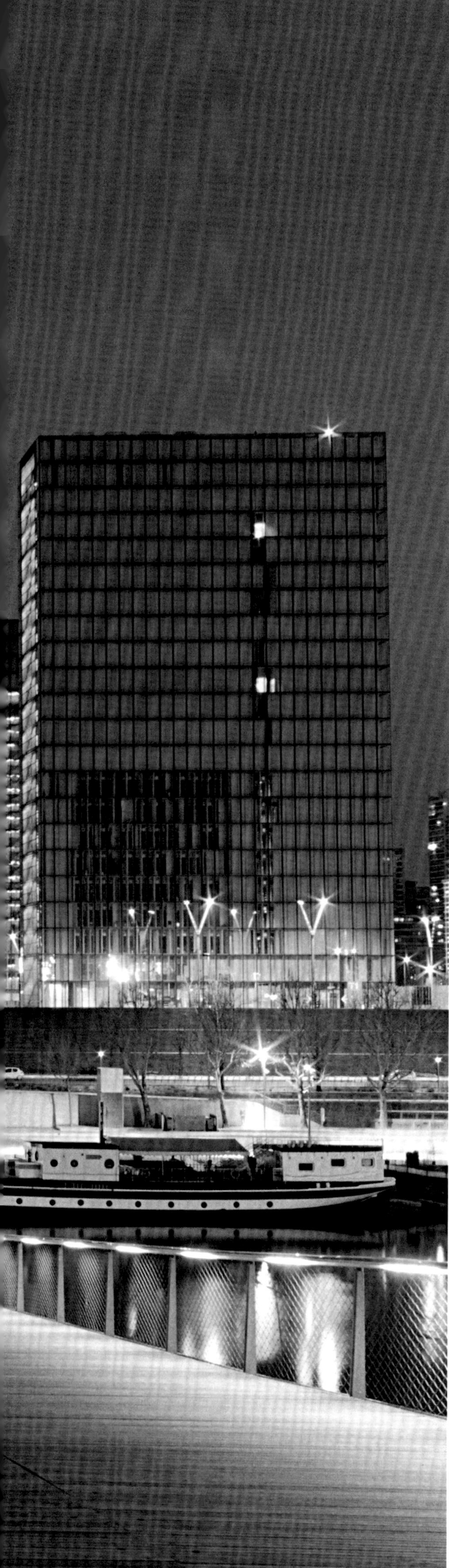

Passerelle Simone de Beauvoir

Opened to the public on July 13, 2006, the Passerelle Simone de Beauvoir is the newest bridge crossing the Seine. Named after the renowned feminist writer Simone de Beauvoir (1908–1986), it is the only Paris bridge named for a woman.

The Passerelle Beauvoir is one of only four passerelles (pedestrian bridges) in the sequence of the thirty-five Paris bridges; at 304 meters (997 feet) it is the longest of the four. Its flowing design and ability to interconnect to different levels on each side of the river give the Passerelle Beauvoir a unique identity.

Because of the distance between the Pont de Tolbiac upstream and the Pont de Bercy downstream, the need for another bridge had been obvious for some time. It became even more evident following the construction in 1998 of the new Bibliothèque Nationale de France on the left bank. Nevertheless,

Passerelle Simone de Beauvoir:
View of the four towers of the Bibliothèque
Nationale de France from the right bank.

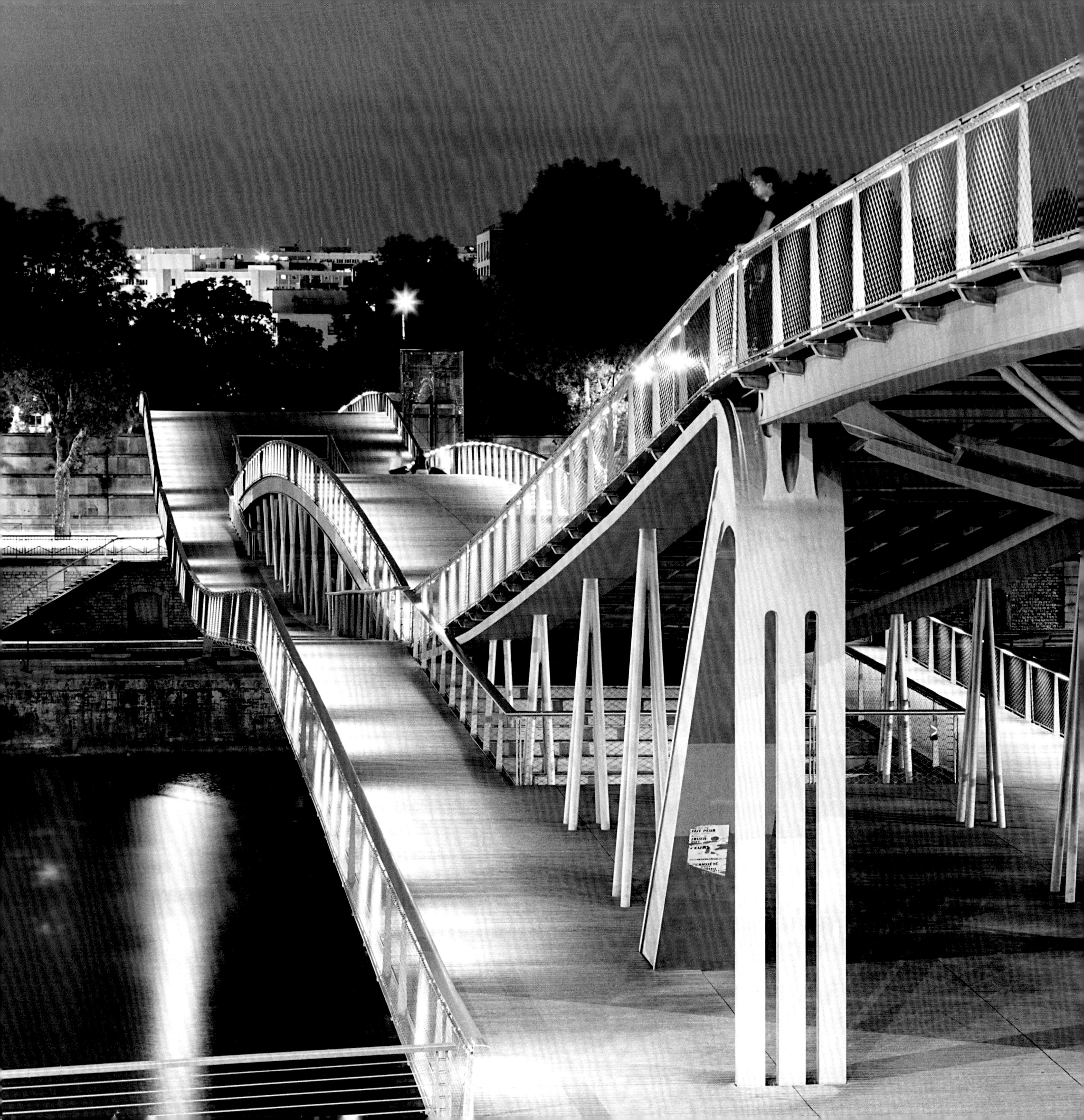

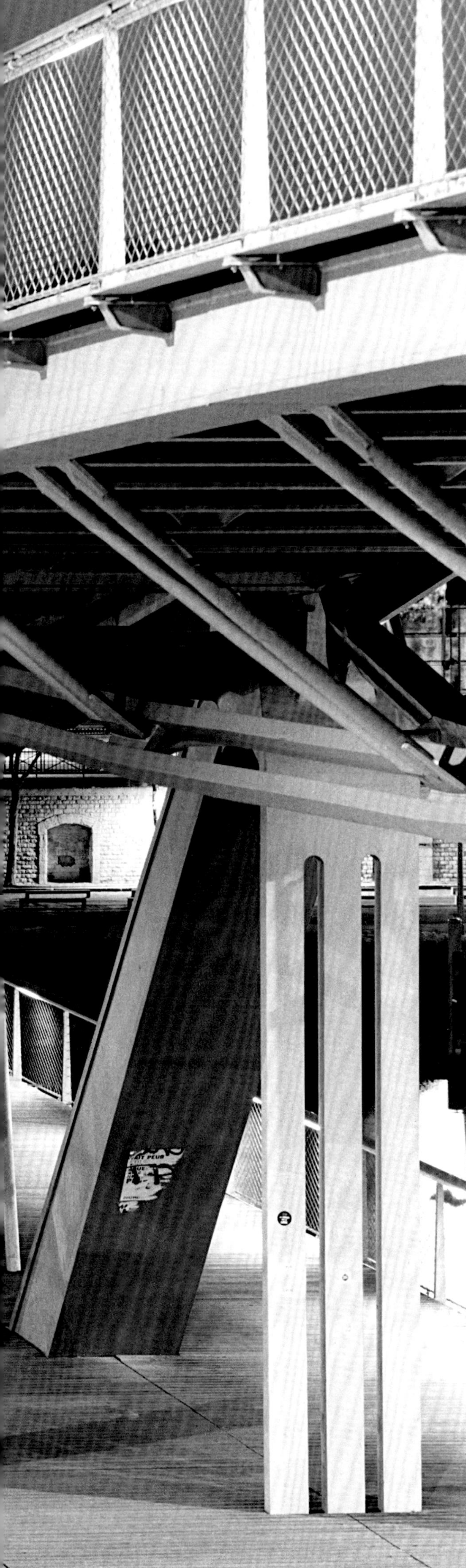

it took ten years from the time the project was launched in 1996 until it was finally opened in 2006. The final cost was €21 million, substantially more than the projected cost of €15 million.

An international competition to select a designer was held, with eighty firms responding. After narrowing the choice to eight firms, the committee finally chose a thirty-seven-year-old Austrian architect named Dietmar Feichtinger. Some years earlier he had competed for the design of another Paris bridge, the Passerelle Solferino (later renamed Passerelle Léopold-Sédar-Senghor), but had lost out.

His design of the central span consists of one convex arc interlacing with one concave arc. They form a graceful lenticular structure in the center of the two arcs. On each side of the main walkway of the central span are two parallel walkways that intersect, creating crossover points for pedestrians. Unlike most of the other Paris bridges, the passerelle has no support structure in the river. Viewing it from one bank to the other, it resembles a roller coaster.

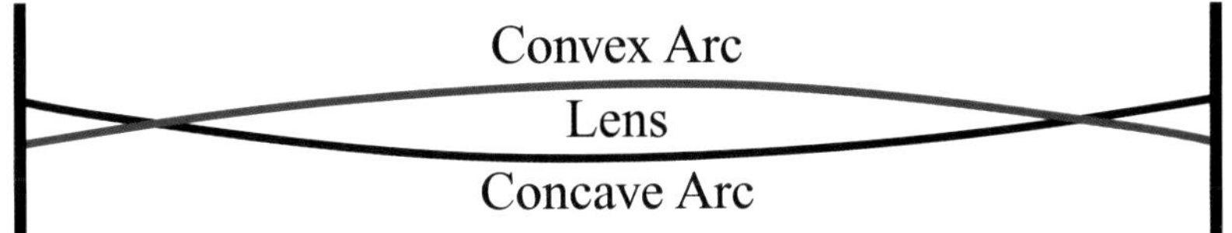

The steel for the bridge was produced in the Dillinger Hutte factory in Germany, and Eiffel Constructions Métalliques performed the fabrication in its factory in Lauterbourg, France. Two barges transported the pre-welded central span, as a single unit, from Lauterbourg to the site. They followed the Rhine River north, through Germany and eventually into the North Sea, then south through the English Channel to Le Havre, and finally up the Seine to Paris. The on-site installation of the center span was accomplished in a single night.

The passerelle connects to three levels on each side. On the right bank it connects to the riverside level, then to the street level, and topside to the Parc de Bercy. Similarly, on the left bank it connects to the riverside level and to the street level, and then topside to the esplanade of the Bibliothèque Nationale de France.

The 4,000-square-meter deck surface is nonslip wood planking. The unique night lighting consists of horizontal bulbs integrated into the handrails. When lit, the bands of light trace the unmistakable silhouette of the bridge in muted sepia tones.

Unlike the more industrial shoreline of the preceding upstream bridges, the left bank of the passerelle features the Josephine Baker floating swimming pool in the river, along with a number of permanently moored boats housing discotheques and clubs.

Passerelle Simone de Beauvoir:
View from Bibliothèque Nationale de France
toward parc de Bercy on the right bank.

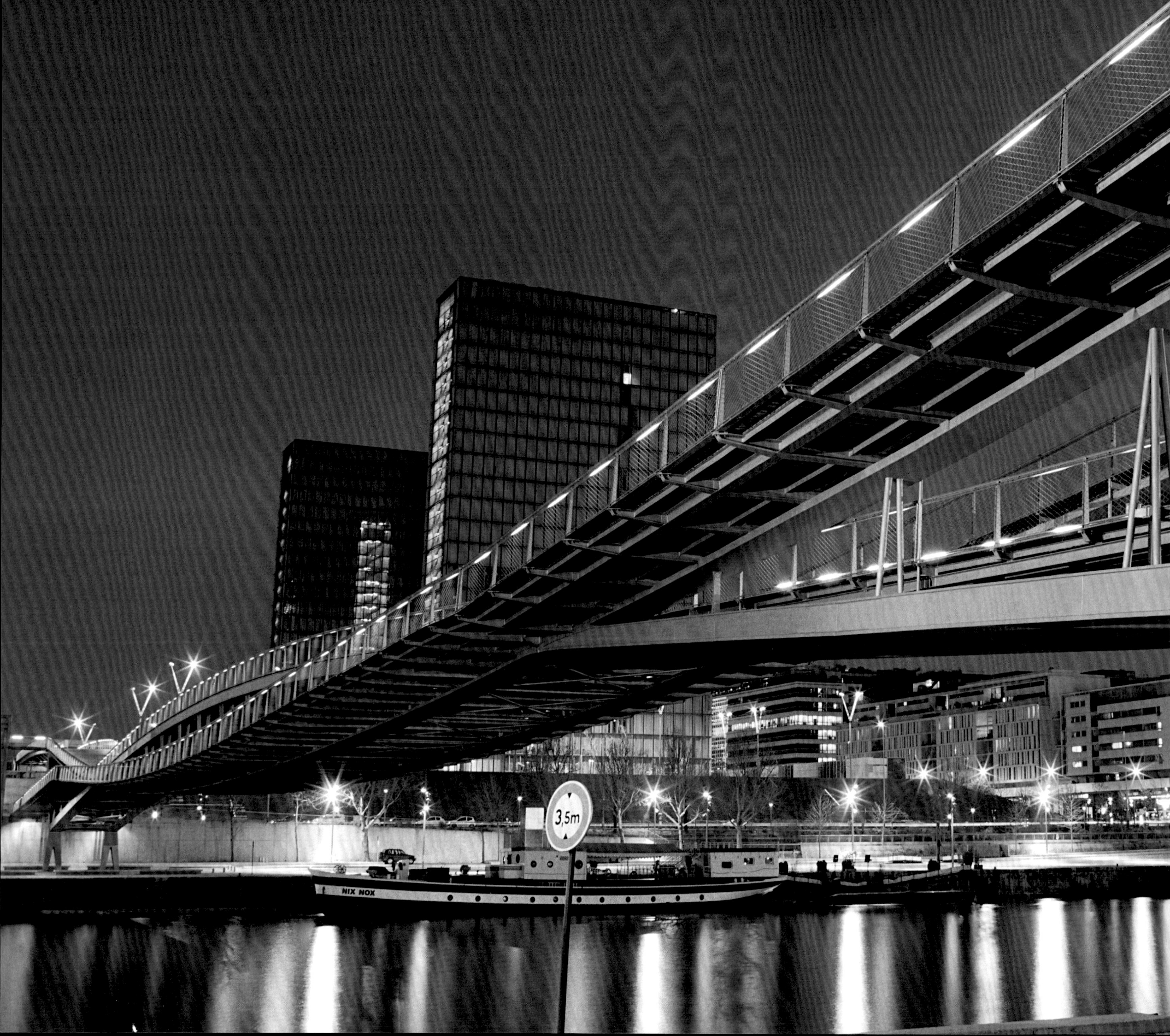
NIX NOX
3,5m

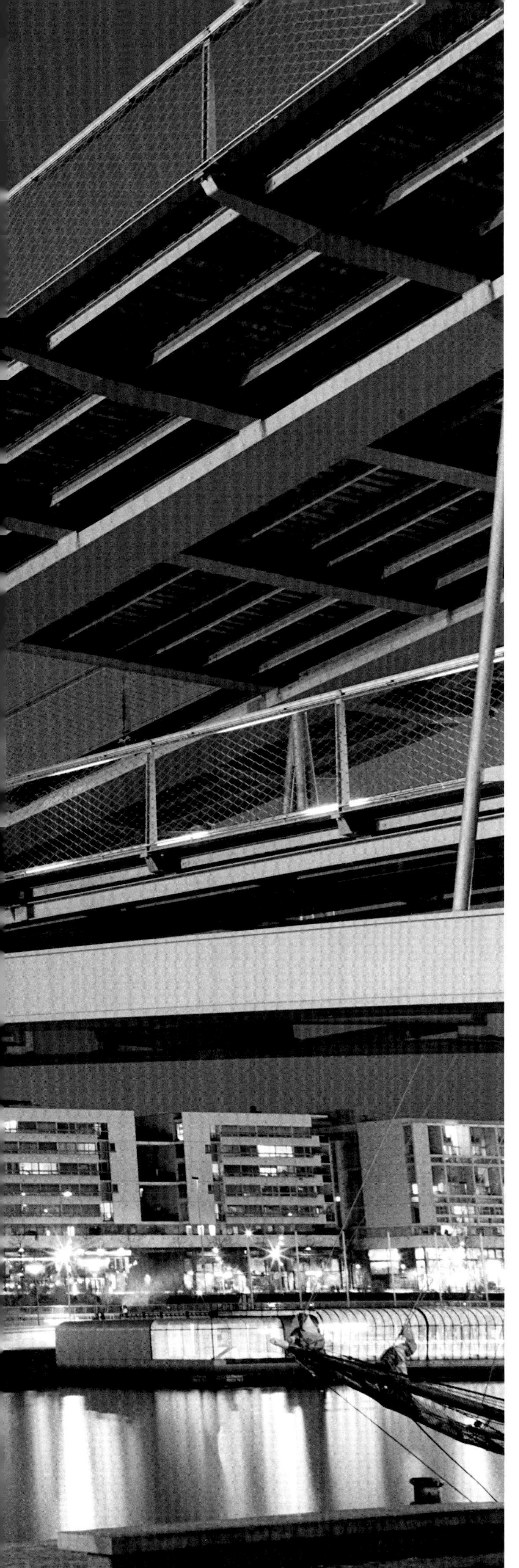

Passerelle Simone de Beauvoir:
The passerelle spanning the Seine with
no intermediate supports.

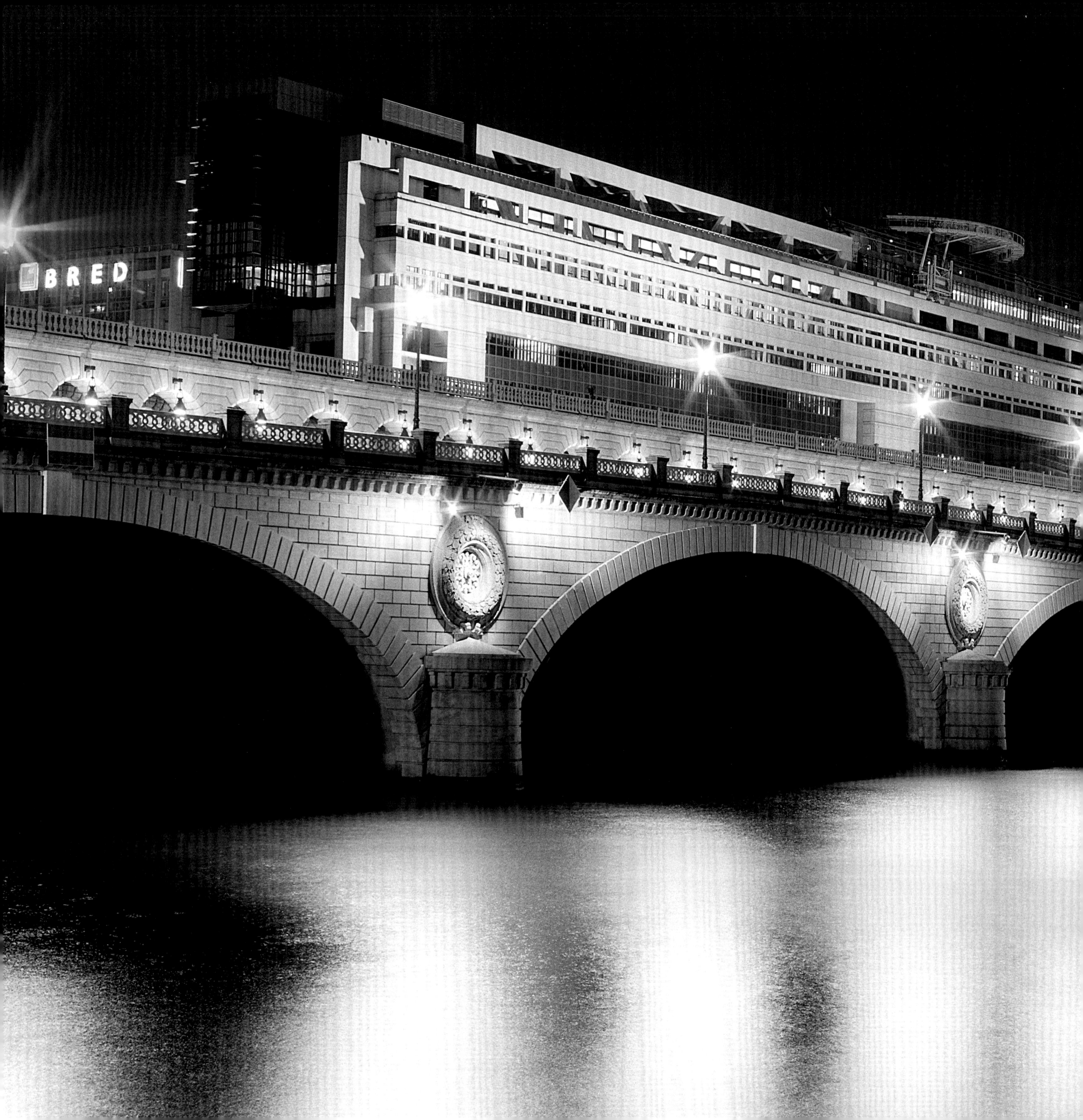
BRED

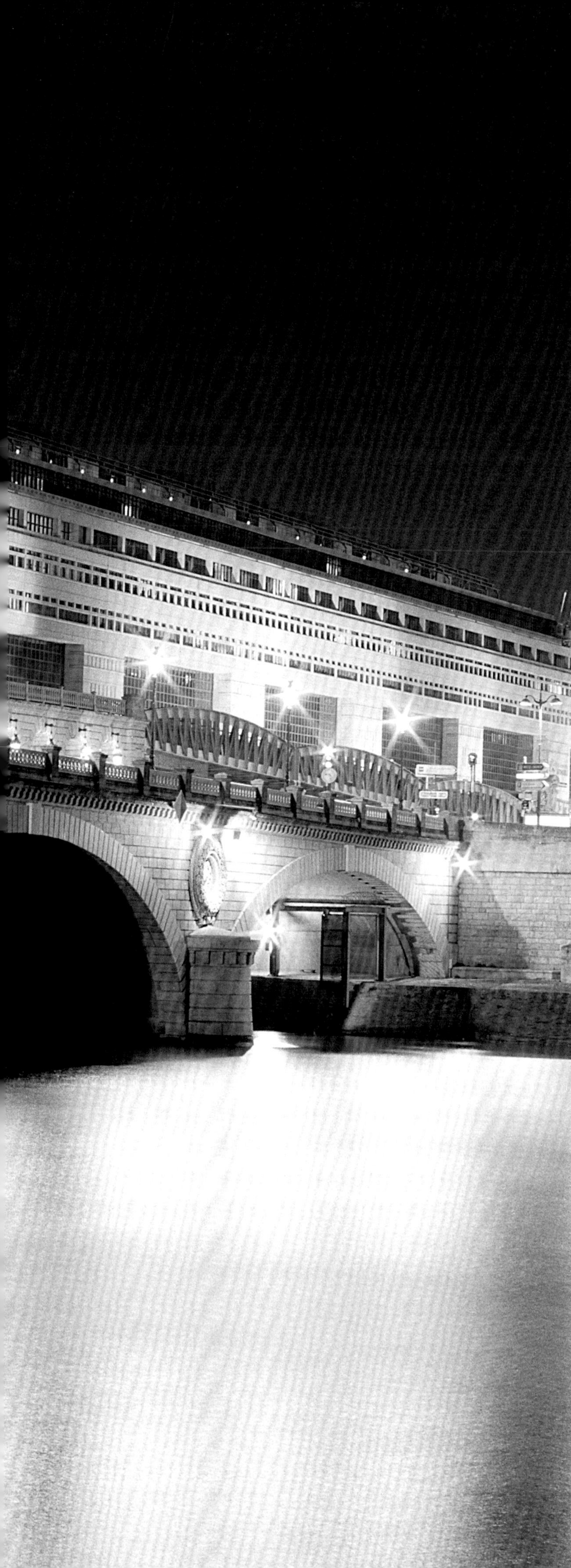

PONT DE BERCY

One can cross this bridge on foot, by automobile, by Paris Metro, on a bicycle, or, in past days, on horseback. Only two of the thirty-five Paris bridges accommodate all these means of transportation: the Pont de Bercy and the Pont de Bir-Hakeim.

Prior to the building of the first Pont de Bercy, the only means of crossing the river at this location was by ferry. In 1831 it was decided that a bridge would be built. After six months of construction, King Louis-Philippe inaugurated the first Pont de Bercy—a steel suspension bridge—in January 1832. Shortly thereafter, structural problems were discovered and weight restrictions were imposed that reduced the capacity of the bridge.

Many of the Paris bridges were built granting the builder the right to collect tolls for a period of time; in the case of Bercy the allotted period was thirty years, from 1832 to 1862. At the end of the concession, in 1863 (during the reign of Napoleon III), construction finally began on a new bridge. The design was identical to the design of the Pont Louis-Philippe, which is located farther downstream. The new Pont de Bercy, completed in 1864, still stands, though some additions have been made to the structure.

Pont de Bercy:
Building of the French Ministry of
Finance behind the arches of the bridge.

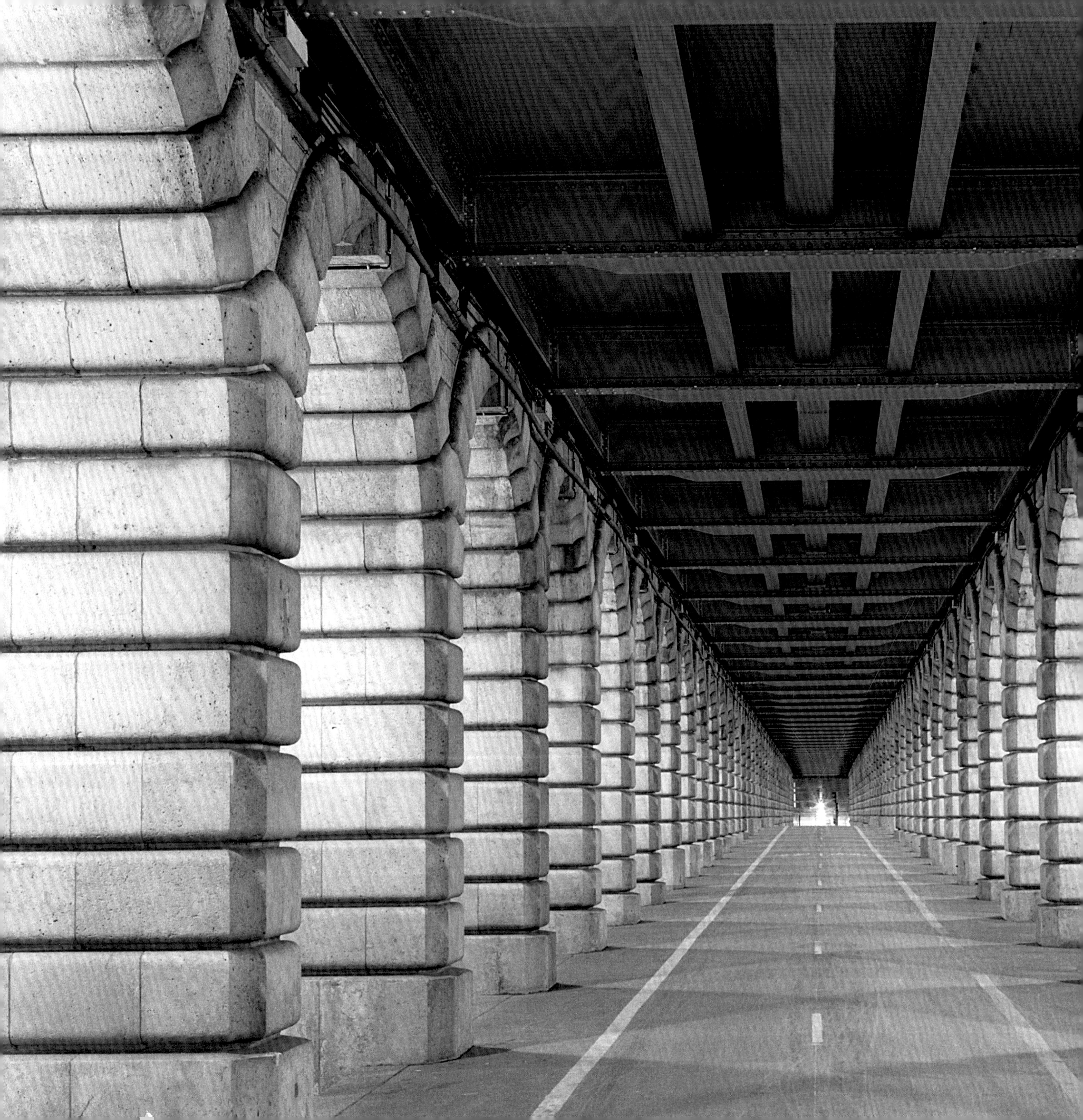

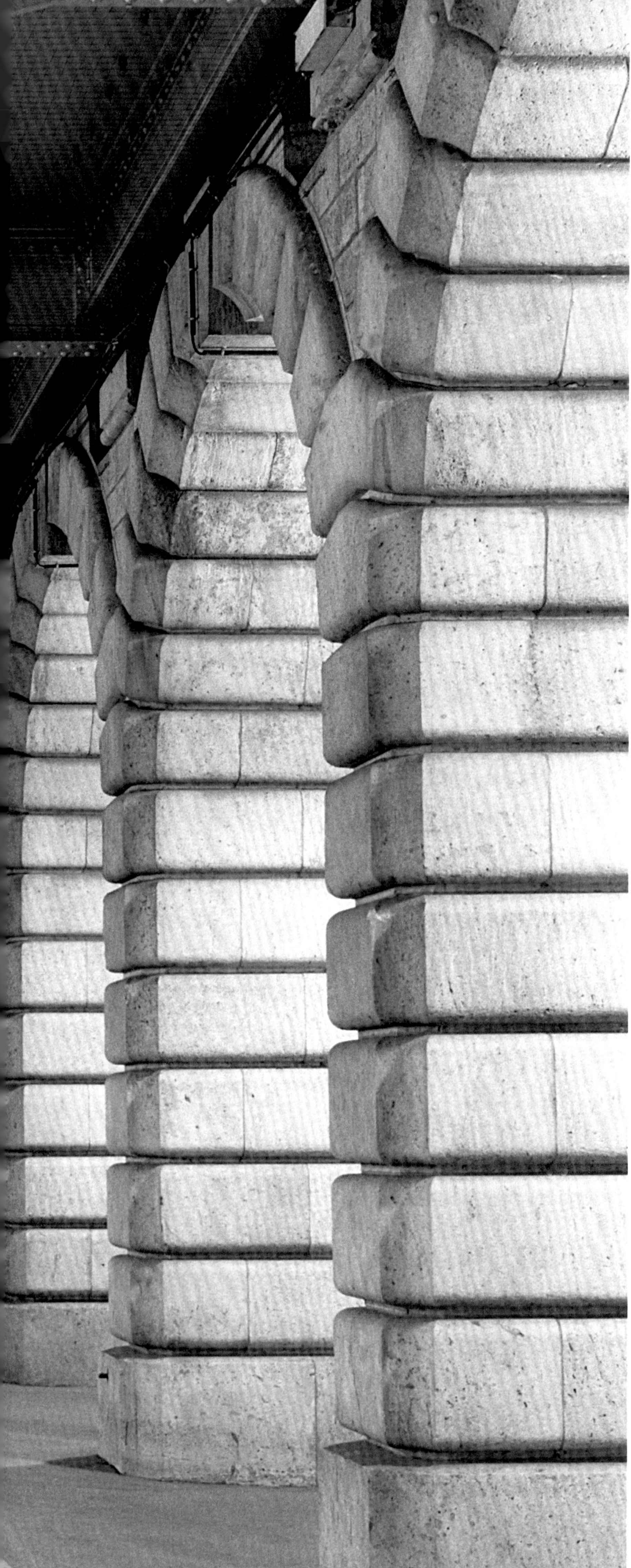

In 1904 the bridge was widened by 5½ meters (18 feet). At the same time a second, upper level was added to carry the Paris Metro. A pedestrian and bicycle passageway runs underneath the elevated Metro and is bordered by forty-one support arches on the upstream side and the same number on the downstream side.

In 1986 three traffic lanes and a sidewalk were added, doubling the capacity of the bridge. To avoid transferring any load to the existing bridge, the addition is structurally independent. Reinforced concrete was used for the addition, unlike the prior work that was a combination of masonry and limestone. The enlarged facility opened to the public in January 1992.

It is interesting to note that from underneath the bridge the three phases of work—1863, 1904, and 1992—are clearly delineated and can easily be seen.

On the left bank the bridge connects to the Boulevard Vincent Auriol; it also carries the Metro into the adjacent Quai de la Gare Metro station.

On the right bank the bridge provides access to two important buildings. One is the Palais Omnisport/Paris Bercy, a multi-purpose indoor arena in the same category as Madison Square Garden in New York, the Staples Center in Los Angeles, and the O2 Arena in London.

The other is the headquarters building of the Ministère des Finances, the French National Treasury building. The immense and impressive edifice is 370 meters (1,214 feet) long and incorporates two giant arches, one of which dips into the Seine. From a viewpoint upstream and across the river, the Bercy finance building looks like a gigantic train roaring across the bridge.

It is interesting that these two buildings are accessed by crossing the Pont de Bercy, going to the intersections of the Boulevard de Bercy and the rue de Bercy, and then taking the allée de Bercy.

Pont de Bercy:
Bicycle lanes under the main structure.

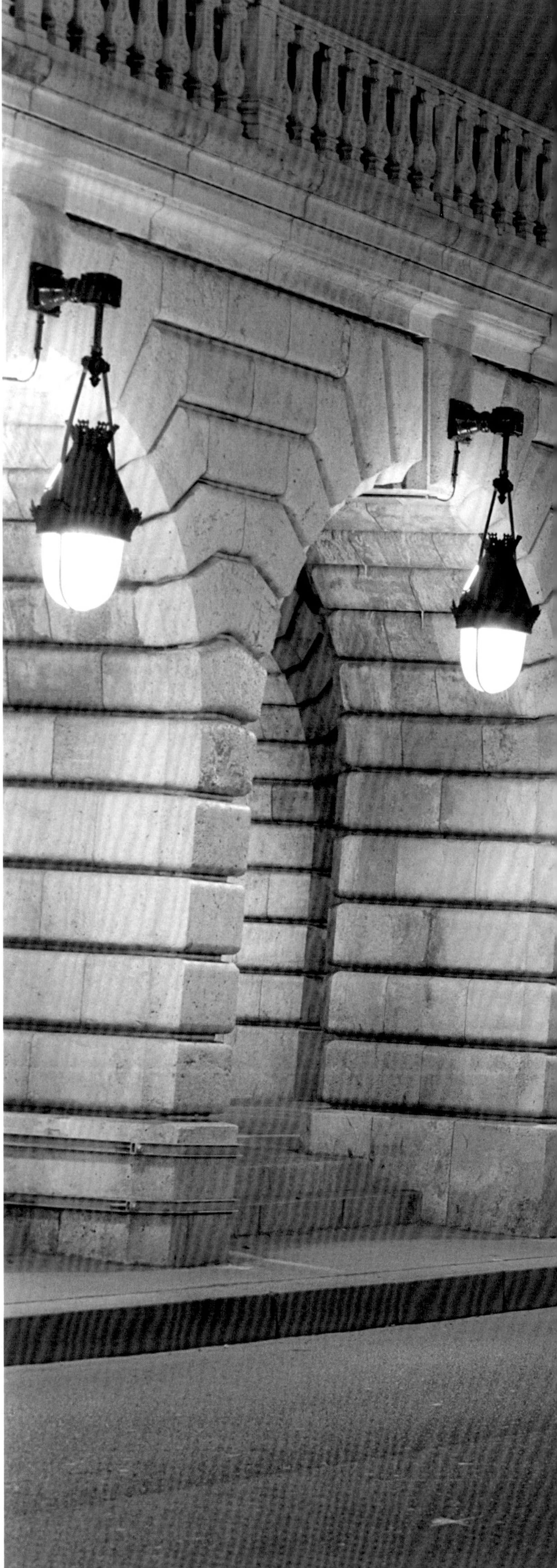

Pont de Bercy:
Lights of the Metro crossing
on the upper level.

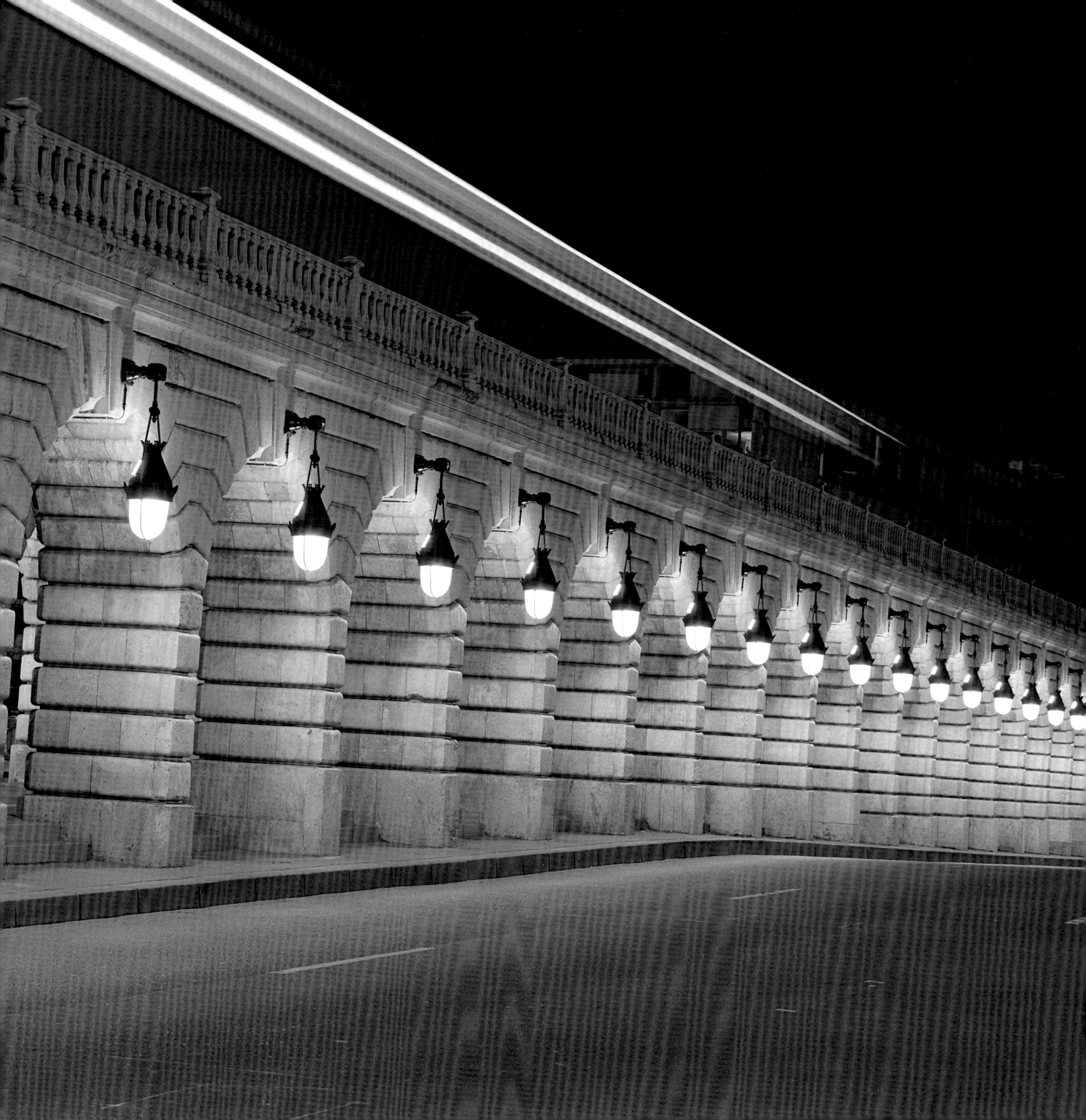

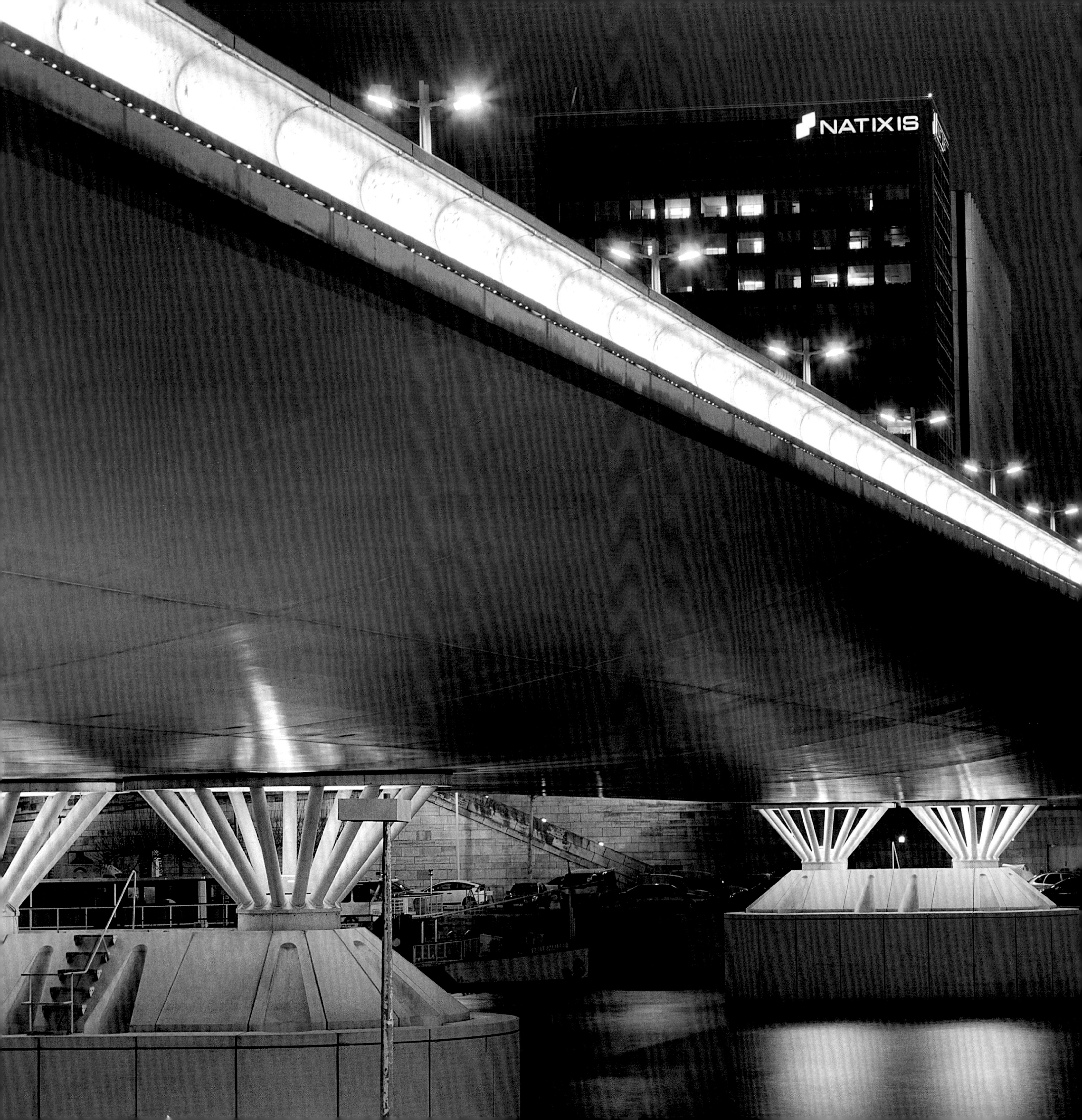

NATIXIS

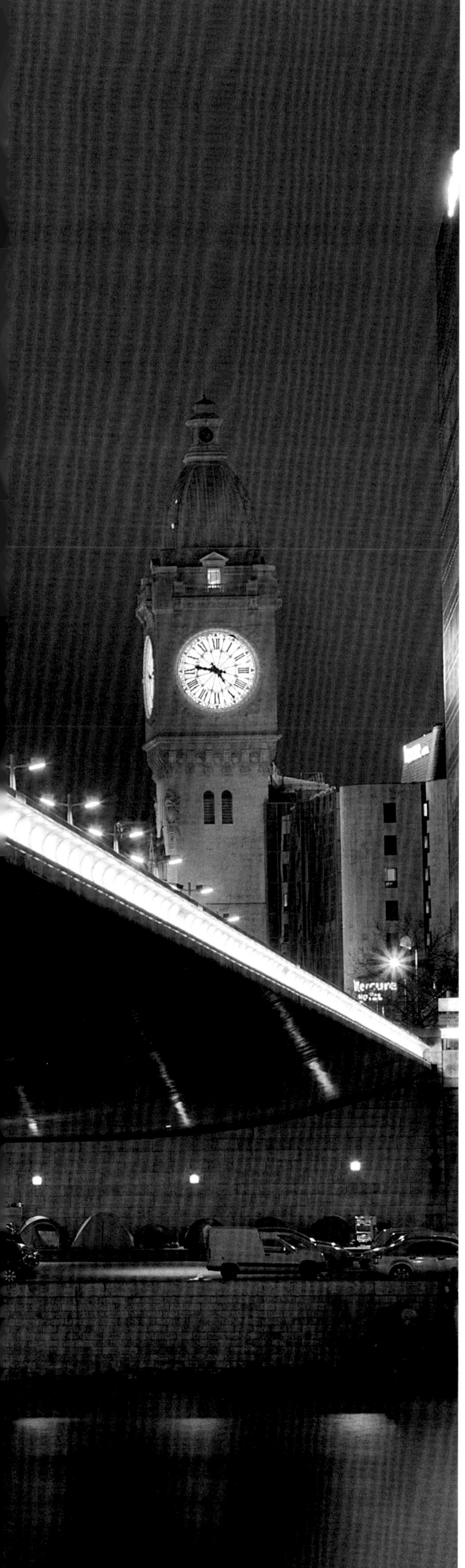

PONT CHARLES DE GAULLE

T he Pont Charles de Gaulle was the last bridge built for automobile use during the twentieth century.

Before the bridge was opened in 1996, its downstream neighbor, the Pont d'Austerlitz, was the busiest bridge in Paris, plagued by traffic jams. The objective of the new bridge was to lighten the load on Austerlitz and provide a more efficient traffic flow, as well as give direct access to the Gare de Lyon, the busiest passenger train station in the capital. The new bridge would also provide a direct link between the Gare de Lyon and the Gare d'Austerlitz on the opposite bank, a link that did not previously exist.

The Pont Charles de Gaulle was inaugurated as a one-way bridge, taking traffic from the left bank to the right bank. At the same time, the Pont d'Austerlitz was changed to one-way traffic in the opposite direction. The resulting, smoother traffic flow helped ease the congestion.

Pont Charles de Gaulle:
Design that resembles an aircraft wing.

The Pont Charles de Gaulle provides four lanes of automobile and bus traffic, two cycle lanes, and two sidewalks, one on each side, allowing pedestrians to connect directly between the two train stations.

The fabric of the bridge is a mixture of steel and reinforced concrete. The clean, dynamic design features a sweeping, slightly convex, aerodynamic structure in the form of an aircraft wing. It sits on two large pylons in the river. Each pylon has two flower-shaped cones with fifteen ribbed support bars. The design, with its predominating color of matte white, is light and airy. Now often referred to as a work of art, the bridge attracted frequent criticism when first opened. At night the lighting emphasizes the graceful, flowing form of the bridge deck.

Looking across the Pont Charles de Gaulle from the left bank, the clock tower of the Gare de Lyon dominates the line of sight; the clock at the top of the tower is the largest in Paris. The clock, built for the Universal Exposition of 1900, is classified as a Monument Historique. Modern office buildings flanking the tower have replaced the district's old docks and warehouses. ❦

Viaduc d'Austerlitz

The Paris Metro crosses the Seine over three Paris bridges, two of which are reserved solely for the Metro. The Viaduc d'Austerlitz is one of the two. It is dedicated solely to Metro line 5, and has no pedestrian or automotive access.

At the beginning of the twentieth century, the challenge to the Paris Metro was to get line 5 across the river at the Gare d'Austerlitz. A tunnel was soon ruled out as being impractical, so a bridge was chosen. However, because of restrictions posed by navigational traffic, the new bridge could not have pillars or supports descending into the river. Furthermore, immediately after crossing the river the bridge had to simultaneously turn and descend. The requirement called for a 90-degree turn and a slope of 40 percent within a 75-meter radius. It would be work considered quite unique at the time.

The engineer, Louis Biette, proposed a single span of 140 meters (460 feet) with the deck suspended from two side-by-side parabolic steel arches. Previously, the longest span across the river had been the Pont Alexandre III with a span of 107 meters.

Viaduc d'Austerlitz:
Fog closing in on the viaduc.

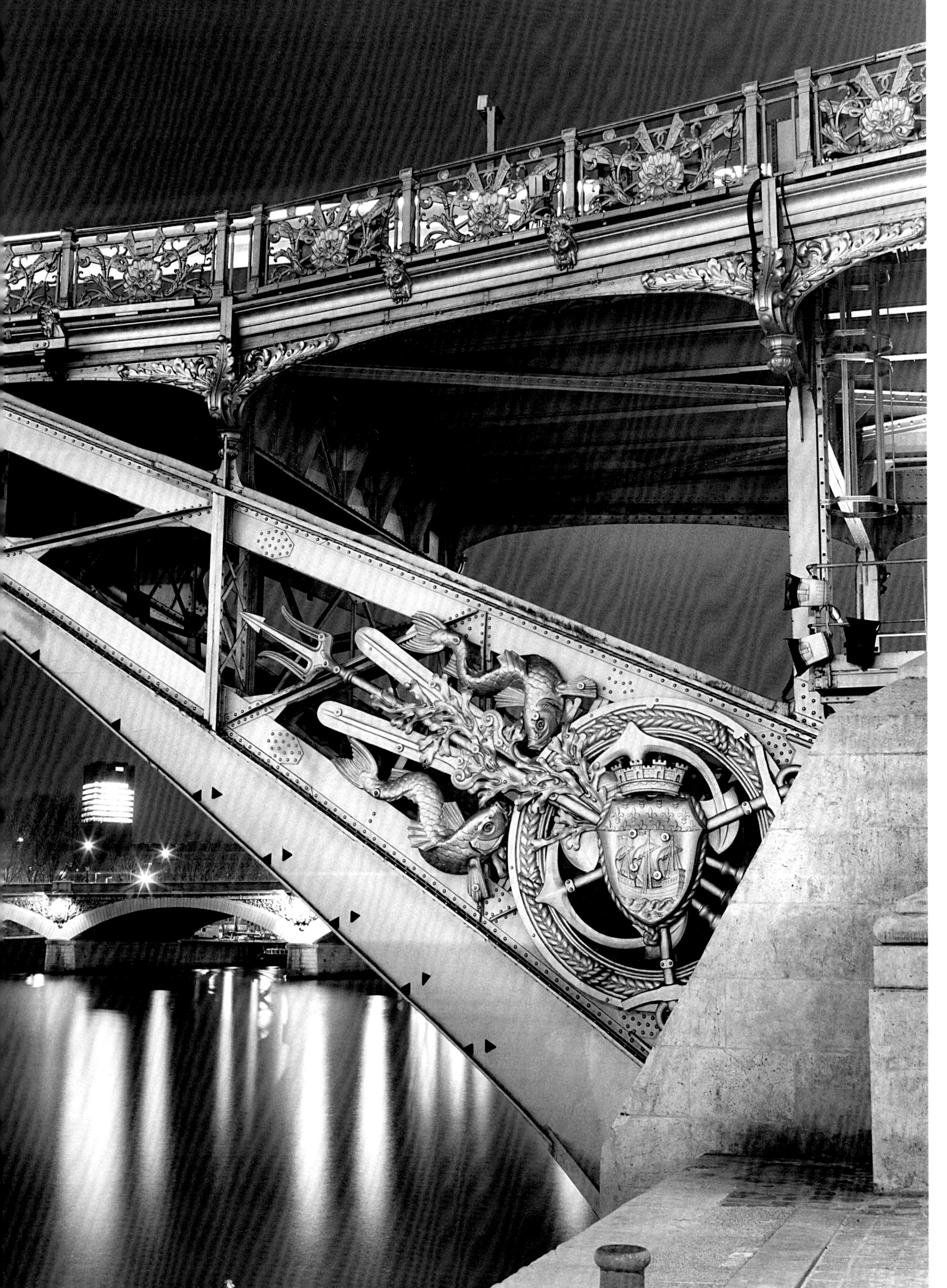

Viaduc d'Austerlitz:
Ironwork designed by Jean
Camille Formigé (1845–1926).

The Société de Construction de Levallois-Perret, previously named Anciens Etablissements Gustave Eiffel (the same company that built the Eiffel Tower), undertook the construction of the river crossing. The manufacture of the turn and descent was given to the firm of Daydé and Pillé, which built the Grand Palais in 1900. The firm specialized in metal construction, particularly bridges. Work on the project began in 1903 and was completed in 1904. In 1936 the viaduct was structurally reinforced to allow it to carry a considerably heavier load.

The Viaduc has been described as "sonically priceless" because of the unique sound created when the Metro passes. The rail cars create a shrill metal-on-metal screech as they make the turn on the short, tight radius on the right bank. This cacophony has been reduced but not eliminated with the newer rail cars, and is still quite evident on the older cars.

On the left bank the Viaduc d'Austerlitz goes directly into the Gare d'Austerlitz and terminates in the Metro station of the same name.

Probably the most pleasing aspect of the Viaduc is the decorative ironwork designed by Jean Camille Formigé (1845–1926). He was responsible for the decorative ironwork on the pillars, the arches, and the abutments of the viaduct. The design consists of dolphins, shells, seaweed, and animal faces, and includes a cast iron design of the coat of arms of Paris attached to anchors, all in varying shades of gray.

In 1986 the Viaduc d'Austerlitz was named a Monument Historique. It has been illuminated at night since January 2000. ❧

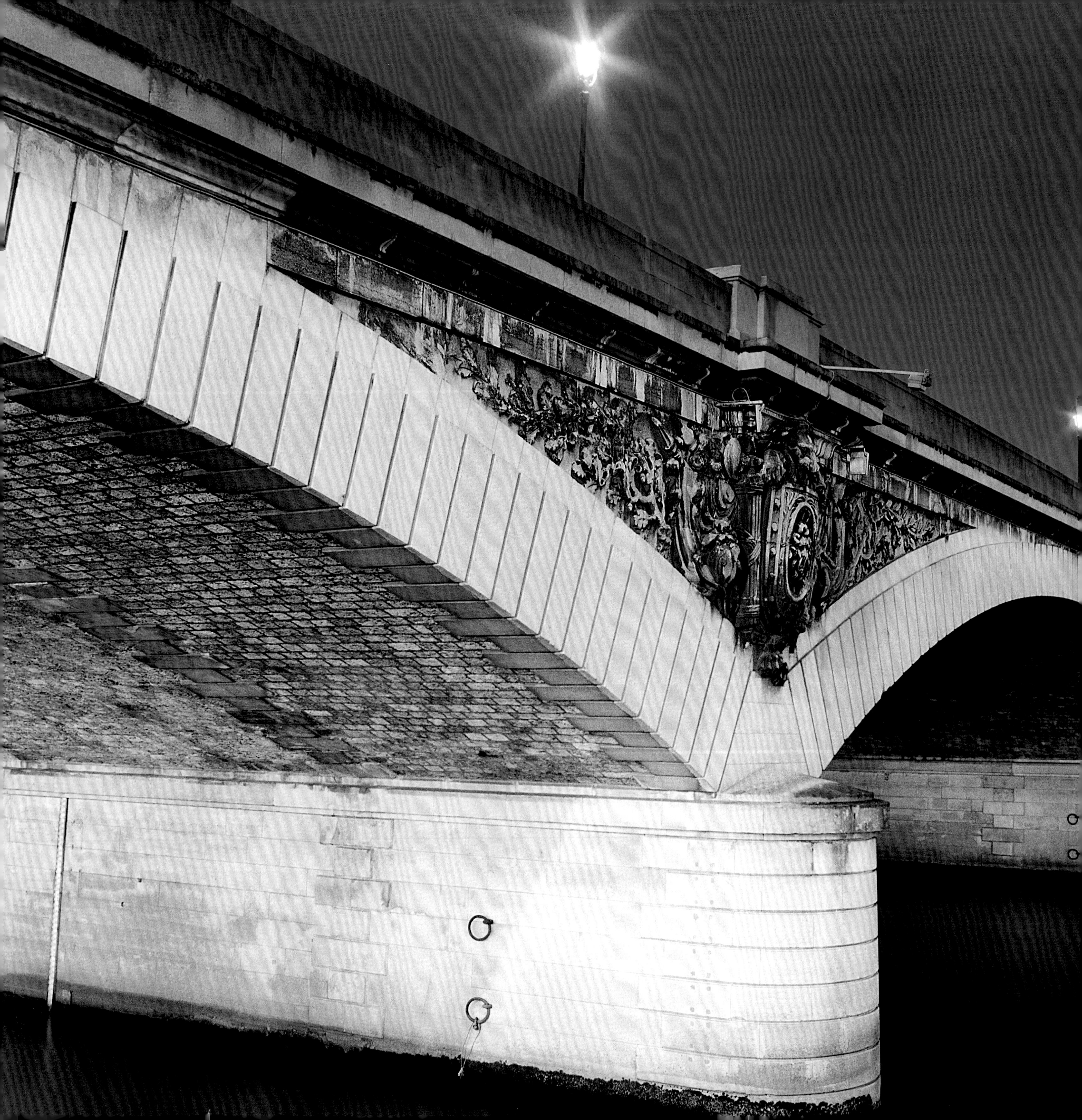

PONT D'AUSTERLITZ

The first Pont d'Austerlitz was built in 1806. It was the largest metal bridge in France and featured five cast iron arches. The cast iron soon developed cracks and became so dangerous that the bridge had to be replaced. It was a toll bridge until 1848 when the City of Paris purchased it and did away with the toll.

The bridge was built to link the Faubourg Saint-Antoine on the right bank to the Jardin des Plantes on the left bank. Prior to that, traffic was carried across the river by ferry.

The Pont d'Austerlitz was named in honor of the famous battle of Austerlitz, where in 1805 Napoleon Bonaparte defeated the Russian and Austrian troops. The battle took place near Austerlitz, which today is a town named Slavkov u Brna in the Czech Republic. The battle of Austerlitz is considered Napoleon's tactical military masterpiece, and is still taught in numerous military schools.

The replacement bridge of stone masonry was built in 1854. It was one of many bridges built or modernized during the Second Empire reign of Napoleon III. The decoration on the bridge included the imperial "N" for Napoleon, surrounded by eagles. After the fall of the Second Empire, a

Pont d'Austerlitz:
View from the left bank looking upstream.

lion positioned above a head of Medusa, and surrounded by flags and weapons symbolizing the Third Republic, replaced the "N." The bridge was widened to its current width in 1885.

Prior to 1996, the Pont d'Austerlitz was the busiest bridge in Paris. The construction of the Pont Charles de Gaulle helped to relieve the congestion, and traffic on Austerlitz became one-way only.

The Pont d'Austerlitz figures prominently in Victor Hugo's novel *Les Misérables* about the June 1832 rebellion. In fact, the title of chapter 2 of book 5 in volume 2 is *Il est heureux que le pont d'Austerlitz porte voitures* (It is fortunate that the Pont d'Austerlitz bears carriages). The bridge is also the subject of the popular song "Pont d'Austerlitz" by French singer Mano Solo (1963–2010).

The bridge was of great importance to the French Forces who entered Paris to retake the city at the end of World War II. The French Capitaine Raymond Dronne, leading the 9th company of General Leclerc's division, was the first to enter Paris. He entered at the Porte d'Italie on the morning of August 24, 1944. Crossing the river at the Pont d'Austerlitz, they reached the Hôtel de Ville (where the Resistance was based) later that afternoon.

The Seine river height is measured on a scale at the Pont d'Austerlitz; a water level 3.5 meters (11 feet) above the average level results in a yellow alert, and 6 meters a red alert. The likely cost of repairing the damage from a red alert flood is estimated at over five billion euros. The famous flood of 1910 peaked at 8.6 meters.

The Thirteen Bridges on the Île de la Cité and the Île Saint-Louis

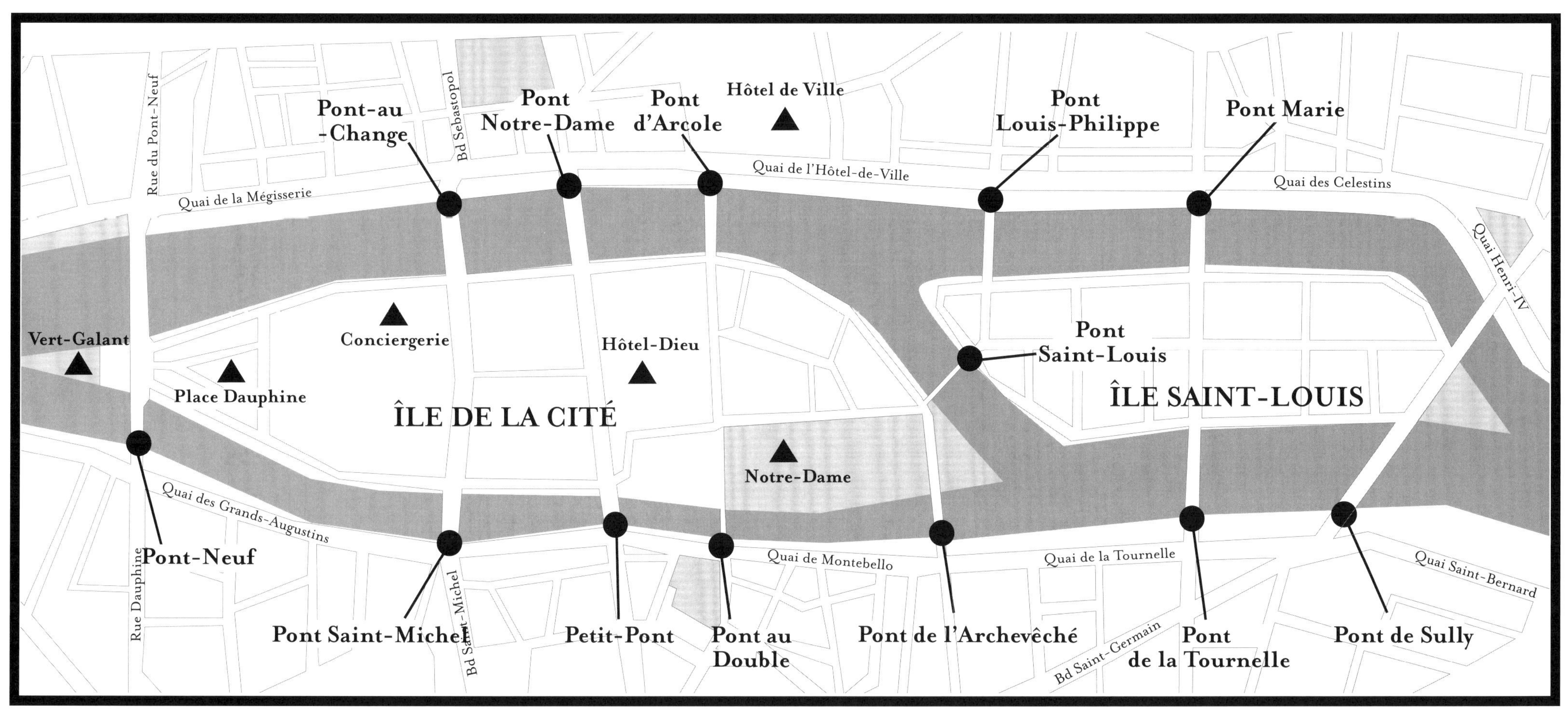

PONT DE SULLY

The Pont de Sully, which is in fact two bridges with the same name, passes across the Île Saint-Louis, one of the three islands in the Seine within the boundaries of the City of Paris. The two bridges are connected by the Boulevard Henri IV, which runs between them on the Île Saint-Louis.

Unlike most of the other Paris bridges, the Pont de Sully makes not one but three connections from the left bank to the right bank. It connects the left to the right bank, and also links the left bank and the right bank with the Île Saint-Louis.

In 1838 people could cross the river at this point by using two footbridges. From the left bank they could take the Passerelle de Constantine to the island and then the Passerelle Damiette from the island to the right bank. The Passerelle Damiette was destroyed in the Revolution of 1848. The Passerelle de Constantine collapsed in 1872 as a result of corrosion in its cables.

In 1866, Baron Hausmann, the Préfet of Paris, opened the new Boulevard Henri IV. The new boulevard led from the Place de la

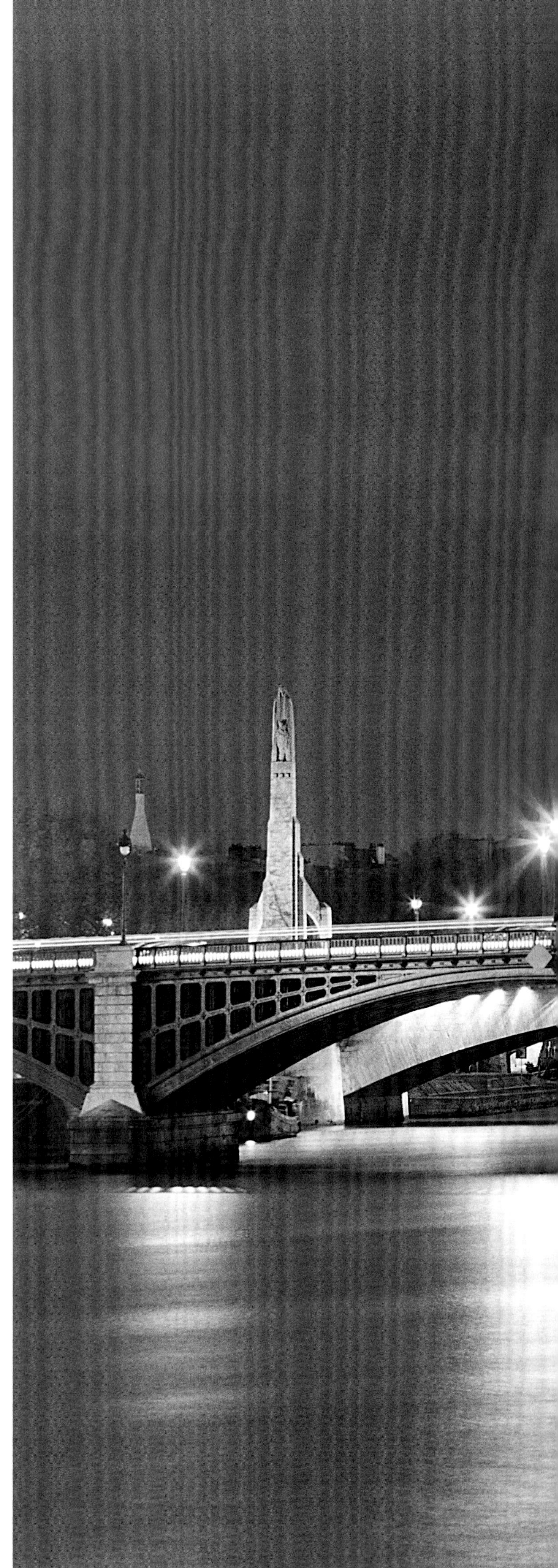

Pont de Sully:
The Grand Bras (large arm)
with Notre-Dame in the rear.

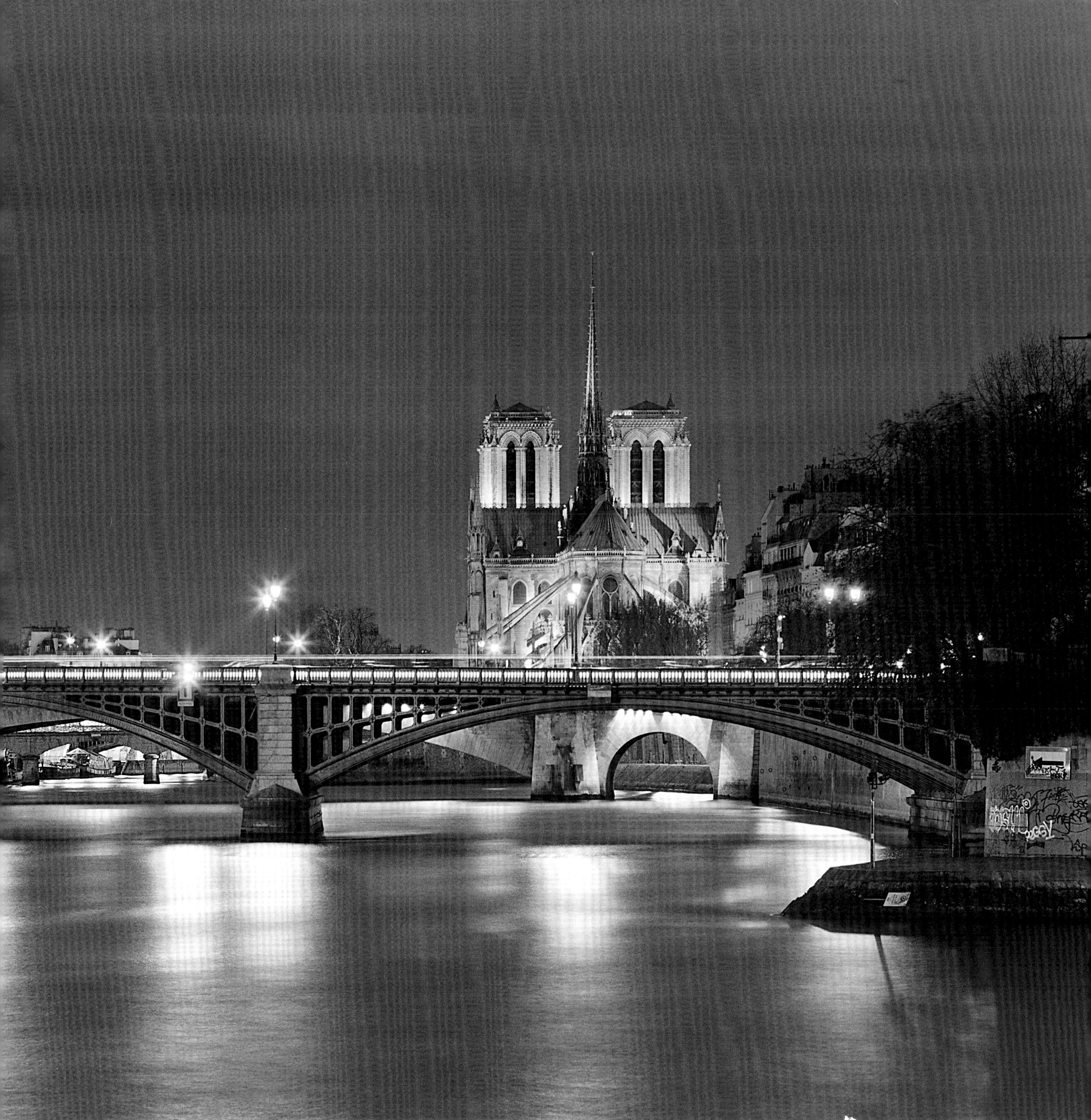

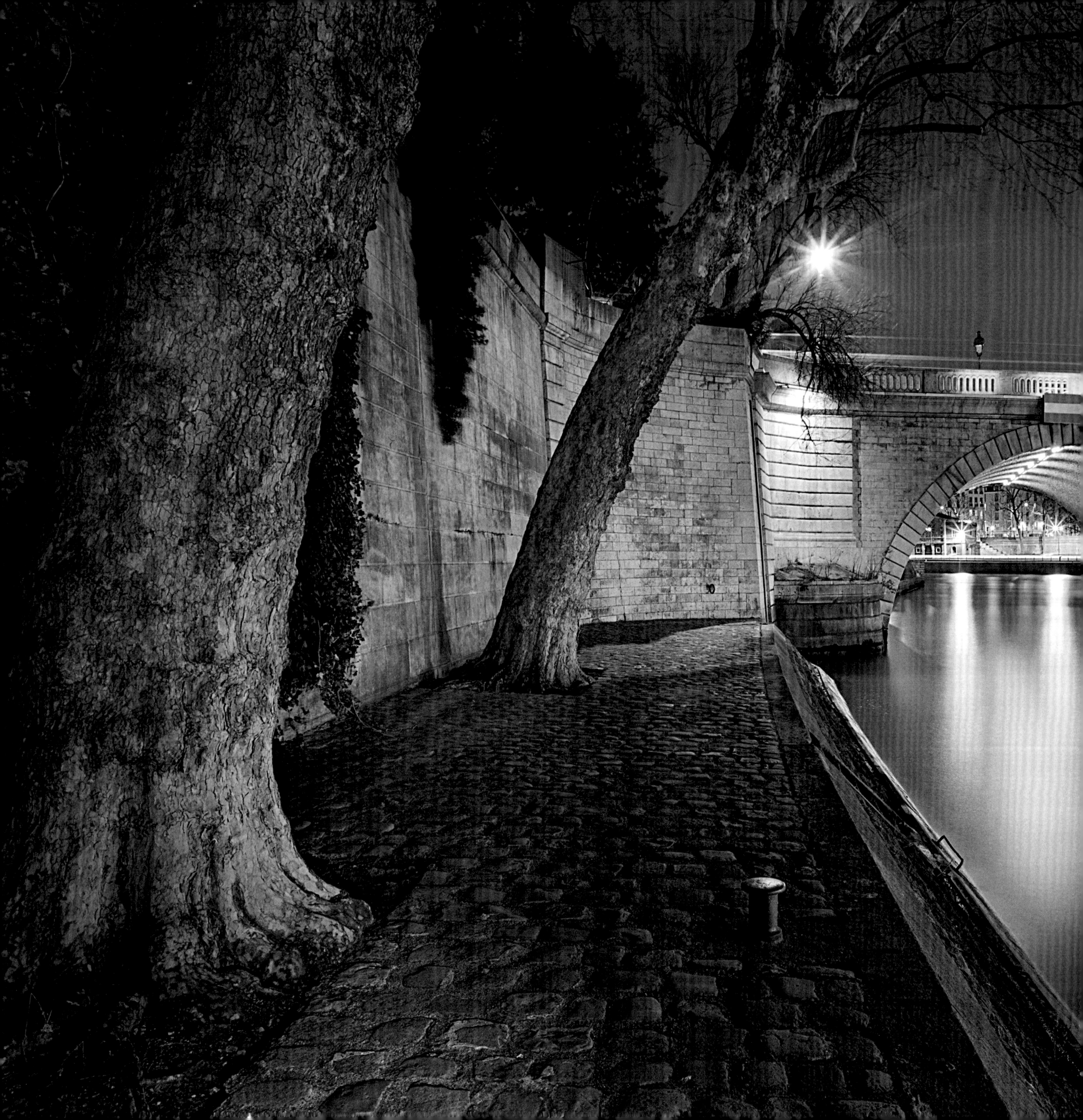

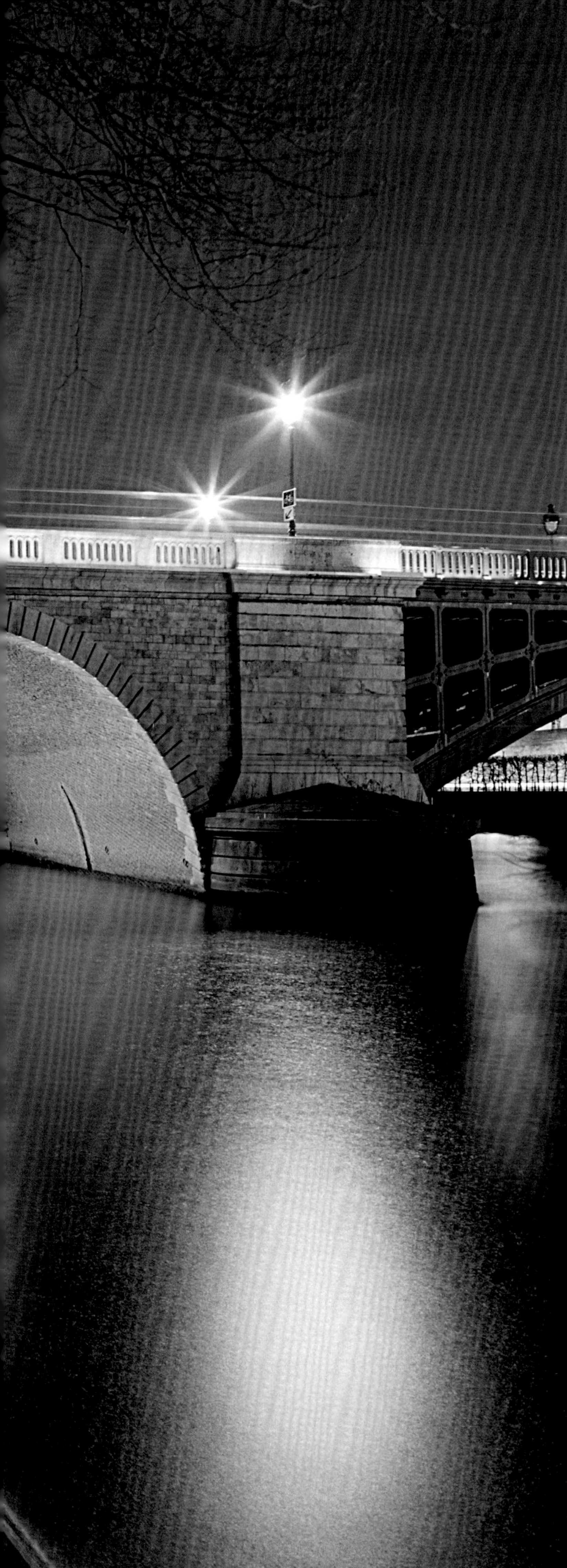

Bastille to the location at the Seine where Hausmann planned to build the Pont de Sully. The plan was to link the boulevard with the proposed new bridge and then connect to the new Boulevard Saint-Germain on the left bank. In 1870, however, plans for the bridge were interrupted when the Second Empire was overthrown during the war with Prussia. It was three days after Napoleon III and his troops surrendered to the Prussians at the Battle of Sedan that the Empire fell.

Work on the bridge finally began in 1876, under the Third Republic, and it opened on August 25, 1877. It was named the Pont de Sully in honor of Maximilien de Béthune, duke of Sully (1560–1641) and minister to Henry IV. This is the bridge that stands today. It crosses the Seine at a 45-degree angle, in contrast to the other Paris bridges, which mostly cross the river at 90-degree angles. The 45-degree angle provides a superb view of the Île Saint-Louis and Notre-Dame.

The bridge is at the far upstream end of the Île Saint-Louis. The two sections of the bridge are the *Petit Bras* (small arm) on the right bank and the *Grand Bras* (large arm) on the left. The Petit Bras consists of one cast iron arch; the Grand Bras consists of three arches, also cast iron. The arches rest on reinforced concrete pillars.

The Square Barye is found at the tip of the Île Saint-Louis on the upstream side of the two arms of the bridge. It is a charming public garden that is part of the Paris system of parks and gardens.

Pont de Sully:
The Petit Bras (small arm) to the right bank.

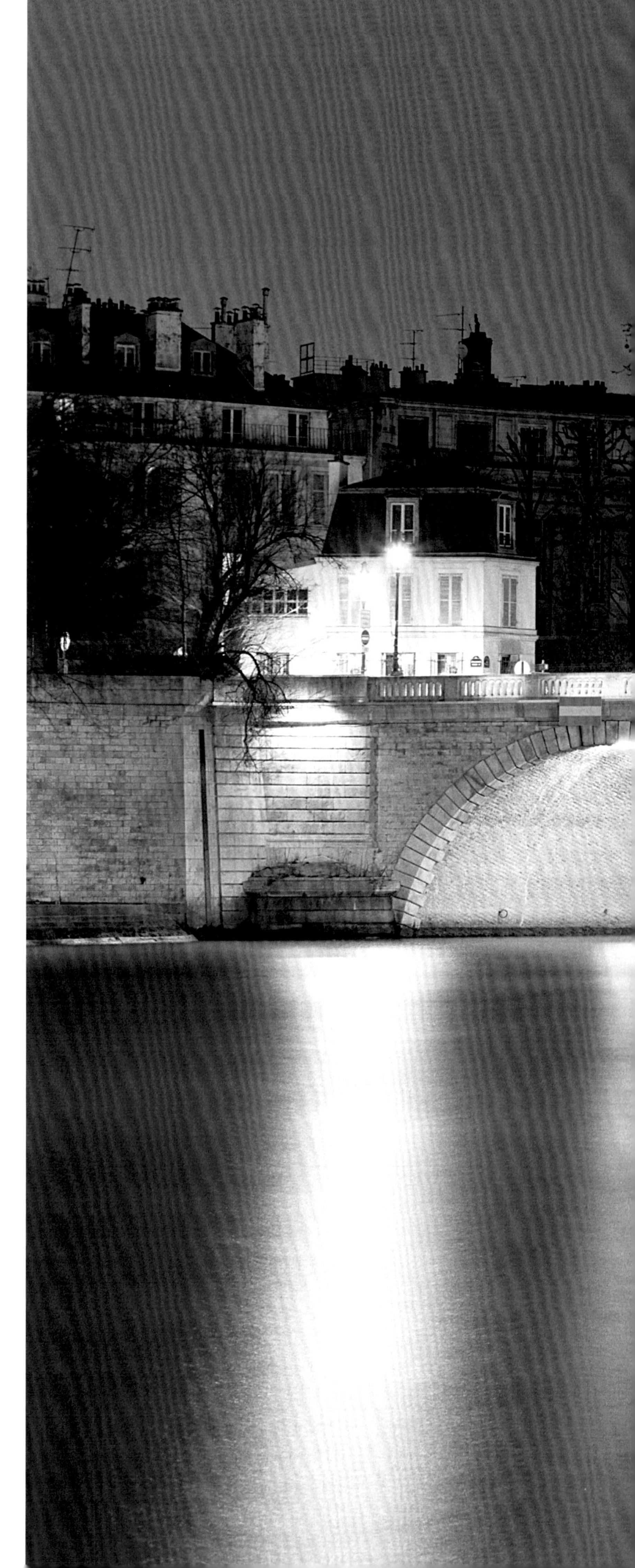

Pont de Sully:
The Petit Bras (small arm) seen
from the right bank.

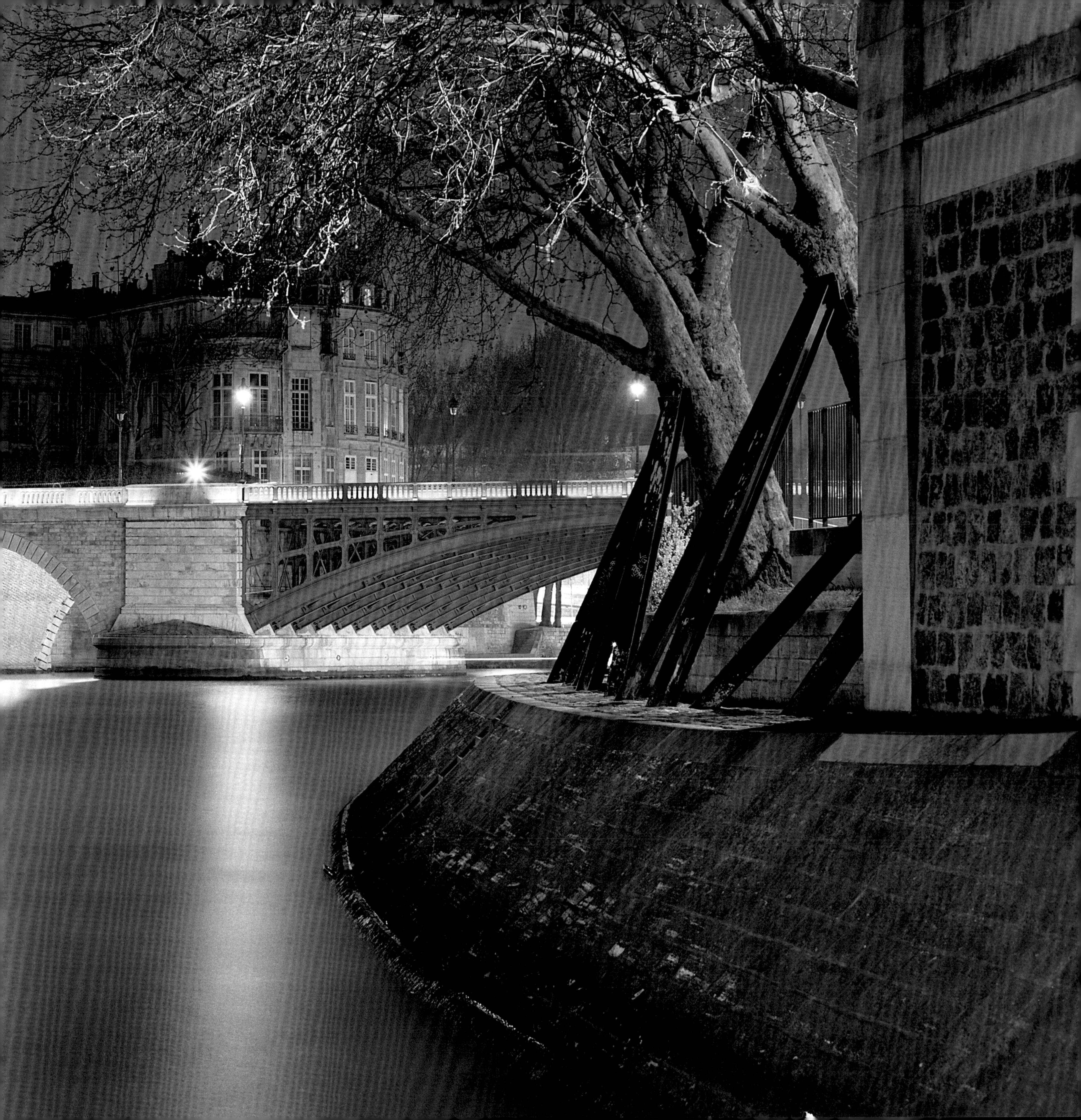

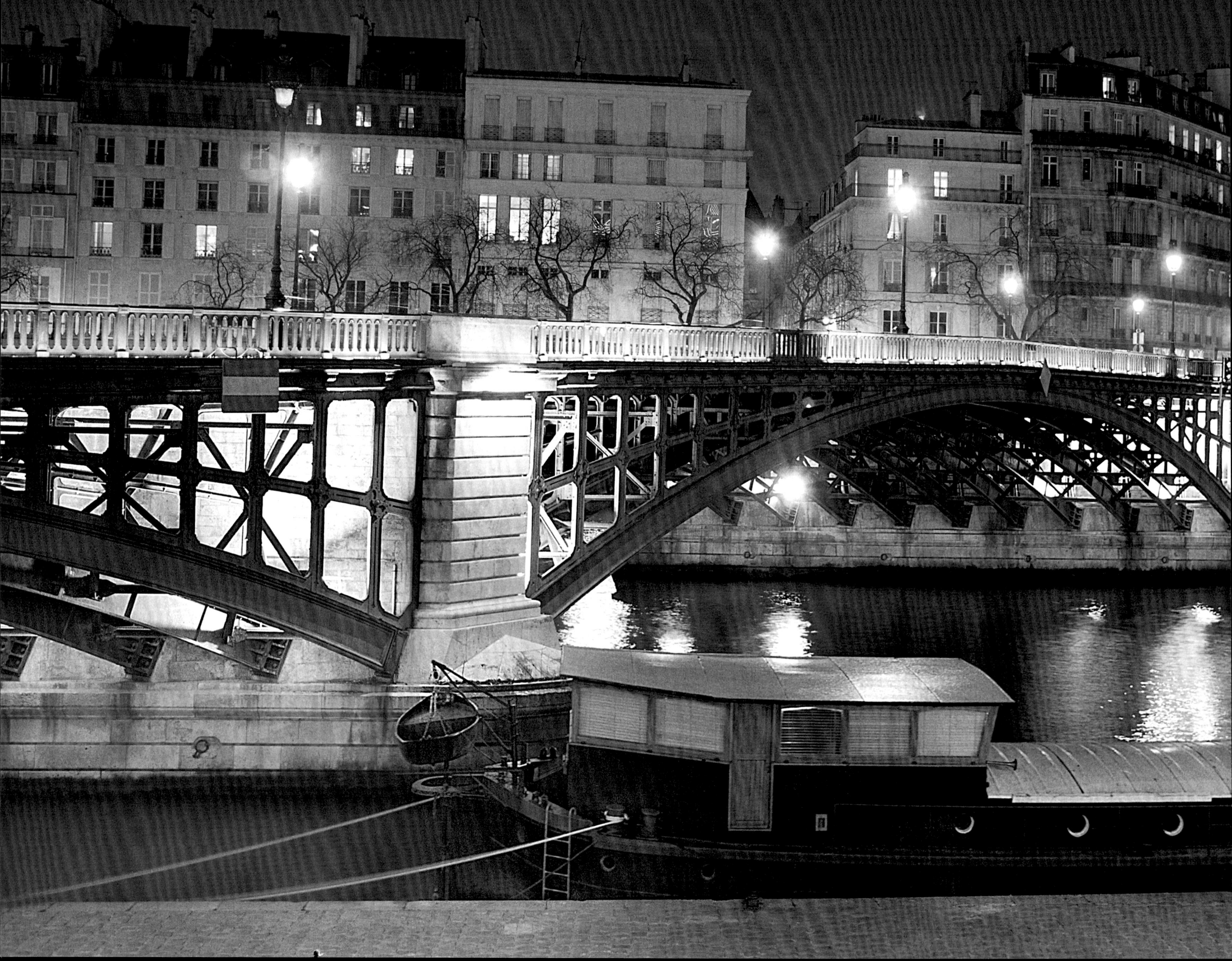

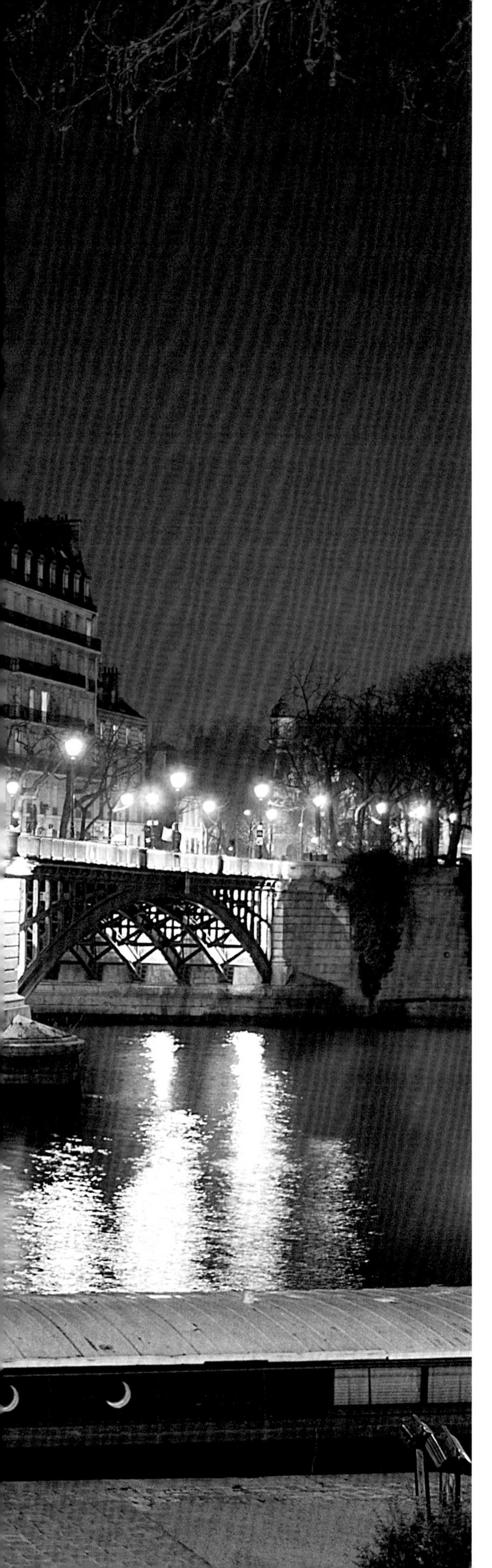

Pont de Sully:
The Grand Bras (large arm)
from the left bank.

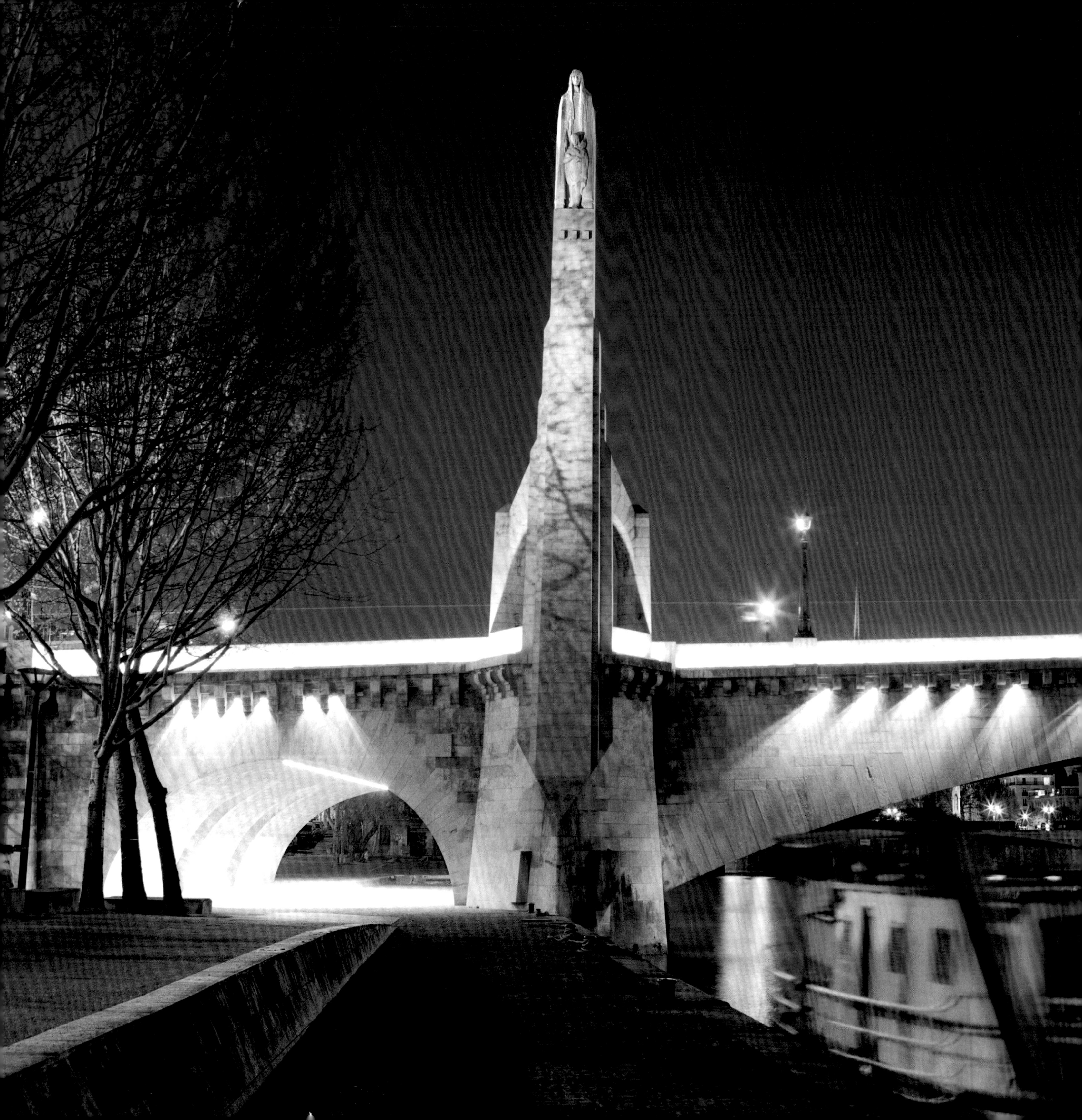

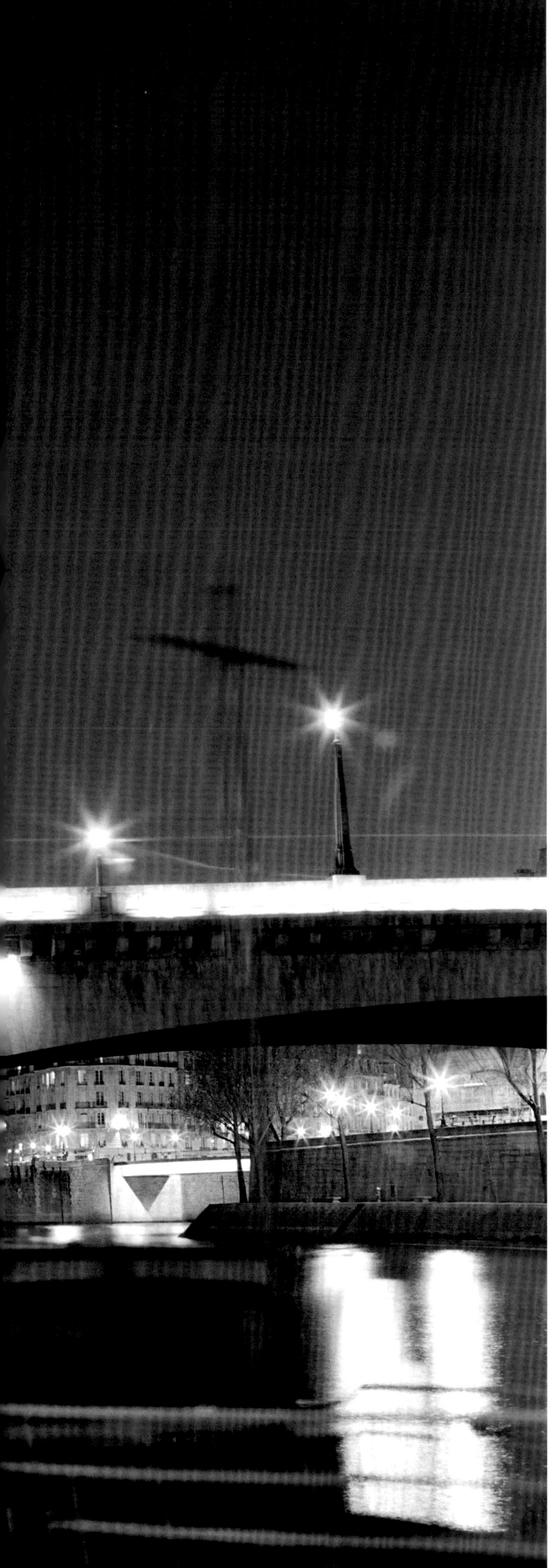

PONT DE LA TOURNELLE

The first Pont de la Tournelle was completed in 1656, some years after the completion of its sister bridge, the Pont Marie. The Pont Marie connected the Île Saint-Louis to the right bank, and the Pont de la Tournelle was built to link the island to the left bank.

The word *tournelle* can be traced to its original meaning of a square turret, constructed at the end of the twelfth century, on the fortress of Phillipe Auguste.

The Pont de la Tournelle of 1656 incorporated six stone arches. The bridge remained in use, with only minor modifications, until 1918 when serious damage caused by the flood of 1910 meant that the bridge finally had to be demolished. During the ten years between the demolition and the opening of the replacement bridge, a temporary wooden footbridge served to connect the island to the left bank.

The bridge in evidence today was constructed of reinforced concrete and finished in 1928. It has one large arch in the middle with a smaller arch

Pont de la Tournelle:
Sculpture of Sainte-Geneviève, the patron saint of Paris by Paul Landowski (1875–1961).

on each side. The smaller arch at the left bank sits on land, while on the right bank the other sits in the water.

The most striking feature of the Pont de la Tournelle is the sculpture of Sainte-Geneviève, the patron saint of Paris, that stands on a very simple pylon between the large and small arches on the left bank side. The pylon is 14 meters (46 feet) tall and the statue of Sainte-Geneviève on top is 5.3 meters (17 feet) tall.

Paul Landowski (1875–1961), one of the most well-known sculptors of the period, created the sculpture. Three years after finishing the statue of Sainte-Genevieve, he completed his most famous work, *Christ the Redeemer*, which sits atop Corcovado Mountain overlooking the city of Rio de Janeiro.

Sainte-Geneviève was born circa 419/422 AD and at the age of fifteen became a nun. According to historical records, in 451 she persuaded the people of Paris to remain and pray instead of fleeing in the face of an invasion by Attila the Hun. She urged Parisians to resist with the famous words that translate as: "Let the men flee, if they want, if they are no longer able to fight. We women, we pray to God as long as He will hear our prayers." The invading Huns subsequently turned in another direction and the people of Paris were saved. At her death in 512, her remains were interred in what became the Abbey of Sainte-Geneviève. Her statue on the Pont de la Tournelle faces east, towards the approaching Attila and the Huns. Landowski would have preferred her to face Notre-Dame, and to represent peace. He also wanted her to be placed at a lower elevation so she could be more easily seen. However, his wishes did not prevail. The year 1928 marks the last time a statue was placed atop a Paris bridge.

In 1744, the ailing King Louis XV vowed that if he recovered from his illness he would replace the ruined church of Sainte-Geneviève with an edifice worthy of the patron saint of Paris. He did recover, and the monument he ordered to be constructed is now the Pantheon. ✎

Pont de la Tournelle:
Upstream view with Pont de
Sully in the rear.

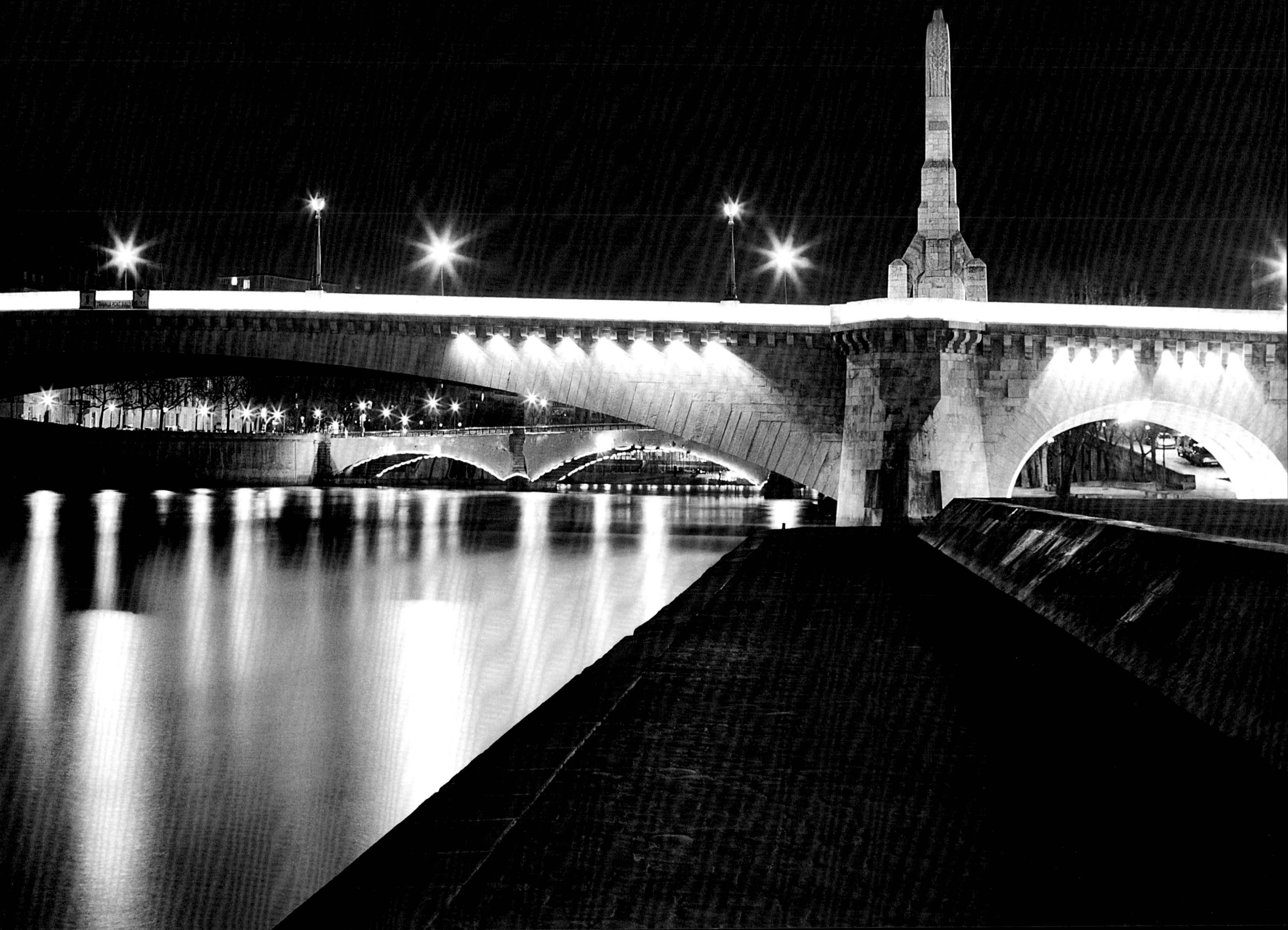

PONT MARIE

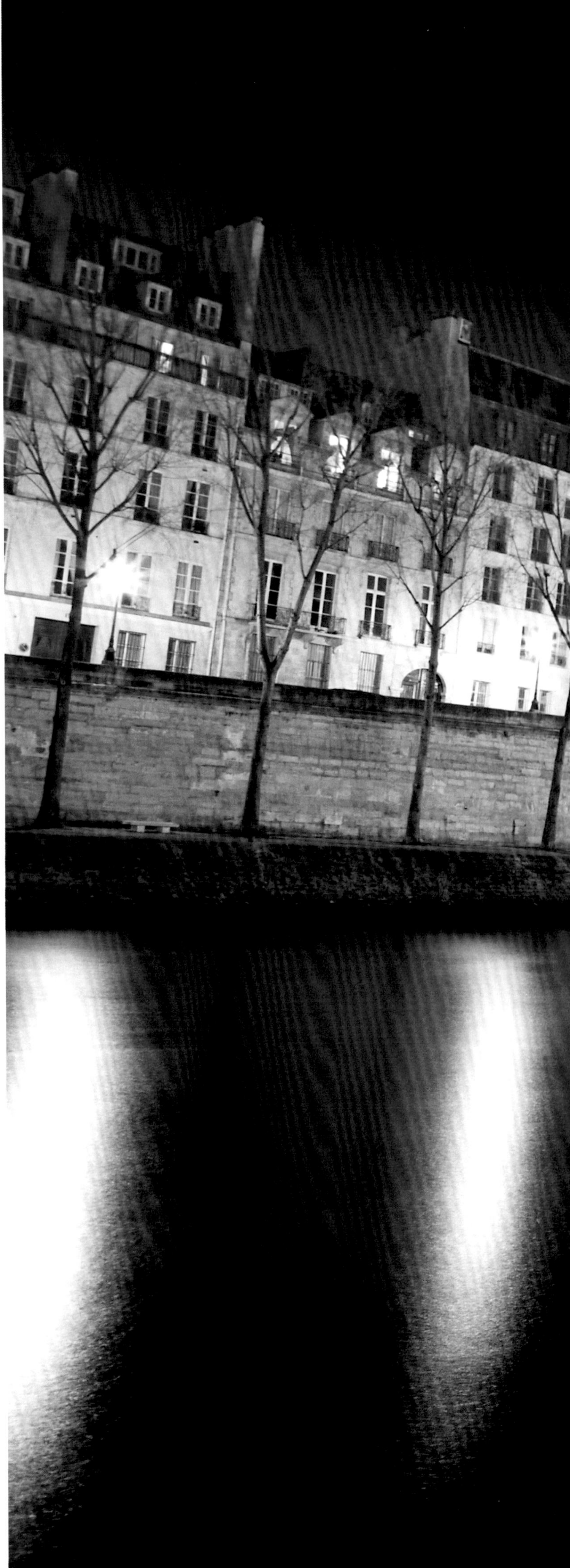

The Pont Marie is the second oldest Paris bridge. It lies between the Pont de Sully upstream and the Pont Louis-Philippe downstream. The bridge links the Île Saint-Louis to the right bank.

The Pont Marie was initially proposed to King Henri IV by the developer Christophe Marie in 1608. The objective was easy access to the island, then called *L'Île aux Vaches* (island of cows), which had been used primarily for grazing cattle. Unfortunately, Henri IV was assassinated in 1610 and the project languished for another four years. In 1614 Christophe Marie finalized a contract with the new King Louis XIII who had succeeded his father to the throne. In October of that year, at the age of thirteen, King Louis XIII laid the cornerstone for the future bridge, which would be named for the developer.

Because of disputes, red tape, and lawsuits, as well as the opposition of the priests of Notre-Dame, the bridge was not finished until 1635, twenty-seven years after it was first proposed.

Pont Marie:
View from the right bank
toward Île Saint-Louis.

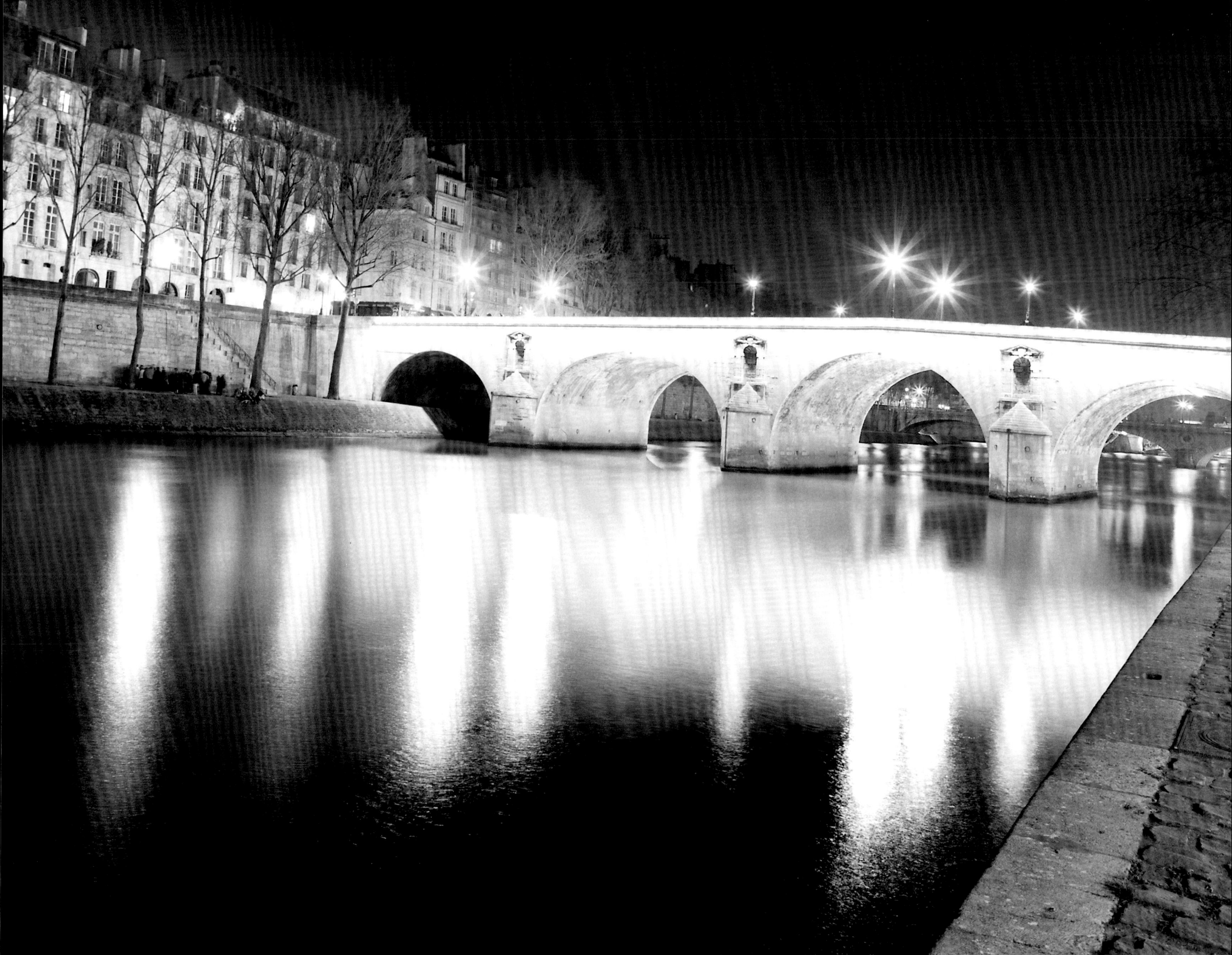

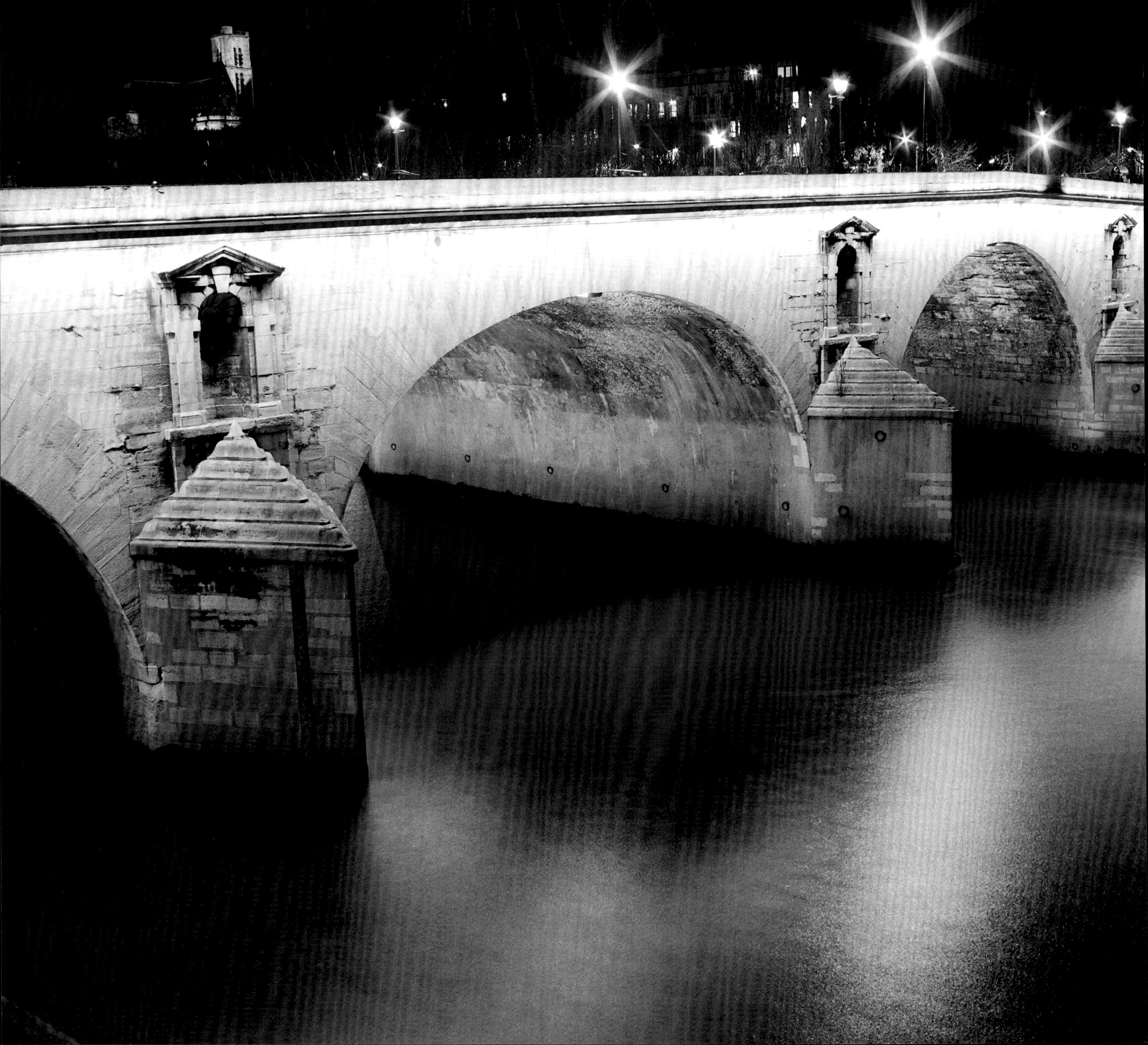

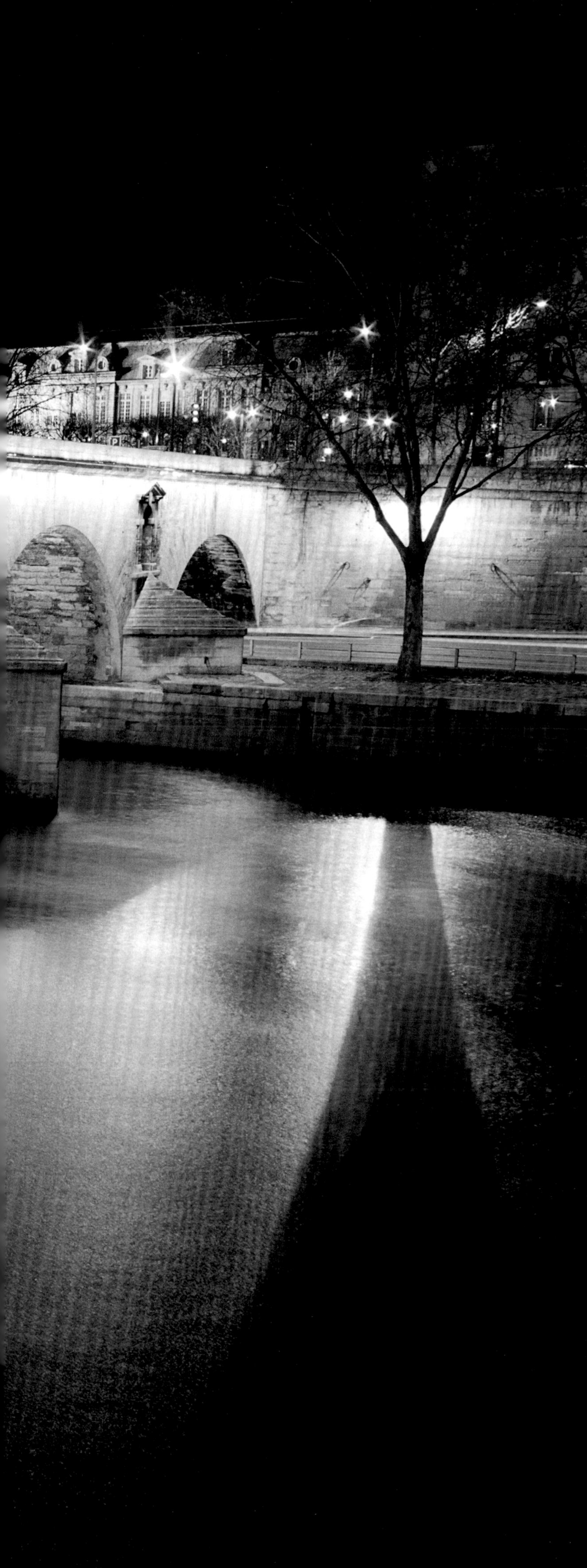

The bridge is constructed of five masonry and stone arches, with an inset niche at the intersection of each leg of the arches. The niches, designed to house statues that were never placed, still exist, and are still empty.

The design of the bridge incorporated a *dos d'âne*, which roughly translates to humpback, a structural approach often used in bridge construction in earlier days. The humpback rise in the center of the bridge has been gradually leveled out, most notably in 1850–1851 when the bridge underwent a restoration. Today the appearance of the bridge is much the same as it was at its debut in 1635.

Following completion, and against the wishes of Christophe Marie, fifty wooden houses were built on the bridge. Later, because of a disagreement about maintenance between the homeowners and the authorities, they began to deteriorate. In late February or early March of 1658 the pressure of frozen ice against the bridge caused a collapse of the two southern arches. Twenty-two houses fell, and sixty people died.

In 1660 the two arches were replaced by a temporary wooden structure and a toll was instituted to finance the reconstruction of the masonry and stone arches. These were completed in 1670. In 1740, following an official edict, some of the remaining houses on the bridge (judged to be in a poor state of repair) were demolished.

In 1750, during the attempted kidnapping of an infant from one of the remaining houses on the bridge, the incensed crowd apprehended a man who, despite the arrival of the police, was murdered.

In 1769 a decree by Louis XV banned all houses on the bridge and finally, in 1788, the last house was removed.

The Pont Marie was classified as a Monument Historique in 1887.

On the upstream side of the bridge a plaque commemorating the high-water level of the 1910 flood can be found.

Pont Marie:
Niches, designed for statues, which
have never been installed.

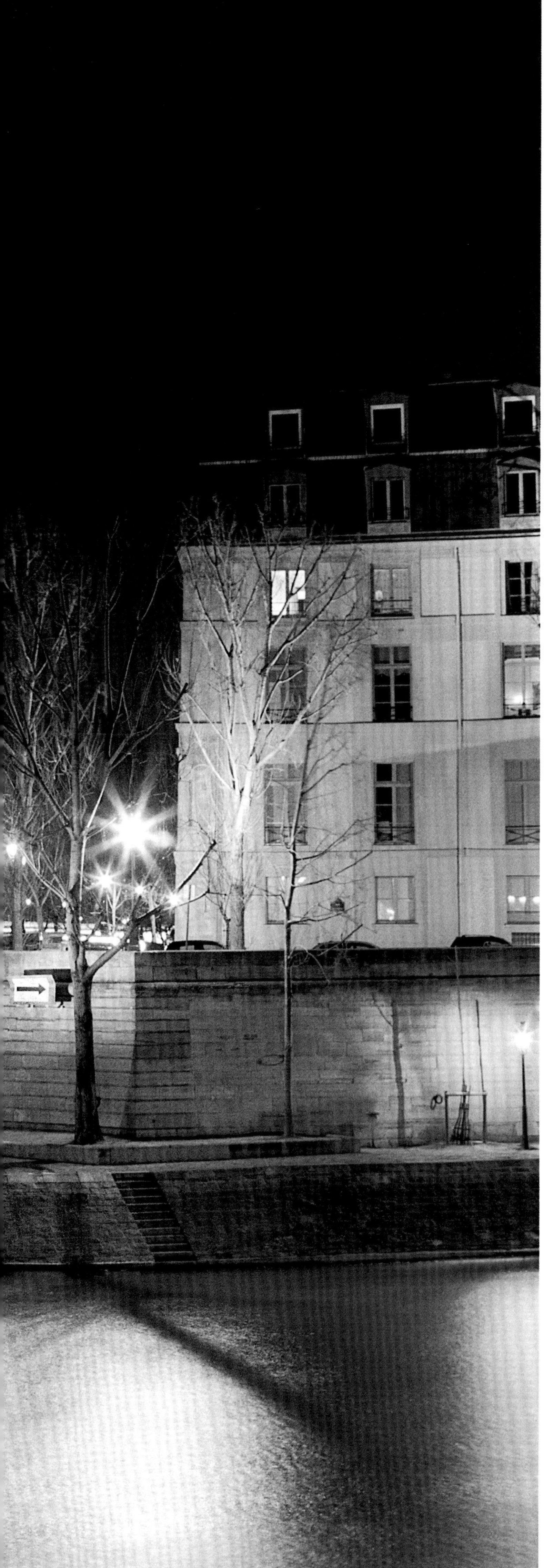

PONT LOUIS-PHILIPPE

The Pont Louis-Philippe is named for King Louis-Philippe, who laid the first cornerstone in July 1833. It was opened a year later, in July 1834.

Like many bridges at that time, it was a suspension bridge with tollbooths. It ran at an angle from the right bank across the Île Saint-Louis to the Île de la Cité, connecting the two islands to the right bank.

During the revolution of 1848 a fire destroyed a portion of the bridge and all the tollbooths. The fire caused some of the suspension cables to melt, throwing about twenty victims to their death in the water below. After the revolution the name was changed to Pont de la Réforme. Repairs were subsequently made, and in 1852 the bridge got its old name back.

In 1860, during the reign of Napoleon III, the decision was taken to tear down the original suspension bridge and replace it with two new bridges. The first, the Pont Louis-Philippe, would run from the right bank to the Île Saint-Louis. The second, the Pont Saint-Louis, would connect the Île-Saint Louis to the Île de la Cité. A new street connecting the two bridges was to be built on the Île-Saint Louis.

Pont Louis-Philippe:
Tip of Île Saint-Louis downstream
from the Île de la Cité.

A suspension bridge as a replacement was out of the question: in August 1850, in the city of Angers, the Basse-Chaine suspension bridge over the River Maine collapsed and 226 soldiers fell to their death. It was the deadliest bridge collapse in French history. For the next twenty years there was an official moratorium on suspension bridge construction, and many existing suspension bridges were demolished. The moratorium was finally lifted in May 1870. By that time, however, technological superiority in the construction of iron cable suspension bridges had passed from France to North America.

The new Pont Louis-Philippe was inaugurated in April 1862 and, except for minor modifications in 1996 and 1997, it is the same now as it was then.

The bridge is 100 meters (328 feet) long and has two columns in the river and three arches. Decorative *oeil de boeuf* (bull's eye) windows in the columns light interior galleries that house various water and gas mains equipment.

At the foot of the last arch on the right bank a door can be seen; above it is the number 16. It looks like the entrance to a house. An ex-Legionnaire has called this his home since 1989. He served seven years in the French Foreign Legion and then decided to settle here, in the 50-square meter space that previously served as a storage area for road maintenance equipment. It is a "tolerated squat," a rent-free residence in a bridge, with a beautiful view, in the center of Paris.

Pont Louis-Philippe:
Both Pont Louis-Philippe and Pont Saint-Louis seen from downstream.

PONT SAINT-LOUIS

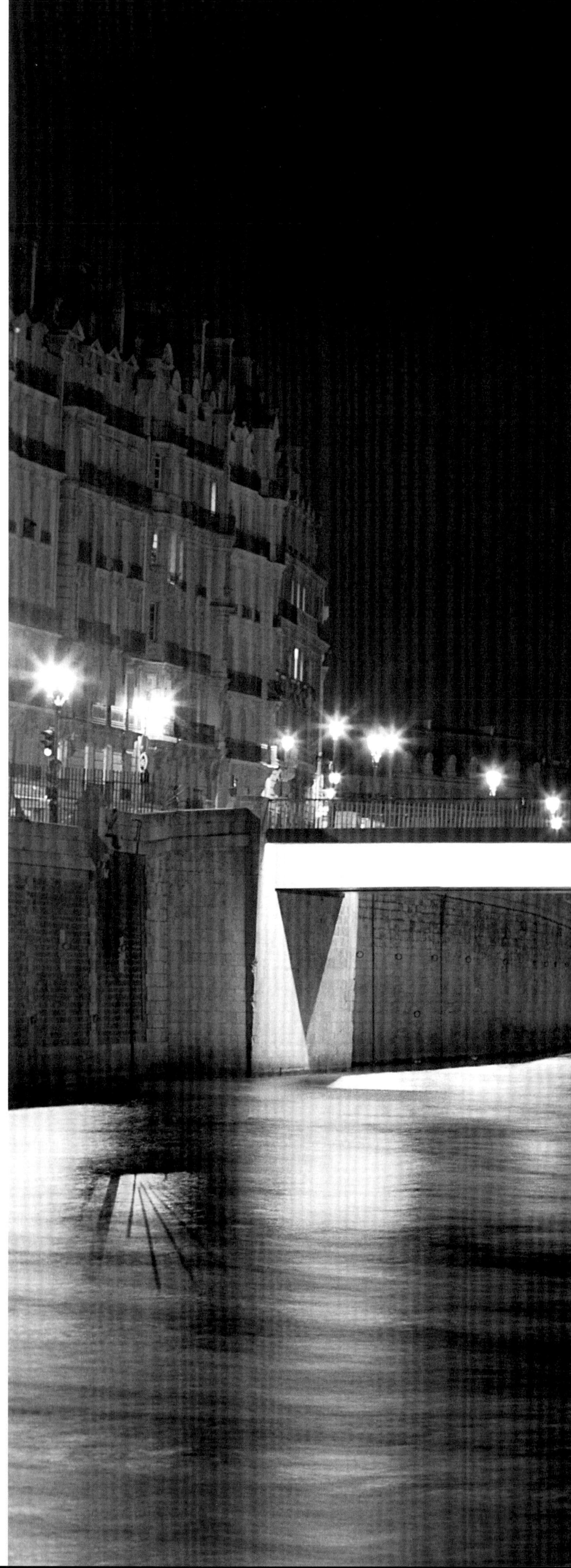

The Pont Saint-Louis, which links the Île de la Cité with the Île Saint-Louis, is the only bridge that connects the two islands.

Built in 1970, it is the most recent of the many bridges that have been built in this location since the beginning of the seventeenth century. The previous bridges had a checkered past: they were plagued by collapses, construction failures, riverboat collisions, and devastating floods.

The Pont de Bois, built in 1630, collapsed only four years later. Weighted down by hundreds of walkers crossing at the same time, the bridge fell. Twenty people lost their lives and another forty were injured. In 1656 it was replaced by a nine-arched structure that had to be abandoned after only a year due to flood damage. Reopened after repairs in 1667, it was again damaged by flooding in 1709 and finally taken down in 1710.

In 1717, the Pont Rouge was built. The name came from the red paint used to preserve the wooden structure. It survived the seventy-three-day flood of 1740, but was subsequently swept away in the flood of 1795.

Pont Saint-Louis:
The only bridge connecting Île
Saint-Louis and Île de la Cité, the
Hôtel de Ville sits in the background.

A new bridge, the first Pont Saint-Louis, was built in 1804. Constructed mainly of oak protected by copper plates and tar, it began to slowly sink soon after being erected. It finally had to be removed in 1811 and was replaced by a temporary simple wooden footbridge.

In 1842 a suspension bridge named the Passerelle de la Cité was built. It is interesting to note that no disaster befell this construction. It was replaced solely because of the fear of suspension bridges engendered by the collapse in 1850 of the Basse-Chaine suspension bridge in Angers, when 226 soldiers fell to their death.

The replacement, built in 1862 and once again named the Pont Saint-Louis, was a single-arch metal bridge. It stood for seventy-seven years. After surviving the infamous flood of 1910, it succumbed on December 22, 1939, when it was struck by a 1,200-ton river barge. The collision caused the rupture of several gas lines and the resulting explosion threw twenty people into the river, three of whom drowned.

On July 7, 1941, during the German occupation, a replacement footbridge was "temporarily" installed. Built like an old railroad trestle, it looked like a horizontal birdcage. It was an eyesore that Parisians complained about incessantly. A permanent bridge was supposed to be built soon thereafter but the project had to wait almost thirty years.

The current bridge, a simple, modern design without embellishments, was inaugurated in 1970. It uses the walls on each side of the river as its supports.

The Pont Saint-Louis of today is not a passerelle although it carries only pedestrian and bicycle traffic. It was built to be wide enough for two lanes of automobile traffic, but concrete bollards prevent vehicles from entering. Although not a beautiful bridge, it is a popular gathering place; strollers regularly find jugglers, mime artists, and musicians performing on the bridge, and amateur groups present skits that delight residents and tourists alike.

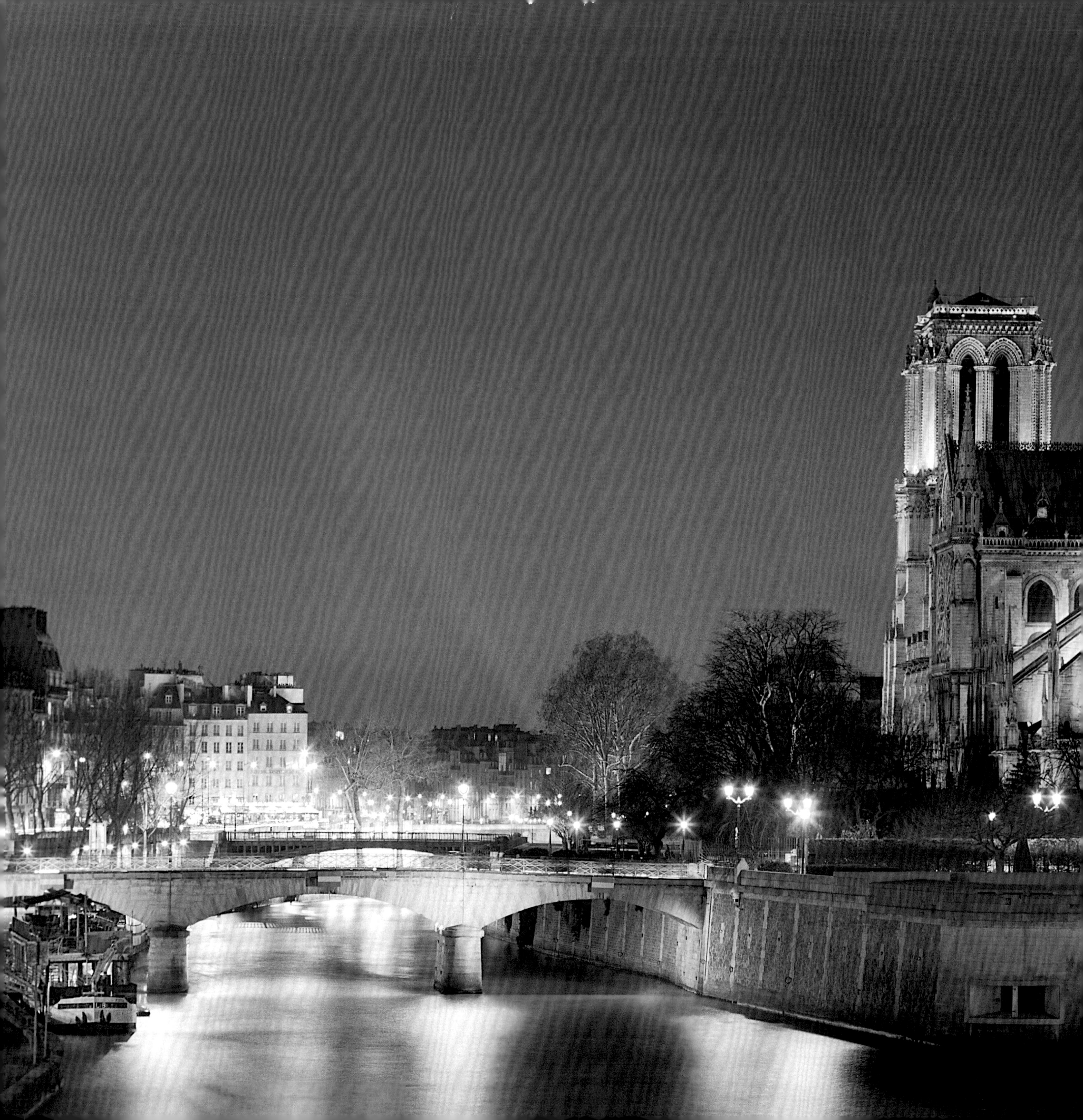

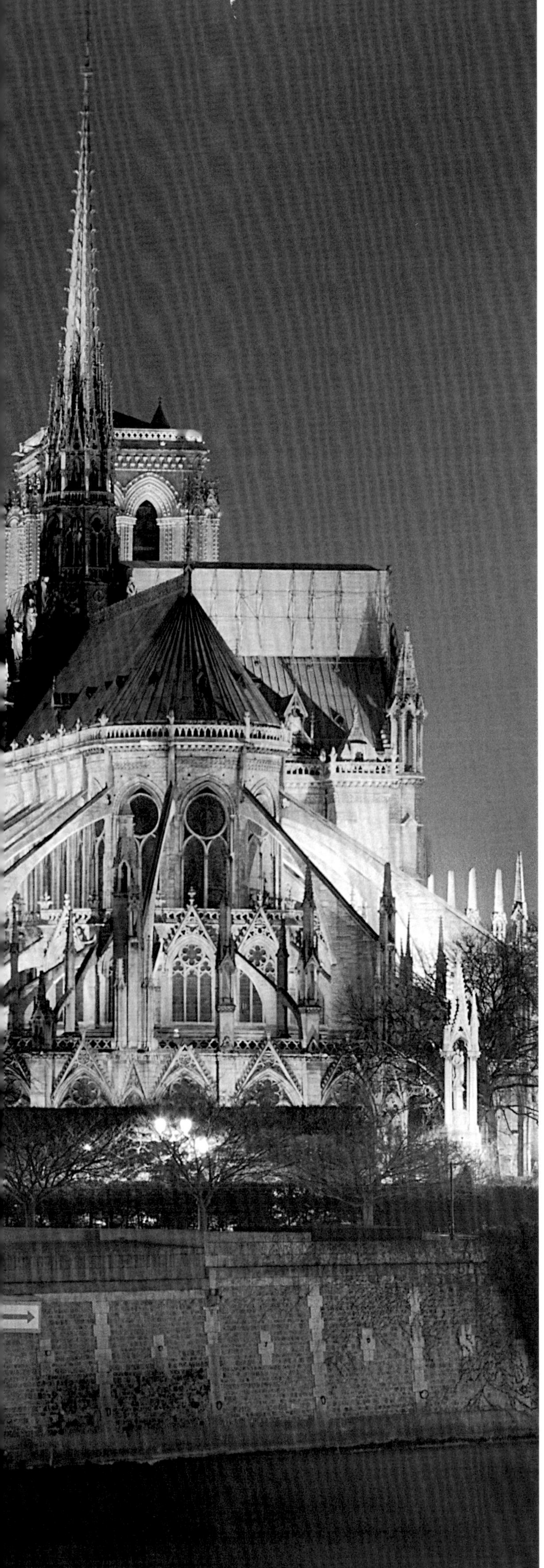

Pont de l'Archevêché

Built in 1828 under the reign of King Charles X, the Pont de l'Archevêché of today has changed very little from its origin.

The name was chosen because the bridge links the left bank to the Cathedral of Notre-Dame on the Île de la Cité, where the Archevêché (Archdiocese) of Paris was located.

The bridge has three masonry arches. The limited clearance of the central arch; the narrowness of the river; and a dangerous, swirling current have made the bridge hazardous to navigation from the outset.

Between 1884 and 1906 twenty-one accidents occurred at the bridge. During the second half of the nineteenth century, sunken boats could be seen gently rocking back and forth.

In September 2008, while passing under the Pont de l'Archevêché, a sightseeing boat with two hundred passengers on board rammed a pleasure boat carrying ten people. The pleasure boat sank. Eight of the passengers were rescued and although they suffered from hypothermia, they survived. A forty-five-year-old man and a six-year-old boy, however, were trapped inside and died.

Pont de l'Archevêché:
Connecting the left bank with the Île de la
Cité and the Square Jean XXIII.

Problems have occurred on the bridge as well as under it. In 1911 two buses collided head-on; one tumbled off the bridge and into the river, killing eleven and wounding a further nine.

Serious discussions for a new bridge took place in 1857, in 1910, and again in 1928, but the only changes undertaken were the widening of the sidewalks and the introduction of one-way traffic.

The Pont de l'Archevêché and the Pont des Arts are bridges overloaded with *cadenas de l'amour*, locks signifying love. Sometime around 2008 (according to the Mayor's office) couples began writing their names on a padlock that they would then lock onto the guardrail fence before flinging the key into the river as a symbol of their undying love. The custom has even generated a new industry: vendors on the bridge selling padlocks.

The Pont de l'Archevêché seems to have the densest proliferation of locks, perhaps because of the French adage that roughly translates as *a lock on the Pont des Arts is your commitment for life and a lock on the Pont de l'Archevêché is your commitment to your lover.*

The sheer number and weight of the padlocks has caused a problem for the City of Paris. It is estimated that more than ten thousand are attached to the Pont de l'Archevêché. From time to time the guardrail fence starts to fail under the weight and has to be replaced, at which point the locks are simply thrown away.

PONT AU DOUBLE

The Pont au Double came into being in the seventeenth century as a result of pressure brought to bear by the administrators of the Hôtel-Dieu on the Île de la Cité. The Hôtel-Dieu, founded by Saint Landry in 651 AD, is the oldest hospital in Paris.

There was no need of a bridge in that location until an annex to the hospital was built on the left bank of the Seine.

The first bridge, a two-story structure built in 1626, was constructed for the use of hospital personnel and patients, who used it as a pleasant walk between the hospital on the Île de la Cité and the annex on the left bank. During that period it was normal for buildings to be erected on the bridges, and Pont au Double was no exception. Hospital rooms took up half the width of the bridge, but by 1835 all of the buildings had been either removed or demolished.

Ordinary pedestrians, who had been obliged to use the very crowded Petit Pont just downstream, were annoyed that they weren't allowed to use the hospital's new bridge. Eventually, after sufficient public pressure, the Pont au Double opened to the public as a toll bridge, although hospital staff and patients were exempt from the charge. The bridge got its name from the toll—*un double denier par homme de pied*—a double denier for a man on foot. The toll was abolished during the French Revolution in 1789.

The original bridge of 1634 was constructed of two semicircular concrete arches. The arches in the water and the insufficient headroom under the bridge were hazards to navigation, and eventually resulted in the demolition of the bridge in 1848. A single arch bridge with a span of 36 meters (118 feet) was built in its place. The masonry replacement was constructed with a product known as cement de Vassy, a new type of cement that had a structural integrity many times greater than cements previously available. It enabled the bridge to be built as a single span resting on each bank of the river with no obstruction in the water.

In March 1879 the municipal council approved the design for a second replacement bridge, to be constructed of metal and steel, and in 1883 the bridge was complete. It is the bridge that exists today. Originally built to accommodate carriages, and later automobiles, its traffic was diverted to the Petit Pont in the 1960s, during redevelopment of the

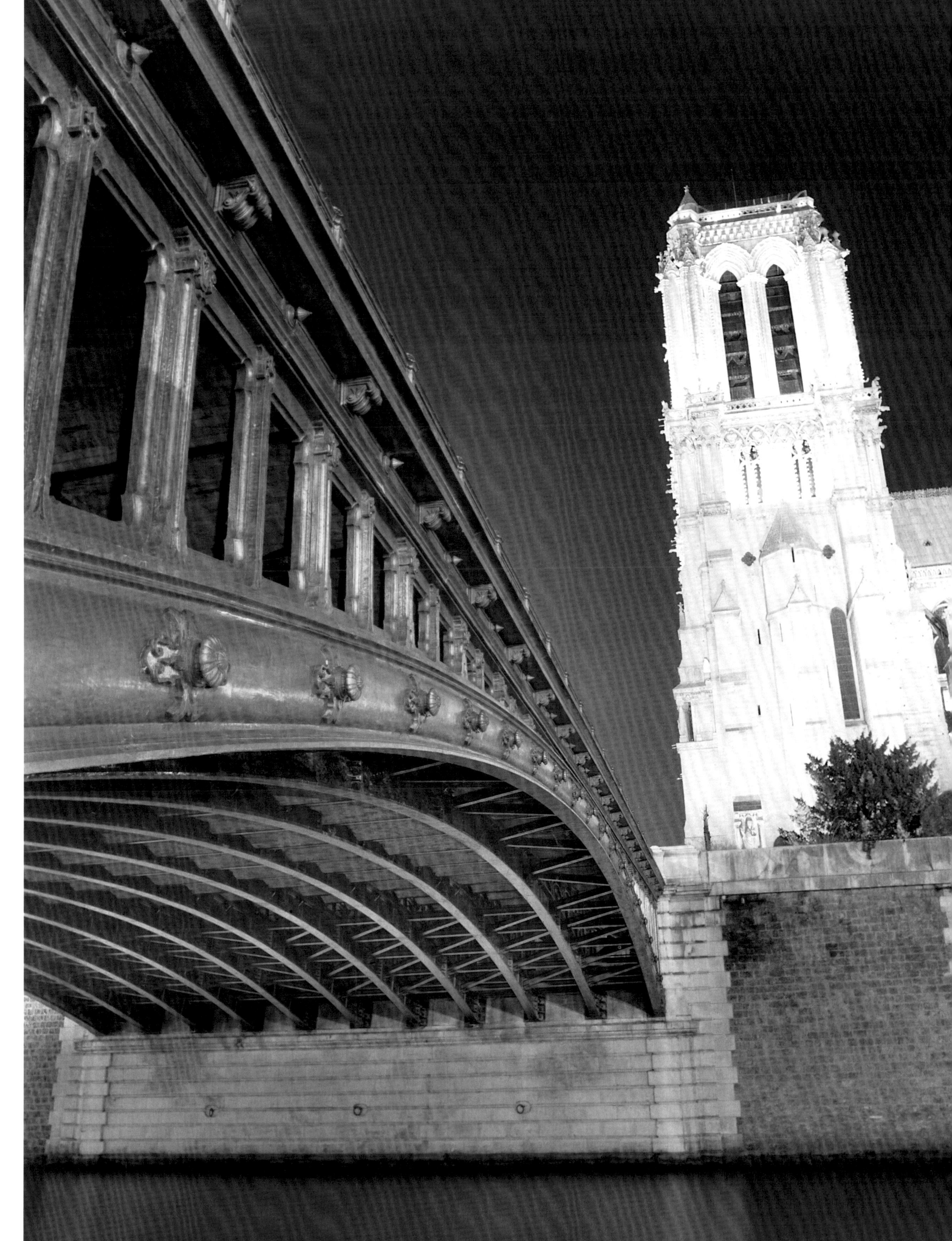

Pont au Double:
Connecting the left bank to
the esplanade of Notre-Dame.

square of Notre-Dame. Retractable bollards and chains placed across the roadway restricted automobile access, and from that time through today only foot traffic can use the bridge. Various restorations have been made, the most recent in 2004 when its greenish-gray color was replaced by its current, stunning copper-red color.

One of the smallest bridges crossing the Seine, the Pont au Double is also one of the most visited bridges of Paris. It leads directly from the left bank Latin Quarter to the esplanade of Notre-Dame on the Île de la Cité, and is visited annually by millions of tourists.

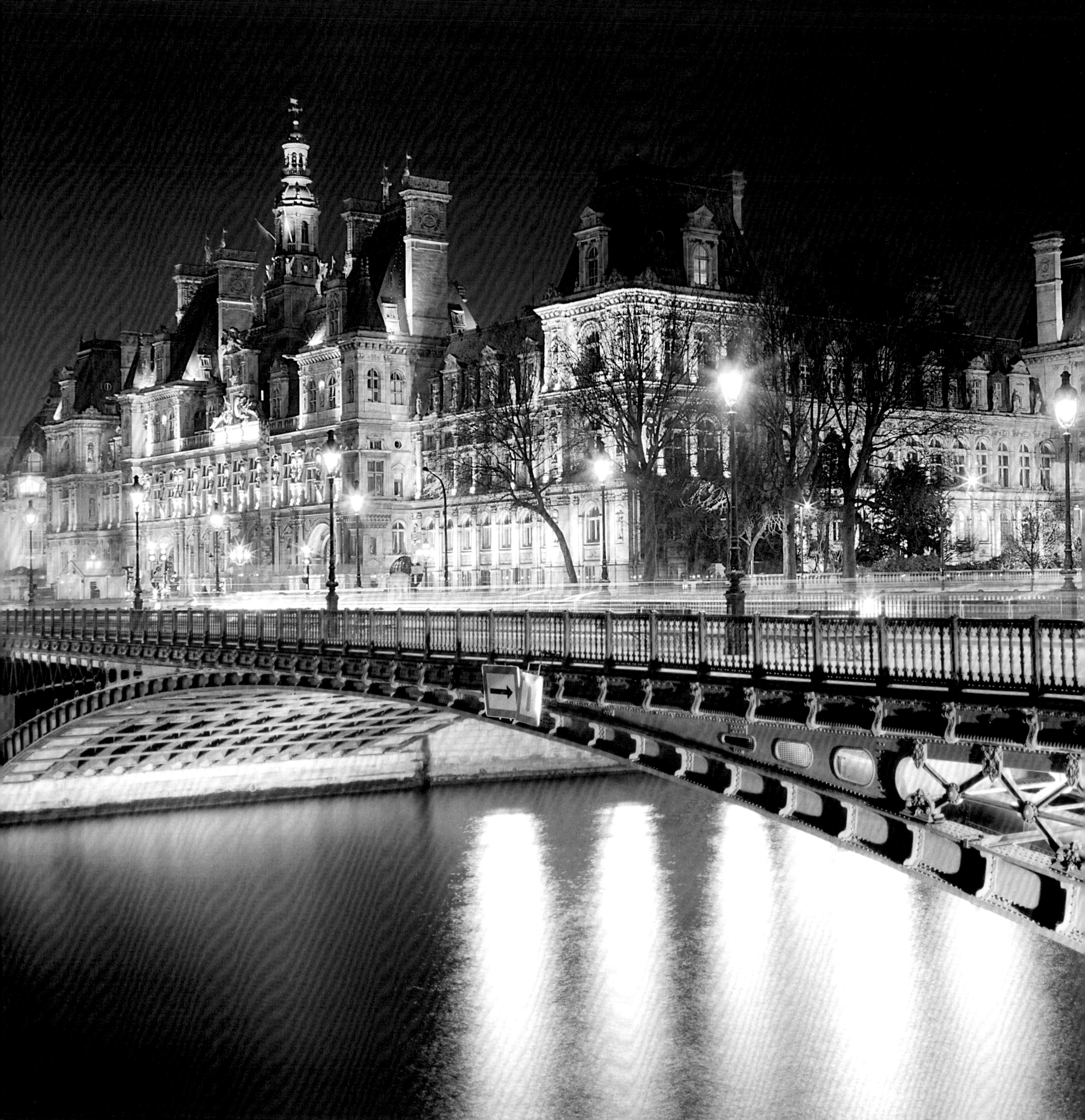

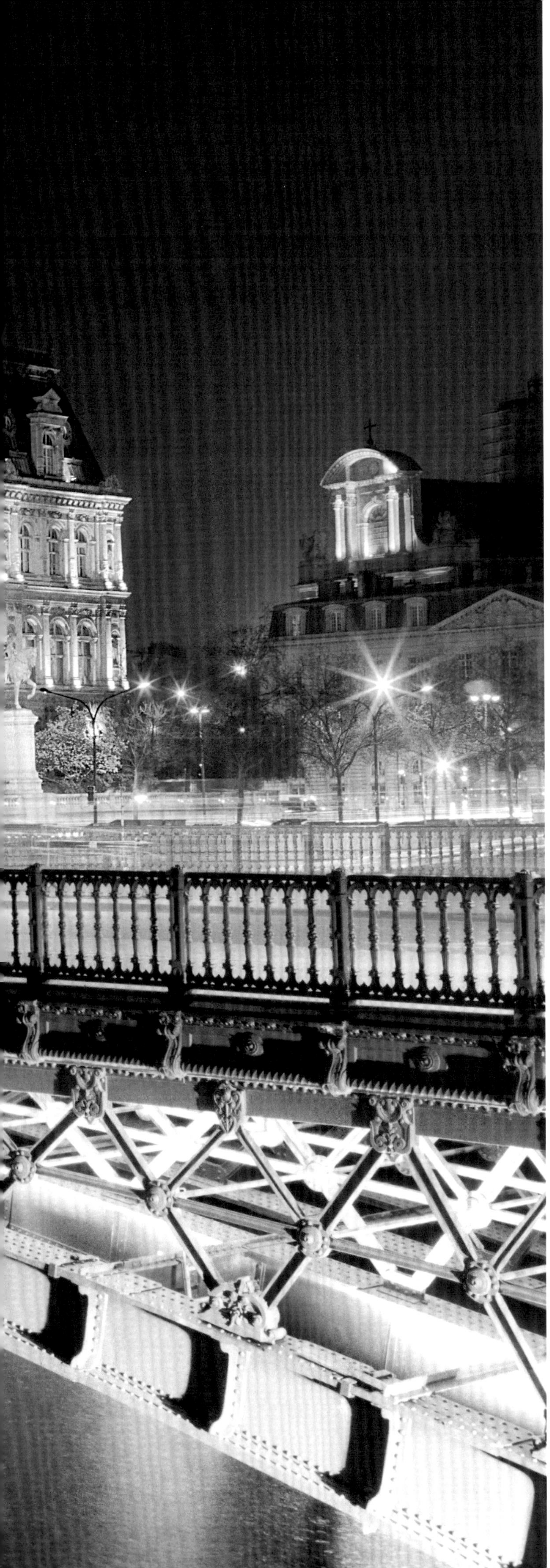

PONT D'ARCOLE

The Pont d'Arcole provides a direct connection between the Île de la Cité and the Hôtel de Ville.

As early as the eighteenth century there was a recognized need for a bridge connecting the Place de Grève (now the Place de l'Hôtel de Ville) and the Île de la Cité. Finally, in 1828, a suspended pedestrian footbridge (passerelle), with a central pier resting in the Seine, was built. It was subsequently demolished in 1854 and replaced by a new bridge for both pedestrians and vehicles, and is still in use today.

Two designs were in competition for the construction of the new bridge. One incorporated three stone arches; the winning design was for a metal bridge, unique at that time. Retired engineer Alphonse Oudry proposed a bridge that consisted of a single arch with a span of 80 meters (262 feet). It would be the first bridge to cross the Seine without support, and made entirely of wrought iron rather than cast iron.

Thirty-four years later, in 1888, the bridge suddenly sagged 8 inches; luckily no one was injured. The following year the wrought iron structure was strengthened and the weight of the deck reduced, which proved successful.

Pont d'Arcole:
Connecting Île de la Cité with the esplanade of the Hôtel de Ville.

In 1967, a tunnel was excavated next to the bridge abutment resting on the right bank in order to allow passage of the new, river-level Georges Pompidou Expressway.

There is some disagreement on where the name of the Pont d'Arcole originated. Some contend it came from Bonaparte's victory at the Battle of Arcole (November 15–17, 1796), where a bold maneuver by his army to outflank the Austrian army cut the Austrian line of retreat and proved to be the key to victory. During the battle, Bonaparte, trying to inspire his men to attack, grabbed a flag and stood in the middle of the Pont d'Arcole, urging his men onward into battle.

This event has been memorialized in many paintings, the most famous of which is titled *Bonaparte au pont d'Arcole* (see below) painted by Antoine-Jean Gros (1771–1835) and which now hangs at the Palace of Versailles.

Others contend the name came from another historic moment: the French Revolution of 1830, also known as *Trois Glorieuses* for the three days of July 27, 28, and 29. Legend has it that as the fighters coming from the Île de la Cité approached the united forces of the Royal Guard and the Swiss Guard at the Place de Grève, they were met by a fusillade that halted their advance. A young man seized the tri-color flag and, charging onto the bridge, planted it on the center pillar before being cut down by army gunfire. His dying words were said to be "*Rappelez-vous que je m'appelle Arcole*" (Remember me, my name is Arcole).

Did this really happen? The 504 who died that day are listed on the Column of July, which stands in the center of Paris's Place de la Bastille. There is no Arcole on that list. In any event, King Charles X was subsequently overthrown and the heretofore-named Pont de la Grève was renamed Pont d'Arcole.

The bridge is also historically notable as it was over the Pont d'Arcole that the first tanks of Général Leclerc's 2nd Armored Division rolled on their way to the Place de l'Hôtel de Ville during the liberation of Paris in August 1944.

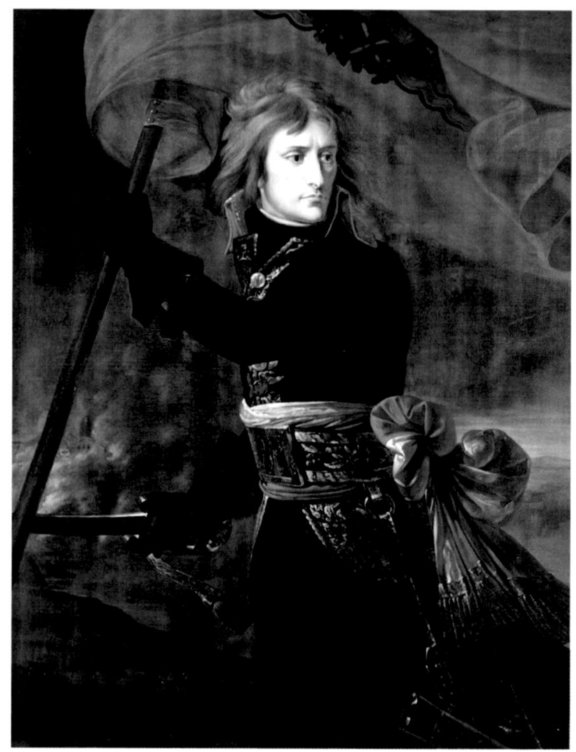

PETIT PONT

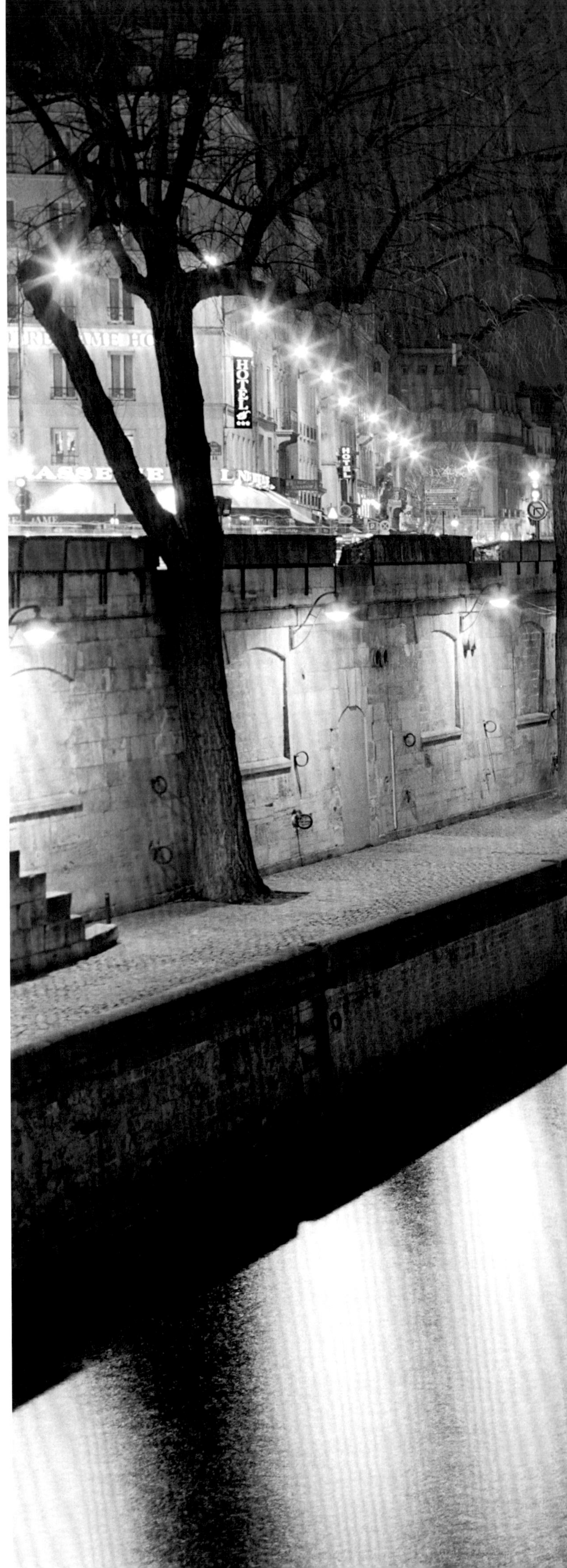

At only 20 meters wide (65 feet) and 32 meters (105 feet) long, the smallest bridge crossing the Seine is appropriately named the Petit Pont. Although the smallest, it has probably the longest history of any of the bridges due to continuing failures and collapses from floods, fires, and ice jams.

The first Petit Pont, which links the Île de la Cité with the left bank, was probably in evidence during the period when the Romans dominated Lutèce (later Paris). Caesar described it in his commentaries on the Gallic wars, and later the Emperor Julien wrote about it in his satirical "Misopogon" written in 363 AD.

One of the bridge's first recorded failures was in 586 AD when it was demolished by fire. The first reported flood that destroyed it was in 885 AD. Subsequently, successive floods carried away the bridge at least thirteen times between 885 and 1658, before it was eventually built of stone in the Middle Ages.

The first structure built with stone piers in 1185 was destroyed in 1196. Throughout the following three centuries, ensuing bridges were

Petit Pont:
View downstream from
Pont au double.

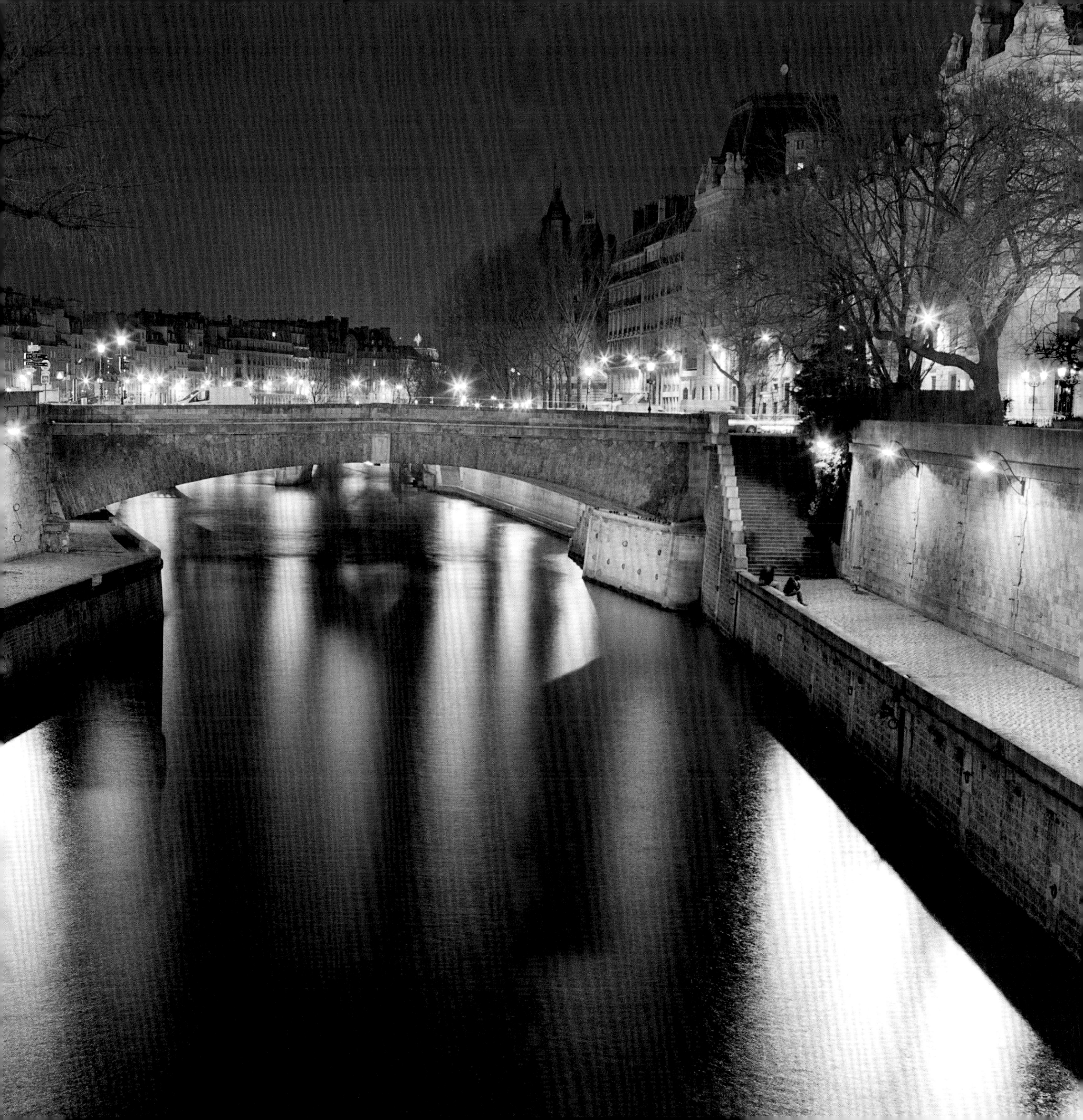

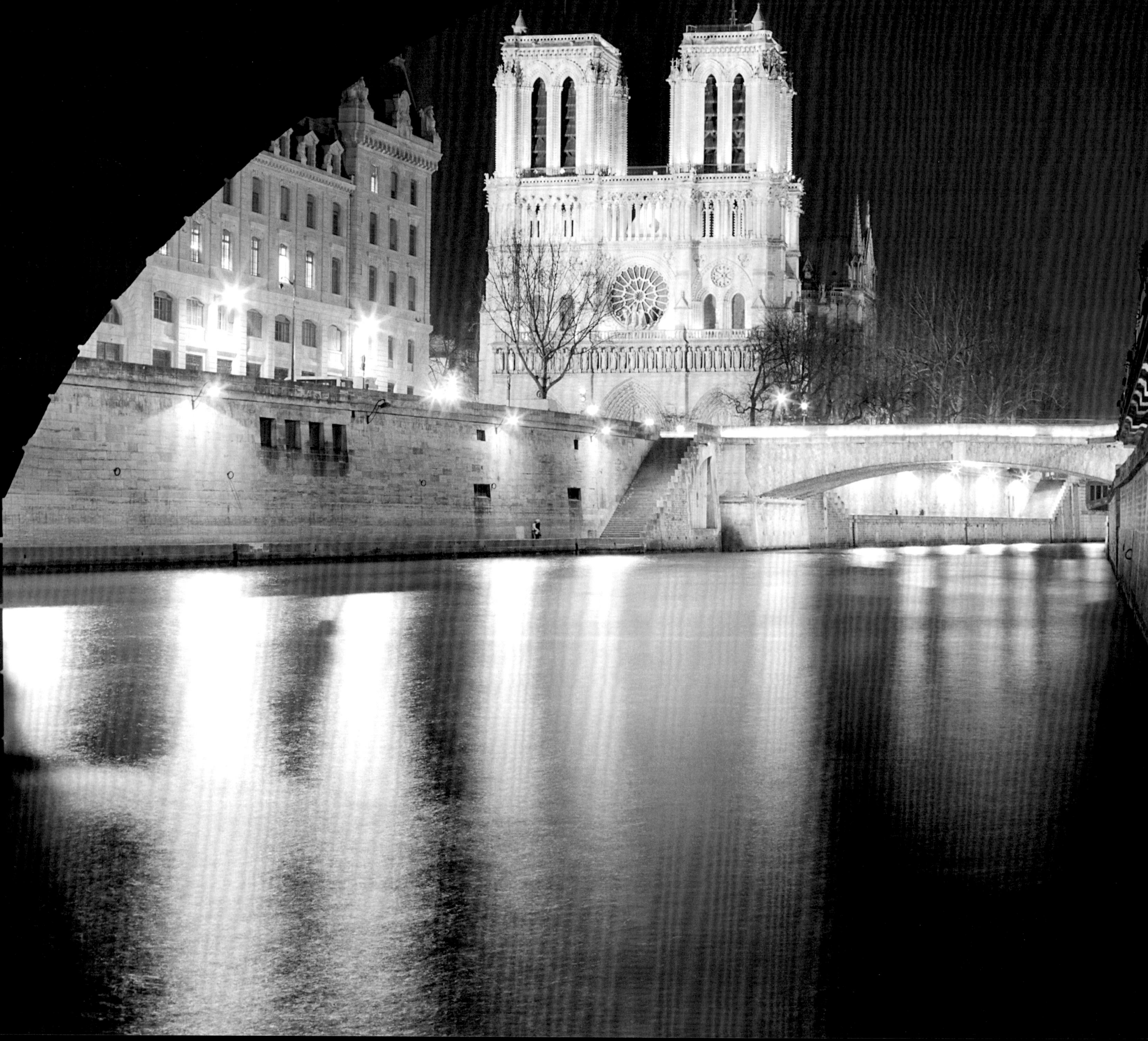

periodically swept away by flooding or by ice. In 1394, under King Charles VI, work started on a three-arch bridge that was completed in 1406. That bridge was swept away by flood waters a few months after completion. It was rebuilt between 1409 and 1416. This bridge managed to survive until the beginning of the eighteenth century. After it suffered from the floods of 1649, 1651, 1658, and 1659 the bridge, then standing in 1718, succumbed to a fate caused by fire and superstition.

As reported by Edmond Jean-François Barbier in his journal of April 27, 1718, fire destroyed the Petit Pont and all twenty-two buildings on it.

A mother had lost her young son to a drowning in the river. She was told that if she placed a lit candle and a piece of bread into a wooden bowl and floated it on the river, it would stop at the location where her son's body could be found. Floating downstream, the candle came to rest against a boat overloaded with hay. The boat, moored at the quai de la Tournelle, caught fire. The other boats moored at the same port were loaded with wood, hay, and coal, and the port itself was loaded with piles of wood. Fearing the fire would spread, the mooring rope was cut; the boat floated into the river and was carried downstream by the current. It became stuck between the wooden supporting piles of the Petit Pont. The bridge and buildings, also made largely of wood, quickly erupted into a spectacular fire that burned for more than eight hours; the embers smoldered for days.

In 1719 the destroyed bridge was replaced with a new Petit Pont. This time the bridge was built of stone, with three arches and two supporting piles in the river and—having learned the lesson—no buildings were erected.

The bridge of 1719 stood for 133 years until it was purposely demolished and replaced. In 1853 a bridge resting on the two opposing river banks replaced it. This bridge had no support in the river and a better overhead clearance height. It remains in service today. ✺

Petit Pont:
View upstream from beneath
Pont Saint-Michele.

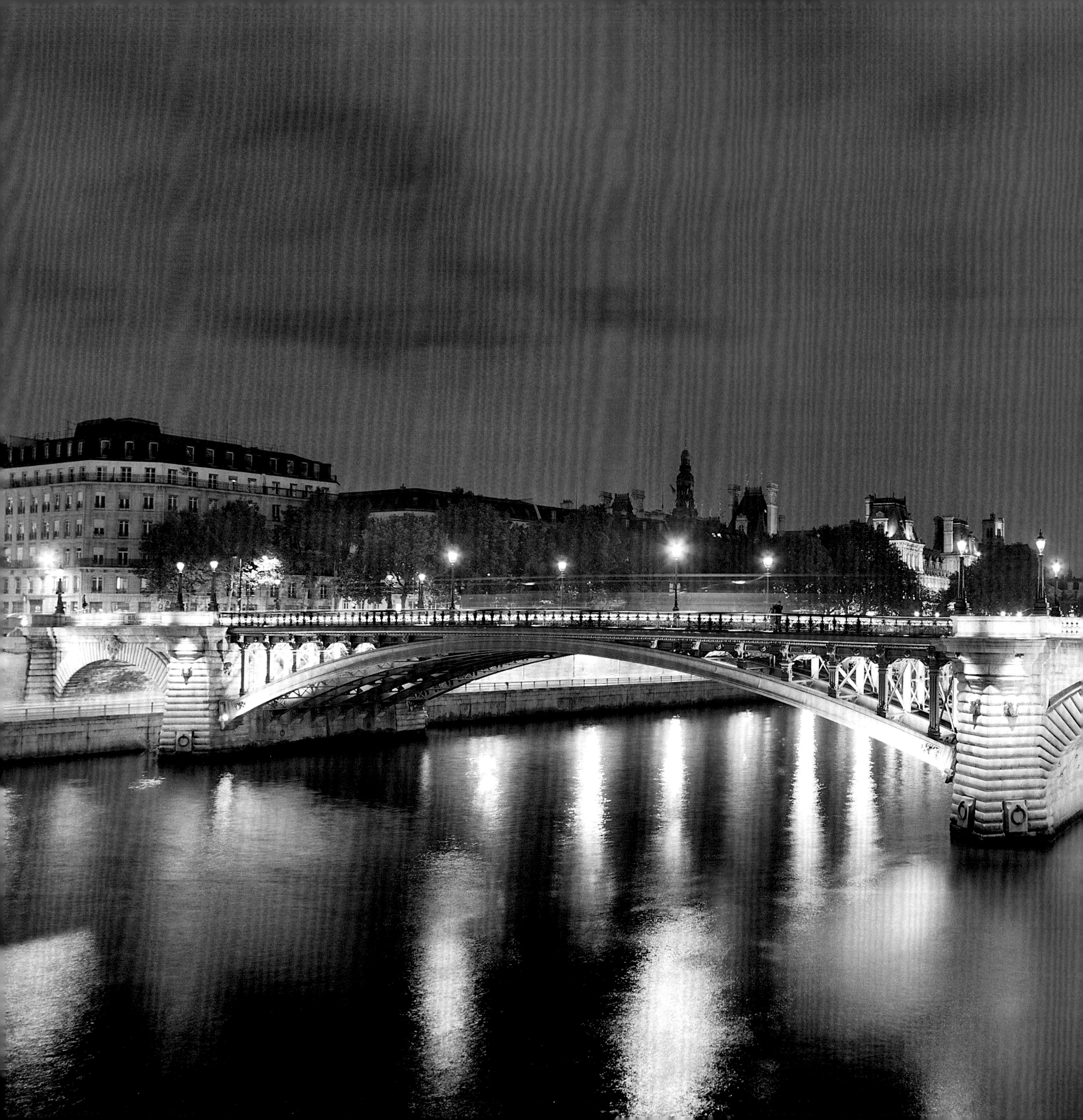

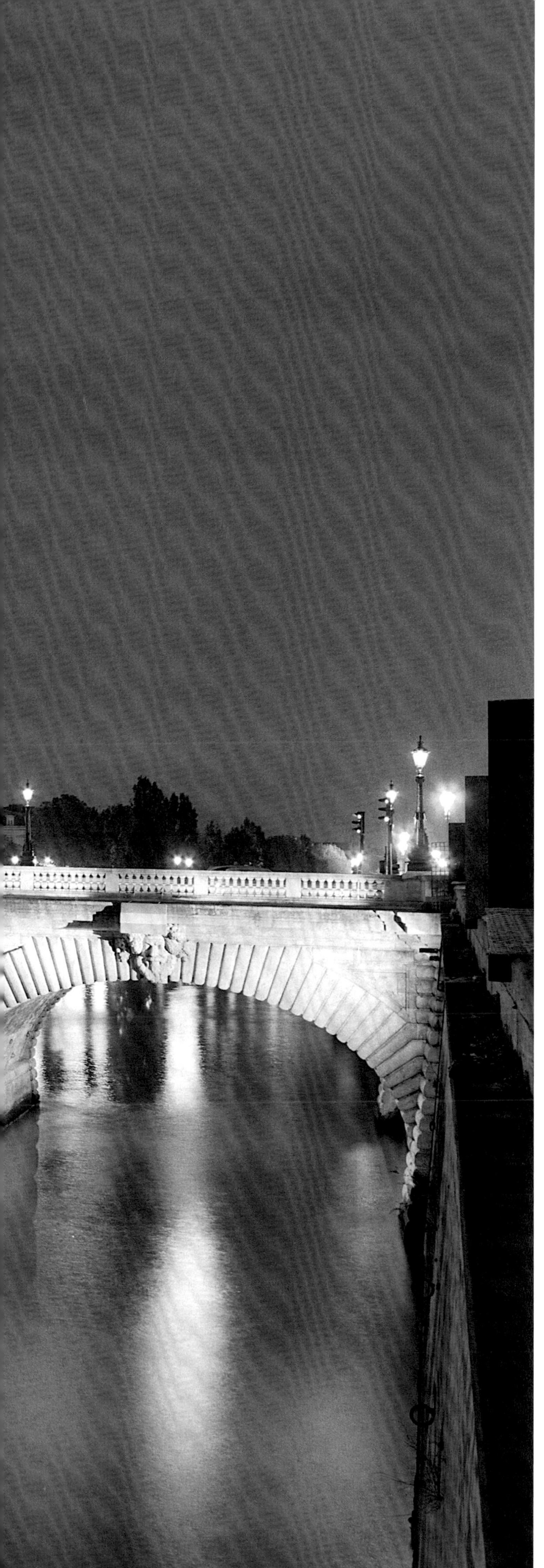

PONT NOTRE-DAME

The oldest Paris bridge—still in its original state—is the Pont Neuf. However, the first Pont Notre-Dame was erected before the birth of Christ and is described in writings by Julius Caesar before his death in 44 BC. In one form or another, the Pont Notre-Dame has existed here for more than two thousand years. It has been variously called the Grand Pont, Pont des Planches-de-Milbray, Pont de la Raison, and, finally, Pont Notre-Dame. It leads to the Petit Pont and creates a straight line connection between the right and the left bank of the Seine, across the Île de la Cité.

Rebuilt at various times, the bridge was swept away by the flood of 1406 and rebuilt again in 1413, this time with sixty houses erected on it. The City of Paris paid for the construction of the new bridge, which was erected under the direction of the municipal officials. The condition of the bridge began to deteriorate, and in 1440 the French Parliament issued an order requiring the bridge to be completely restored. The municipal officials failed to make the needed repairs and during the flood of 1497 it was further damaged.

The following year, a group of master carpenters warned municipal officials that the bridge was in bad shape and in danger of collapsing, but

Pont Notre-Dame:
Looking upstream from Île de la Cité.

the officials paid no attention to the warnings. Then, at dawn on October 15, 1499, one of the master carpenters realized that collapse was imminent. Going immediately to the police, he advised the lieutenant in charge about the danger. The lieutenant went to Parliament where he was given an order to evacuate the bridge. The inhabitants were told to leave as quickly as possible and to take with them what they could.

Shortly before noon, a thunderous roar was heard as the buildings and bridge collapsed. The crash created such a dust cloud that the area around the bridge was *noir comme en pleine nuit* (black as night). In spite of the earlier warning, few were able to save their belongings, and the collapse caused considerable loss of life.

Following the disaster, the city officials were summoned to appear before Parliament, which ordered five of the officials to be imprisoned. Subsequently, on January 5, 1500, they were found guilty of malfeasance and heavily fined. They all died in prison.

In 1512, the construction of a new Pont Notre-Dame was finished, this time with sixty-eight houses built on it. More than 250 years later, in April 1769, an act of Parliament ordered that the houses on the bridge "shall be immediately demolished" and replaced by parapets and sidewalks to create a "suitable width." It wasn't until 1786 that this order was fully executed. After the houses were removed, the bridge stood until its replacement, which had five masonry arches, was built in 1853 during the Second Empire of Napoleon III.

The 1853 bridge became known as the Devil's Bridge because no fewer than thirty-five accidents were recorded there between 1891 and 1910.

Finally, in 1919, to ameliorate traffic problems and facilitate the passage of boats, the three middle arches were torn down and replaced by one large, single, metal arch. Raymond Poincaré, President of the French Republic, inaugurated the new structure that same year, and it has since remained unchanged.

The keystone on each of the arches is a head of Dionysus, carved in stone. On each side the piles are decorated with a ram's head.

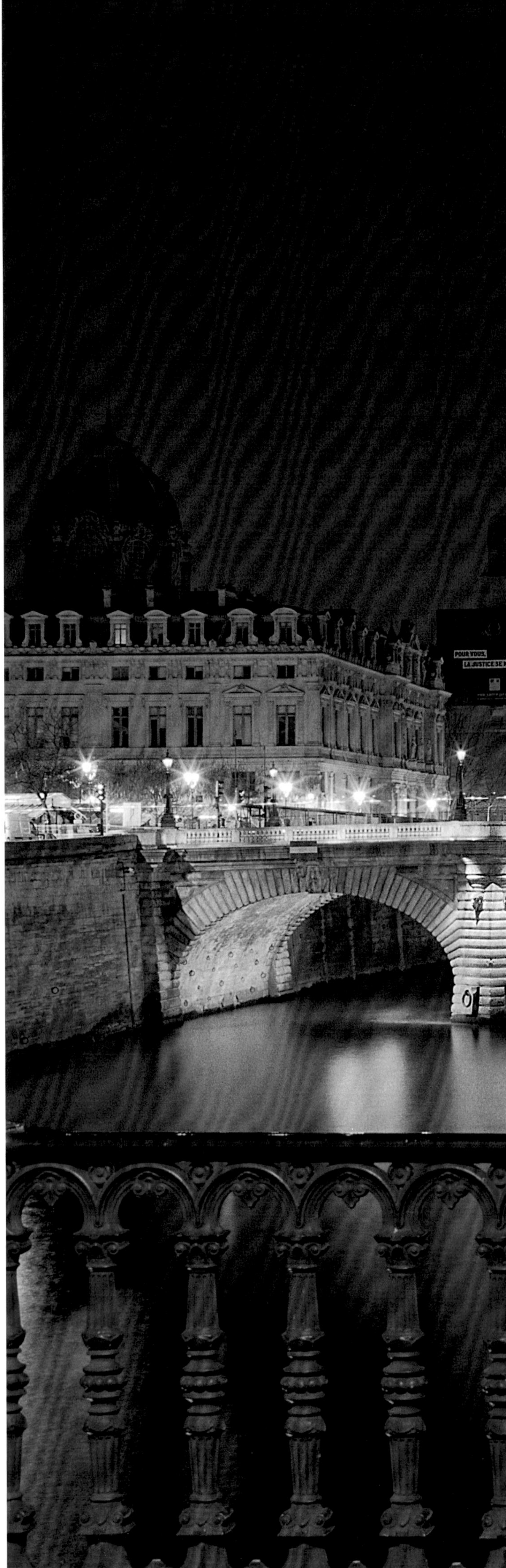

Pont Notre-Dame:
Downstream view from
Pont d'Arcole.

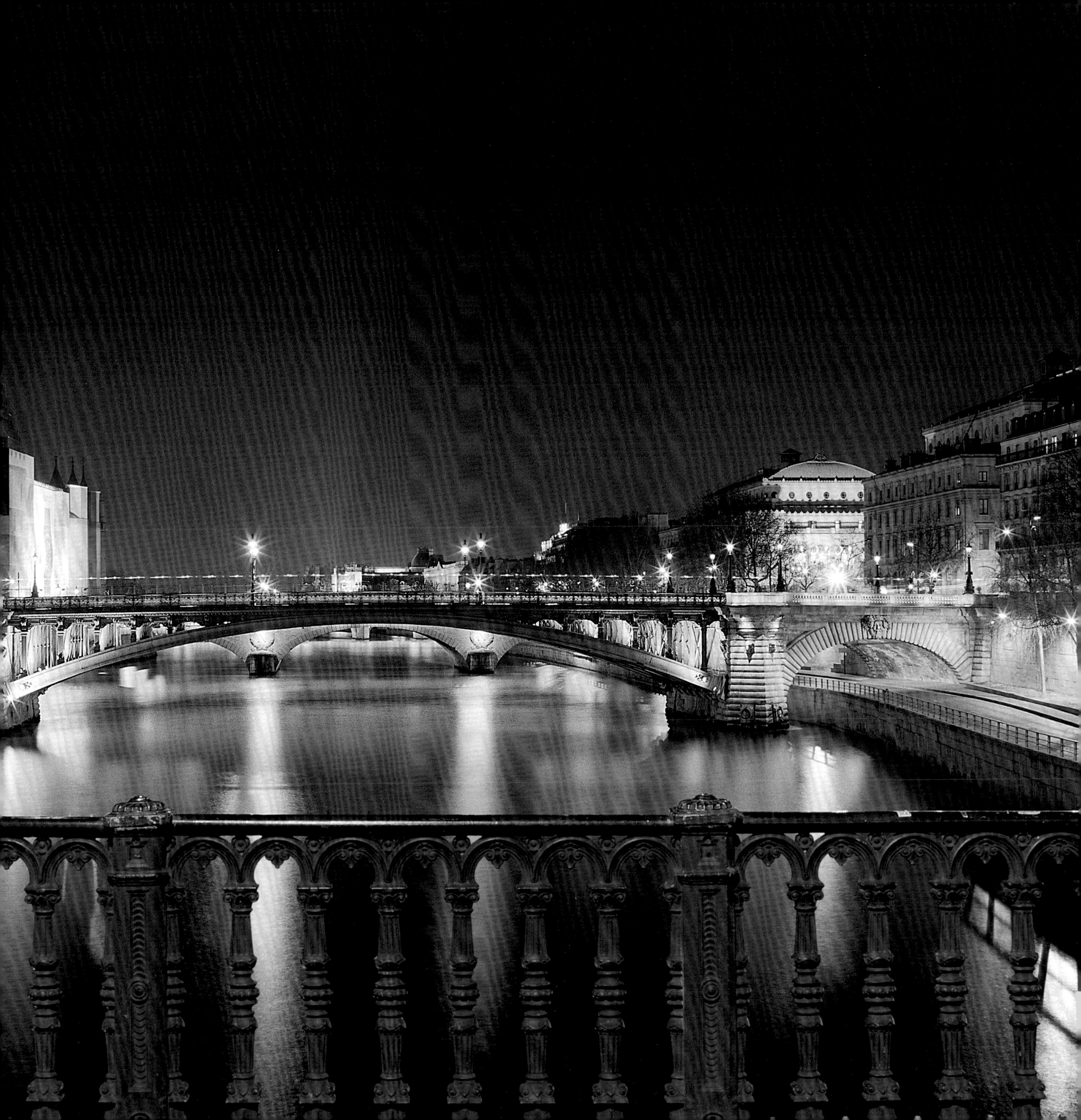

PONT SAINT-MICHEL

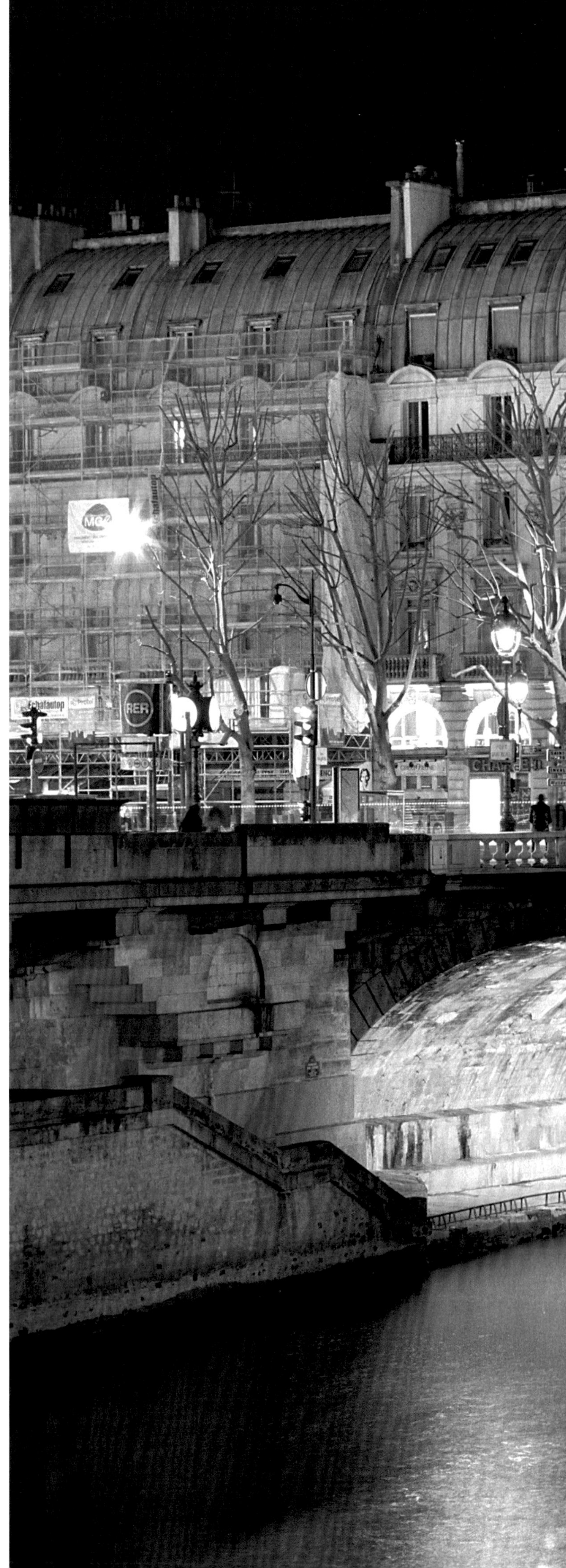

First constructed in 1378, the Pont Saint-Michel has been rebuilt numerous times, the most recent being in 1857 when the existing bridge was constructed.

Like most of the bridges built in the Middle Ages, the first bridge had houses facing each other along both sides. During the severe winter of 1408, ice destroyed the bridge and its houses. A wooden replacement was built in 1416. Eight years later, in 1424, it was named Pont Saint-Michel for the first time due to its close proximity to the Chapel of Saint-Michel. It has kept the name even though the chapel no longer exists.

The 1416 wooden bridge lasted until 1547 when several boats struck it, causing the collapse of the bridge and its seventeen houses. The subsequent bridge, completed in 1549, was again wooden, and had houses along its entire length. First weakened by the floods of 1615, ice floes completely destroyed it in January 1616. The stone replacement, built in 1624 (with thirty-two houses on each side), lasted for 229 years until it was removed in favor of a newer bridge. The Pont Saint-Michel

Pont Saint-Michel:
Napoleon's capital N surrounded by laurel.

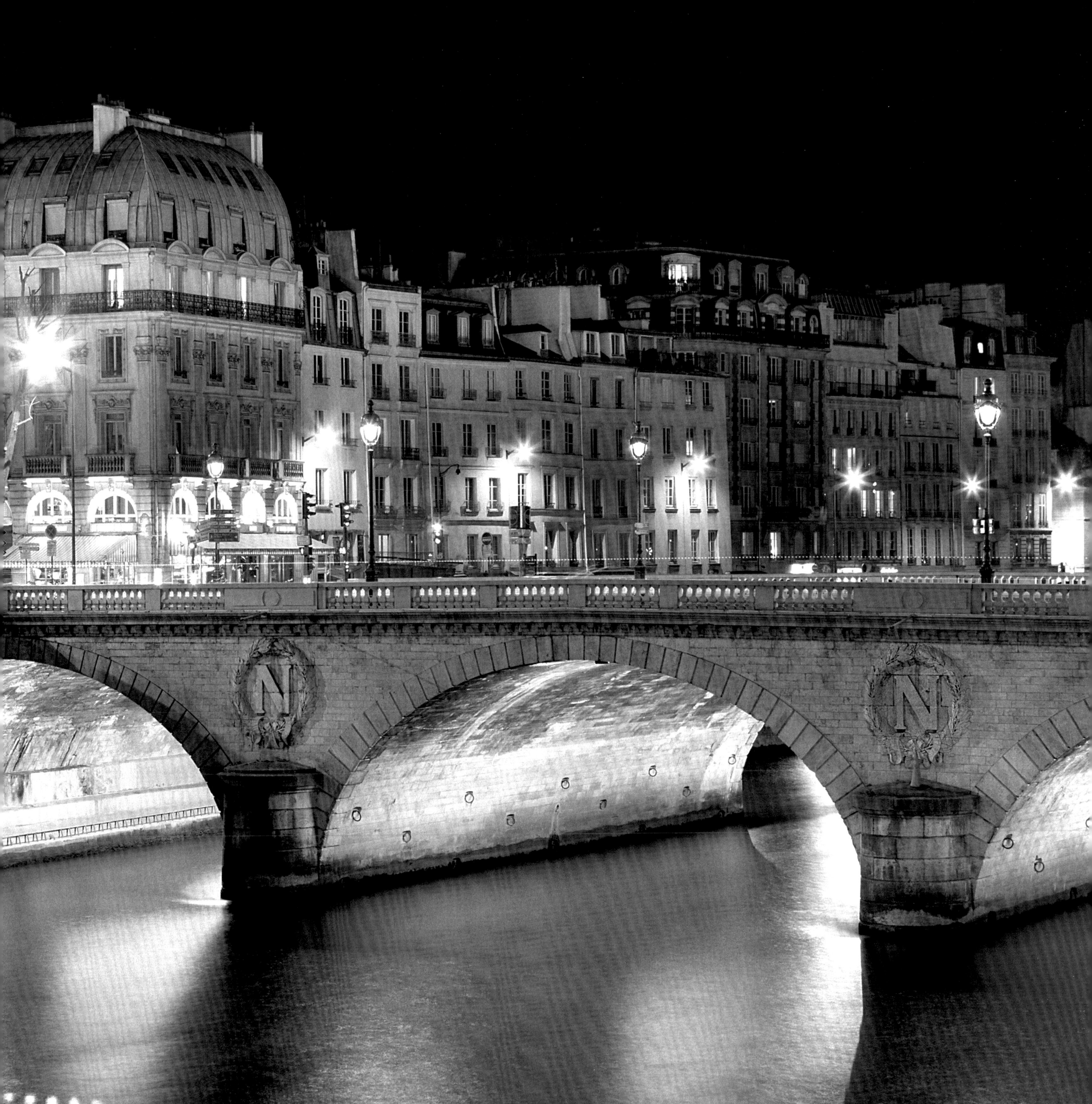

was the last of the Paris bridges to have its houses removed. An order of 1786 required their removal, but compliance took until 1808.

Today's bridge was built during the Second Empire reign of Napoleon III and opened in 1857. The three arches that replaced the previous four-arch design create less of an obstruction and are much safer for river traffic.

During construction, an ancient copper plaque was discovered in the foundations of the old bridge. It had an effigy of King Louis XIII and writing that stated that on September 21, 1617, the King laid the foundation stone for the bridge. The plaque now sits in the Museum of Cluny. The engineers who designed the bridge presented a design that respected the decoration of the previous seventeenth-century bridge. Napoleon III intervened and decided the design would incorporate the emperor's insignia of a capital N surrounded by laurel, which can easily be seen on the bridge today.

It was on, and adjacent to, the Pont Saint-Michel that the Paris Massacre of October 17, 1961, occurred. The events of that day took place during the war in Algeria (1954–1962). It started with a protest march, organized by the Algerian National Liberation Front, with an estimated crowd of 30,000 Algerians. They were protesting in favor of Algerian independence and also against a curfew on Algerians in Paris that the prefect of police, Maurice Papon, had introduced. In 1998, Papon was convicted of crimes against humanity for his participation in the deportation of more than 1,600 Jews to concentration camps during World War II.

The protest was planned to take place in three sectors of the city: Place de l'Étoile, Place de la République, and at the Place Saint-Michel next to the bridge. Police rounded up some of the demonstrators and beat them back into Metro stations, while others were shot or drowned after being thrown into the river from the Pont Saint-Michel. The incidents went virtually unreported at the time.

The day after the events, the police reported two deaths. In the years that followed, the numbers of those who died varied. Historians put the figure at between thirty-two and three hundred. In 1998, the French government acknowledged that the massacre had occurred and that forty people died in the melee. However, the exact number killed by the security forces remains a heavily debated issue. The most famous photograph of the events that day is a shot that shows a white banner draped across the Pont Saint-Michel, on which is written "*Ici on noie les algeriens*" (here we drown the Algerians).

Forty years later, Paris Mayor Bertrand Delanoë placed a plaque on the Pont Saint-Michel commemorating the date. It reads: "*A la mémoire des nombreux Algériens tués lors de la sanglante répression de la manifestation pacifique du 17 octobre 1961*" (In memory of the numerous Algerians killed during the bloody suppression of the peaceful demonstration on 17 October 1961).

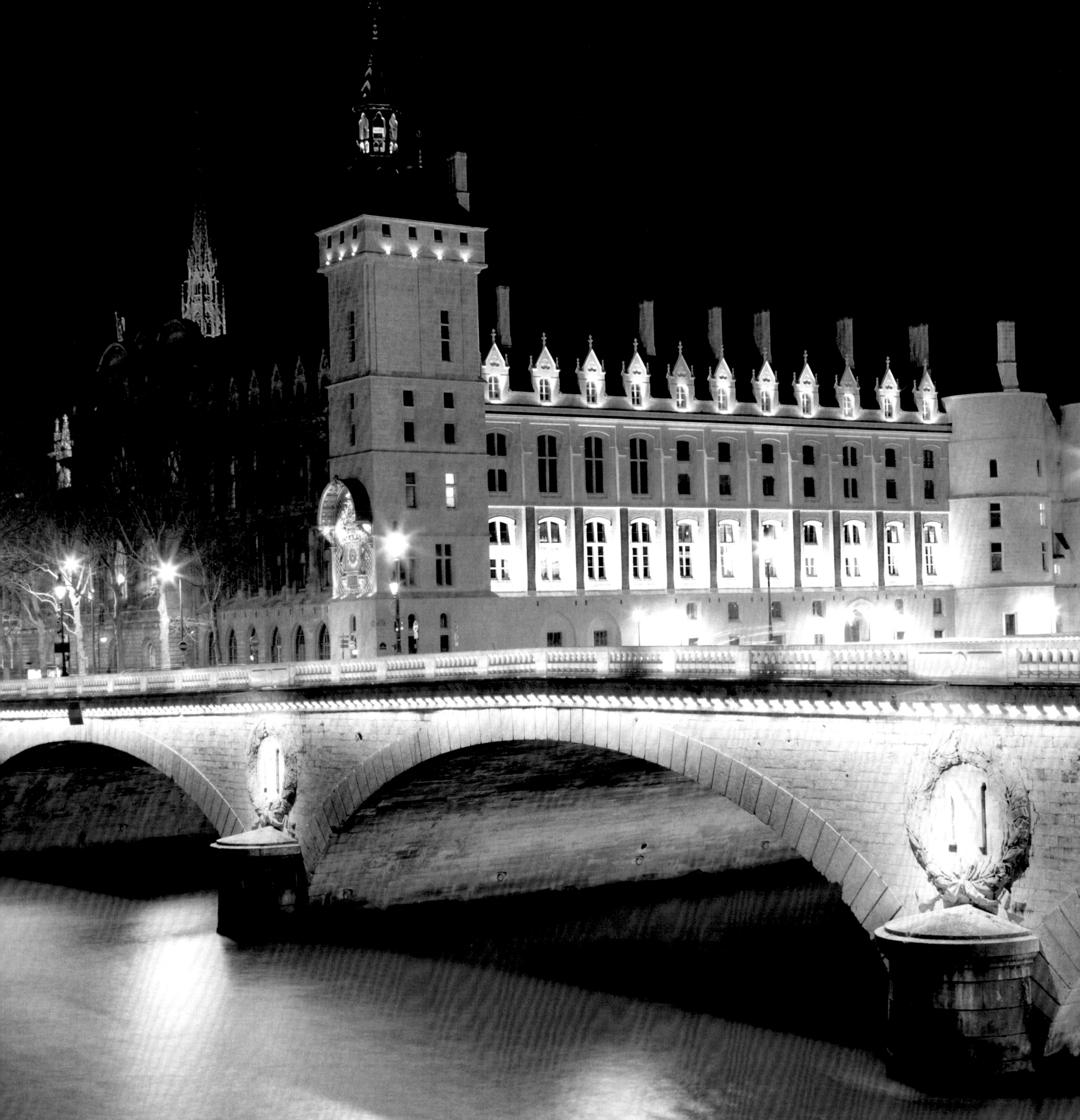

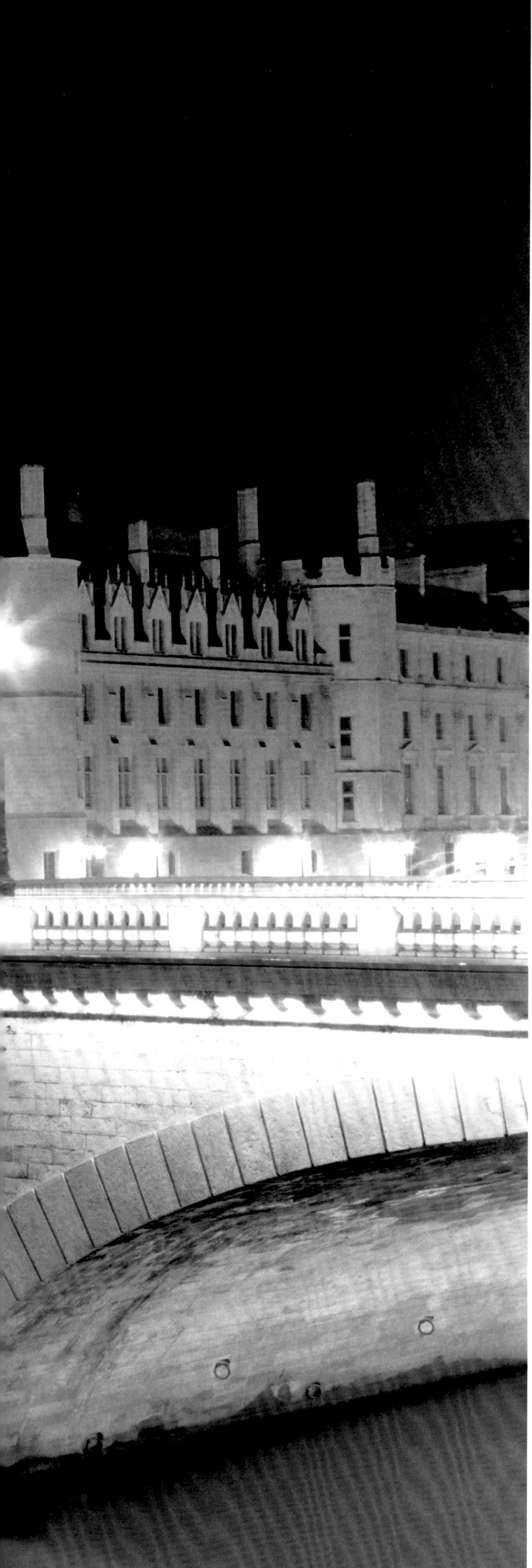

PONT AU CHANGE

For a long time this was the only bridge connecting the Île de la Cité to the right bank of the Seine. There is evidence of a bridge at this location around 50 BC, but the history following that time is somewhat vague until around 872. At that time it was a bridge built of stone and was heavily fortified to serve as a barrier to military invasions by the Normans arriving by river.

The name comes from the time of Louis VII (1137–1180), who in 1141 ordered the moneychangers to locate on the bridge. This allowed visitors entering the city to change money there. Thus the name became Pont au Change. In 1304 Philippe le Bel (1268–1314) authorized gold and silver dealers to join the moneychangers on the bridge.

Later bridges at this location, mostly made of wood, were destroyed by floods, fire, or ice floes in 1196, 1206, 1280, 1296, 1596, 1616, 1621, 1651, 1658, and 1668.

The bridge has also been known as *chemin des rois . . . et de la guillotine* (the pathway of kings . . . and of the guillotine). It was known as such because it was over this bridge that the kings and queens of France would

Pont au Change:
The Conciergerie dominates the view
looking downstream.

pass upon their public entries into the capital. It was also the route taken by royal processions going from Chatelet on the right bank to Notre-Dame on the Île de la Cité. At the other extreme, condemned prisoners, after being judged at the Palace of Justice, were marched across the Pont au Change to their execution on the guillotine.

After crossing the Pont au Change to the Île de la Cité, one is met by the Conciergerie, which is a former royal palace and prison, and part of the larger complex that is the Palace of Justice. During the French Revolution, hundreds of prisoners were taken from the Conciergerie to be executed on the guillotines at various locations around Paris. Marie Antoinette was incarcerated here while awaiting her date with the guillotine. Her cell has been converted into a chapel dedicated to her memory. Much of the building is still in use by the Paris law courts; a small portion is open to the public.

The current Pont au Change is another of the bridges built during the Second Empire reign of Napoleon III, constructed under the aegis of Baron Haussmann. The new bridge, with three elliptical stone arches, was started in 1858 and opened to traffic in August 1860.

The Pont au Change and the Pont Saint-Michel are "sister bridges," having been built to the same conceptual design created by engineers Vaudrey et Lagalisserie. However, the Pont au Change is slightly larger and construction took considerably longer because the foundations of the previous bridge had to be removed before construction was able to begin on the new bridge. Both bridges prominently incorporate the imperial insignia of Napoleon III, which is a capital N surrounded by laurel.

Haussmann's urban development program under Napoleon III included the building of large boulevards; one of the plans included the Pont au Change and the Pont Saint-Michel. The bridges are the keys to the formation of a direct north–south route from the Gare de l'Est train station in the north of the city to the Porte d'Orléans on the far south side of the city. The route begins with a two-mile direct path following the Boulevard de Sebastopol from the Gare de l'Est to the Pont au Change. Then, crossing both the Pont au Change and the Pont Saint-Michel, it follows the Boulevard Saint-Michel on the left bank, heading south for over two more miles, before finally arriving at the Porte d'Orléans. This was a tremendous improvement in traffic flow in the nineteenth century.

The Pont au Change plays a prominent role in the novel and movie titled *Perfume* (2006), starring actor Dustin Hoffman. Of particular interest in the movie is the rendition of the Pont au Change as it may have appeared in the era when shops and houses were erected on the bridge.

The Pont au Change is also featured in Victor Hugo's novel *Les Misérables*, when Police Inspector Javert, who saved the life of Jean Valjean, comes to the Pont au Change and throws himself into the Seine.

PONT NEUF

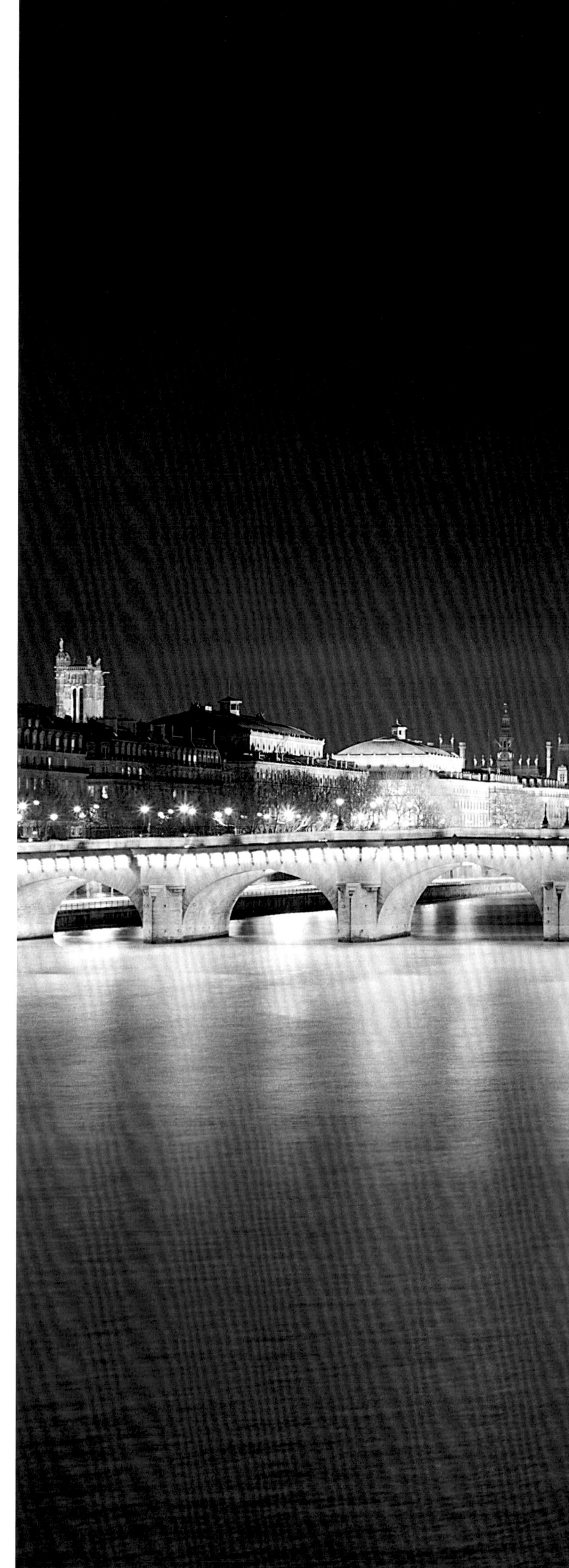

Ironically named the Pont Neuf (New Bridge), this is actually the oldest of the thirty-five bridges that today cross the Seine in Paris. It was first planned in 1556 during the reign of Henry II. His successor, Henry III, laid the cornerstone in 1578. Work was interrupted by his assassination in 1589 and was subsequently restarted and completed in 1607 under the reign of Henry IV. With modifications and improvements the same bridge stands today.

It is located at the downstream tip of the Île de la Cité and was the first bridge to connect the right bank with the left bank by way of the Île de la Cité. It is separated into two parts; the larger section has seven semicircular arches linking the right bank to the Île de la Cité, while the smaller section has five semicircular arches linking the Île de la Cité to the left bank.

Like most of the bridges built at that time, the Pont Neuf was in fact a series of smaller, individual, single-arch bridges connected on top by a common passageway that created one, longer, single bridge. Measuring 238 meters (781 feet) from the right bank to the left bank,

Pont Neuf:
Crossing the Île de la Cité
at Vert Galant.

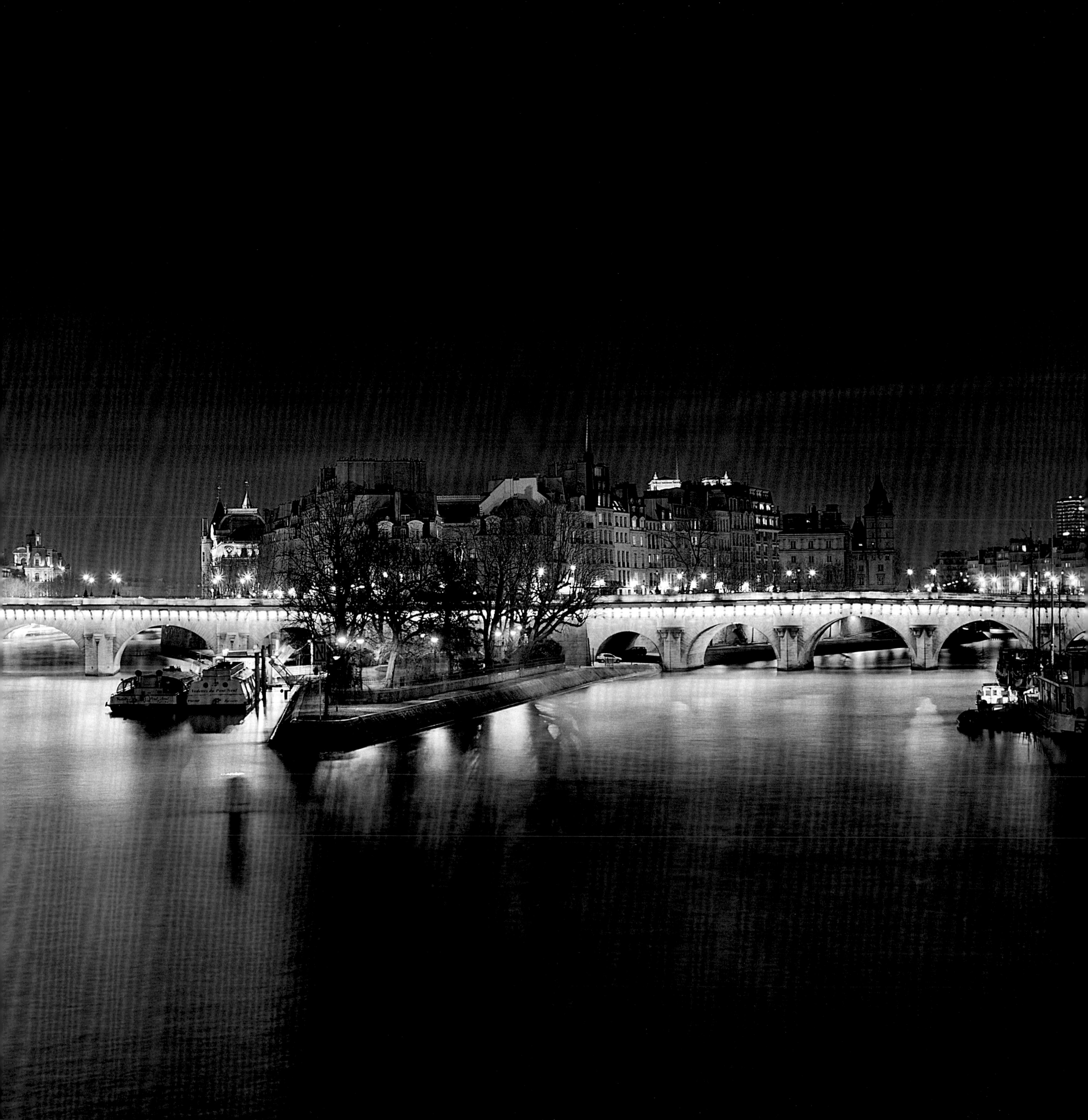

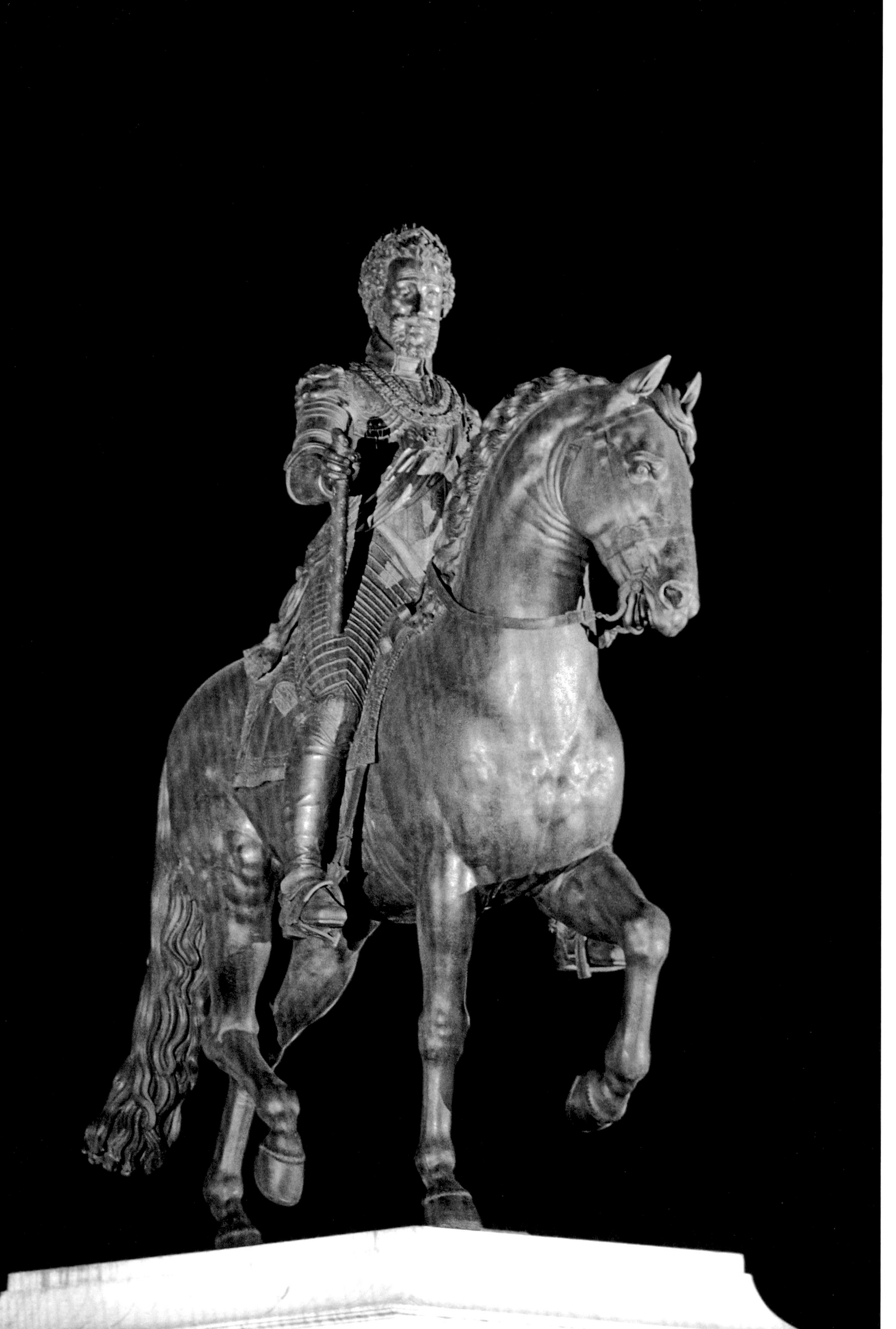

Pont Neuf:
Henri IV.

it is the third-longest of the thirty-five bridges. It was the first bridge to be built without houses. During construction, Henry IV visited the work himself—crossing onto the bridge on wooden planks that were connected to piers. He was warned that some workers had fallen to their deaths from the planks and it is said that he replied, "Ah, but they weren't kings."

The bridge continued in its original state until 1848 when six of the arches on the section toward the right bank were restored. Since then various improvements and modifications have been made. A major restoration was begun in 1994 and completed in 2007, the year of its four hundredth anniversary. The original character of the Pont Neuf remains intact.

The Pont Neuf was classified as a Monument Historique in 1889 and as a World Heritage Site by UNESCO in 1991.

Early on, the Pont Neuf became the most popular spot in the city. It was the center of a permanent fair, a meeting point for all the sophisticated as well as the vulgar pleasures of the capital. At any moment you would find street performers—acrobats, fire-eaters, and musicians—charlatans and quacks, as well as hustlers and pickpockets, not to mention a lively trade in prostitution. Among the many businesses were several famous "tooth pullers." Small business flourished on the bridge, with secondhand booksellers and other itinerant merchants.

Two popular sayings during this epoch epitomized the activity on the Pont Neuf. It was said by the Paris police that if, after watching for three days, they did not see their suspect cross the bridge, he must have left Paris. And the other: "*qu'on était toujours sûr d'y rencontrer à n'importe quelle heure un moine, un cheval blanc et une putain*" (you are always sure to meet, regardless of the hour, a monk, a white horse and a prostitute).

Between 1851 and 1854 all of the boutiques established on the Pont Neuf were finally dismantled and banished.

The central point of the bridge is called Place du Pont Neuf. Here, an imposing, 4.3 meter (14-feet) bronze statue of Henry IV sits astride his horse, his head uncovered, wearing a full suit of armor, and holding the bridle with one hand and a truncheon with the other.

Marie de Médici, the wife of Henry IV, ordered the statue in 1605, before the assassination of the king in 1610. The statue that stands today was erected in 1818 under Louis XVIII, to replace the original destroyed by the revolutionaries in 1792. The new statue was cast from a mold that was made using a surviving cast of the original.

Unique to the Pont Neuf are its mascarons, unique because there are 381 of them. The bridge is decorated with these grotesque, stone masks that are often ferocious in appearance and sometimes disturbing. Their name comes from the architectural term "mascaron"—an ornamental face whose function was to scare away evil spirits. These were widely seen in architecture between the fifteenth and the nineteenth century.

The 381 mascarons are located on both sides of the bridge, upstream and downstream. Each is somewhat larger than an actual human head and each one is different. Some are sticking their tongues out, others are grinning, while still others are making strange, frightening or ridiculously twisted faces. The faces seem to come to life. According to some they are caricatures of Henri IV's mistresses; others liken these devilish faces to the men he cuckolded.

Victims of weather and natural erosion over the centuries, the mascarons have been meticulously reconstructed and replaced from time to time. They were completely restored between 1852 and 1855, and once again during the work performed on the bridge between 1994 and 2007. From the 1855 restoration, the Carnavalet museum has conserved six of the original mascarons dating from the seventeenth century.

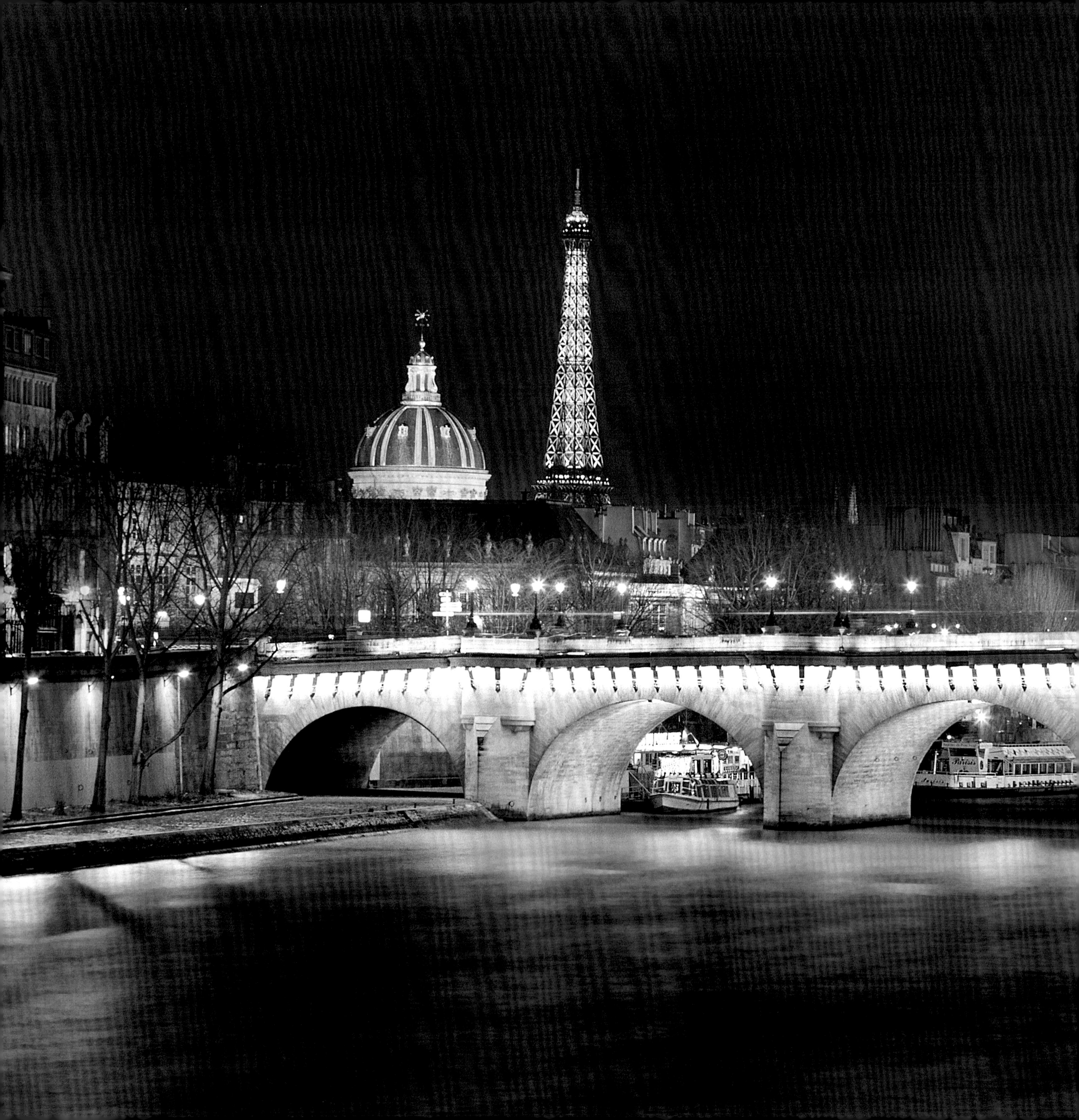

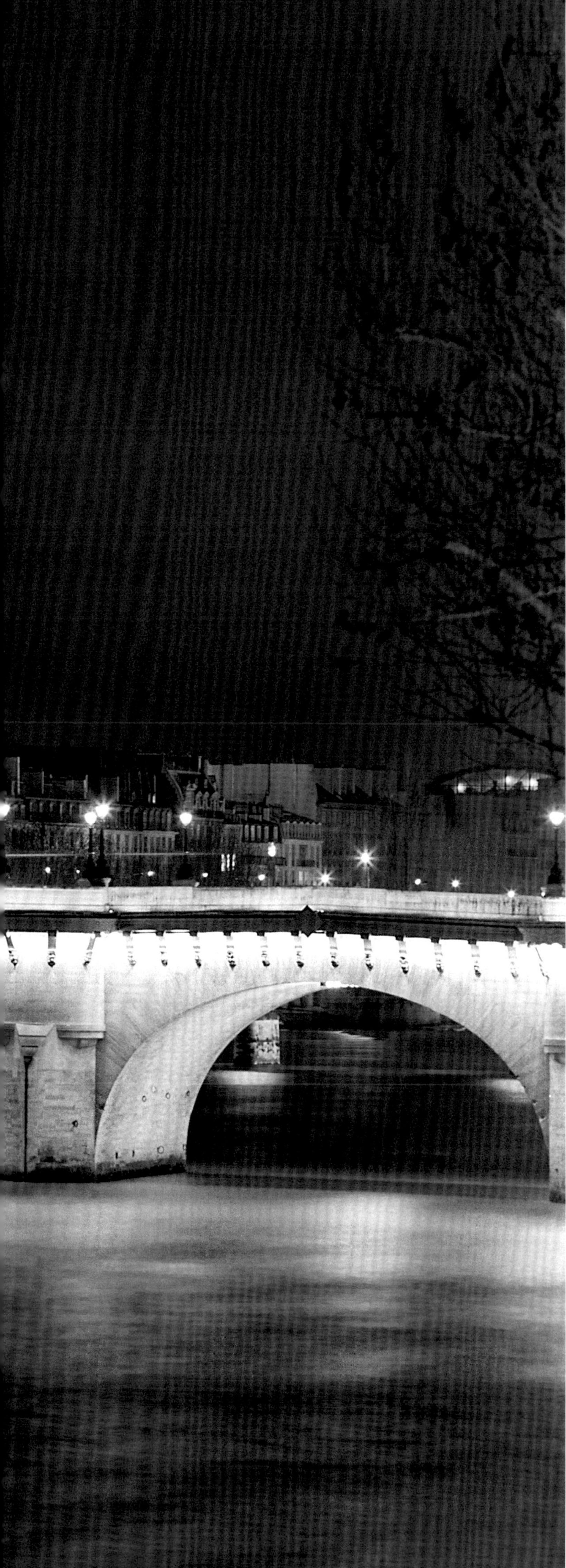

Between 1712 and 1719, a large pump house was built on the bridge and decorated with an image of the Samaritan woman who drew water from the well for Jesus, as described in the Gospel of St. John. It operated from 1609 to 1813 and was known as La Samaritaine. After it was closed, a merchant named Ernest Cognacq erected a boutique on the site and gradually grew his business into what became, in 1869, the department store La Samaritaine.

The famous store, featured in many films, was well known for its rooftop café, which afforded excellent views of the city. The store, which had been operating at a loss since the 1970s, was closed in 2005 because the building did not meet safety codes. La Samaritaine still sits prominently at the right bank terminus of the Pont Neuf.

In 1607 the finished bridge barely grazed the downstream tip of the Île de la Cité. Over the years the Île de la Cité has been extended and a park, the Vert Galant, has been developed. Steps behind the statue of Henry IV lead down to it. The park is located 7 meters (23 feet) below the level of the bridge and is named in honor of Henry IV who was known by this moniker "because of his numerous mistresses in spite of his advanced age."

Although quite small (less than half an acre or one sixth of a hectare), the park, or square, is popular with picnickers, lovers, families, and those who just want to relax and sit on a bench. It offers a beautiful view of the river downstream, the boats, the Pont des Arts, and the buildings on both sides of the river. The square is planted with a mixture of chestnut, yew, black walnut, maple, weeping willow, catalpa, locust, and ginkgo biloba trees.

Famous French photographers Robert Doisneau and Eugène Atget are known for photographing here, and a well-known photograph taken by Doisneau is aptly named *Square du Vert-Galant*.

On living in Paris, Benjamin Franklin famously wrote that one cannot understand "the Parisian character except in crossing the Pont Neuf."

Pont Neuf:
View from right bank with
the Institut de France.

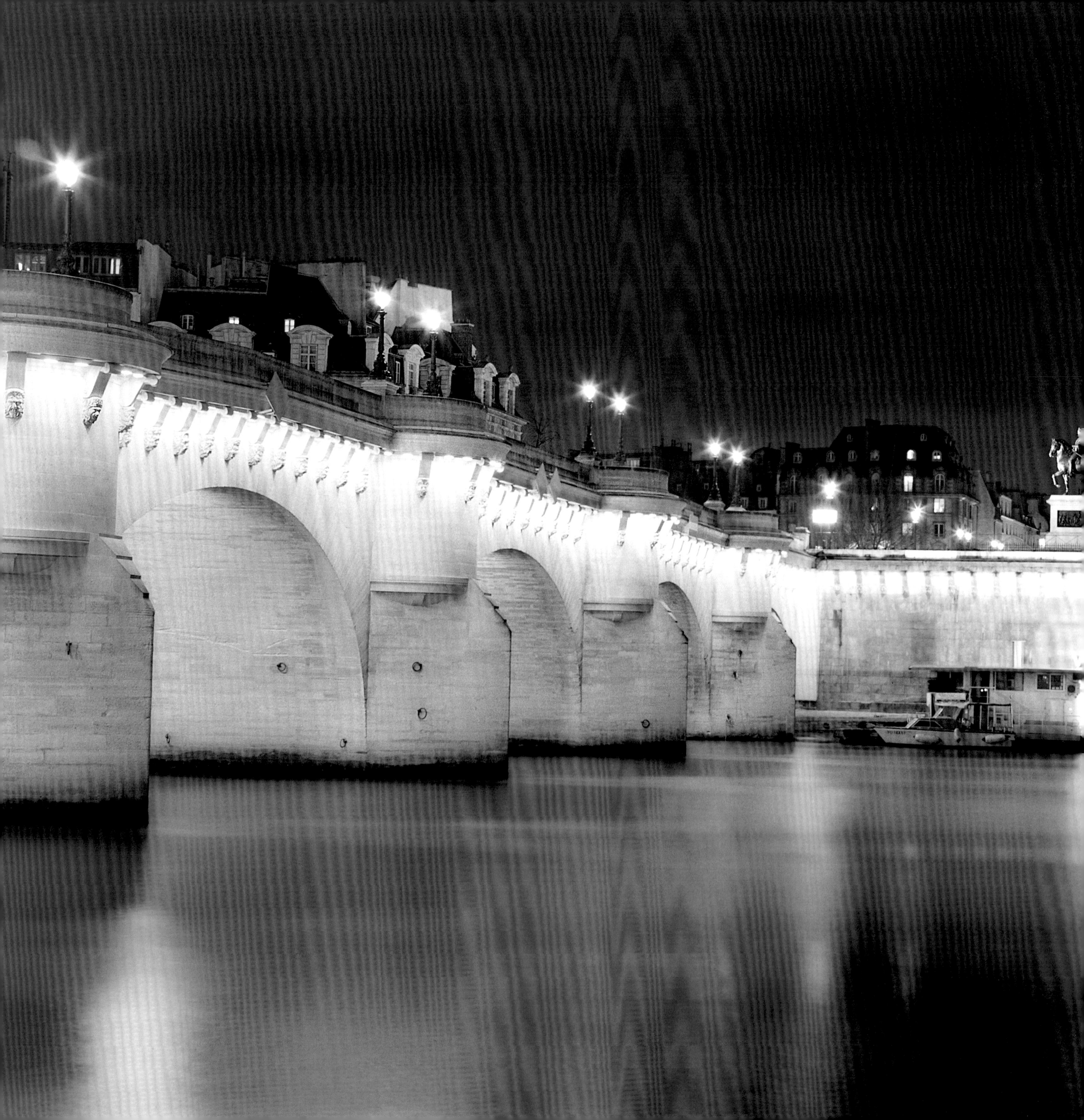

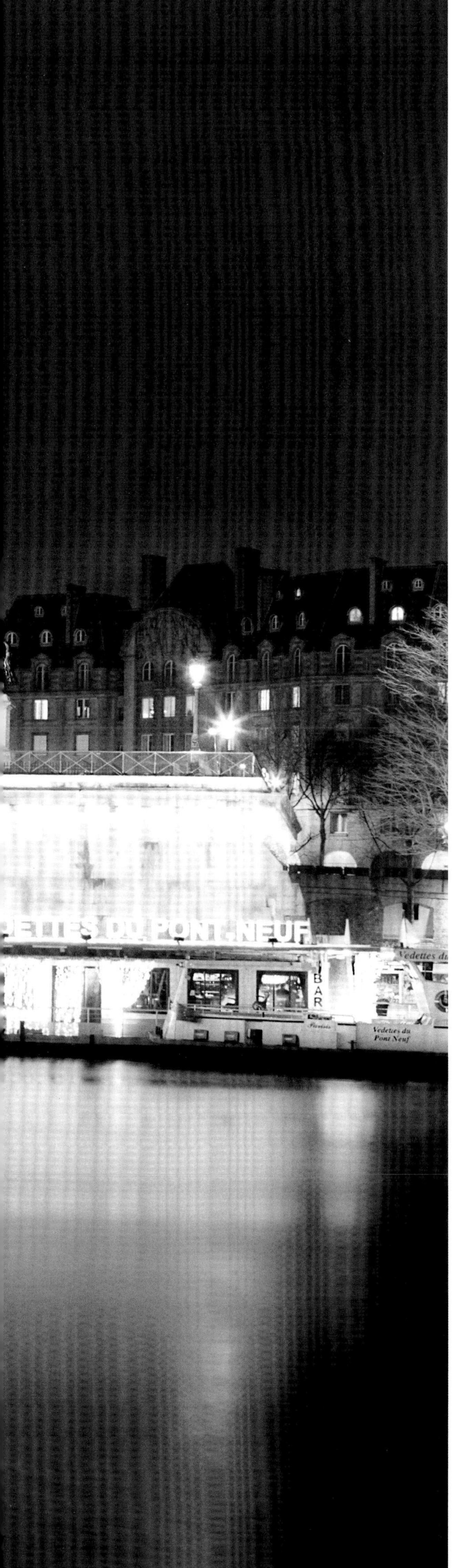

Pont Neuf:
View toward Île de la Cité and Henri IV,
above the Vedettes du Pont Neuf.

Pont Neuf:
View from left bank with La Samaritaine.

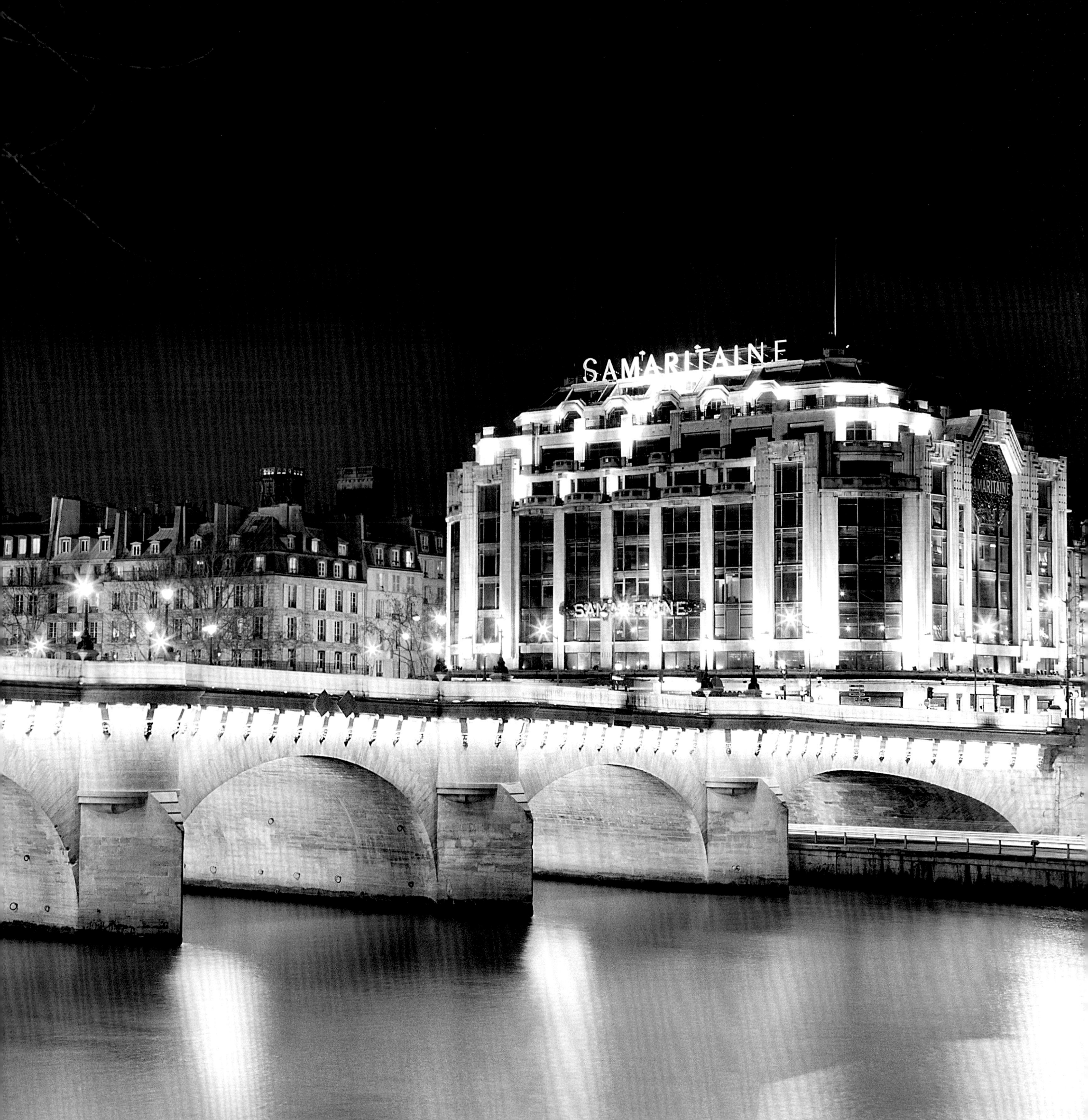

SAMARITAINE
SAMARITAINE
SAMARITAINE

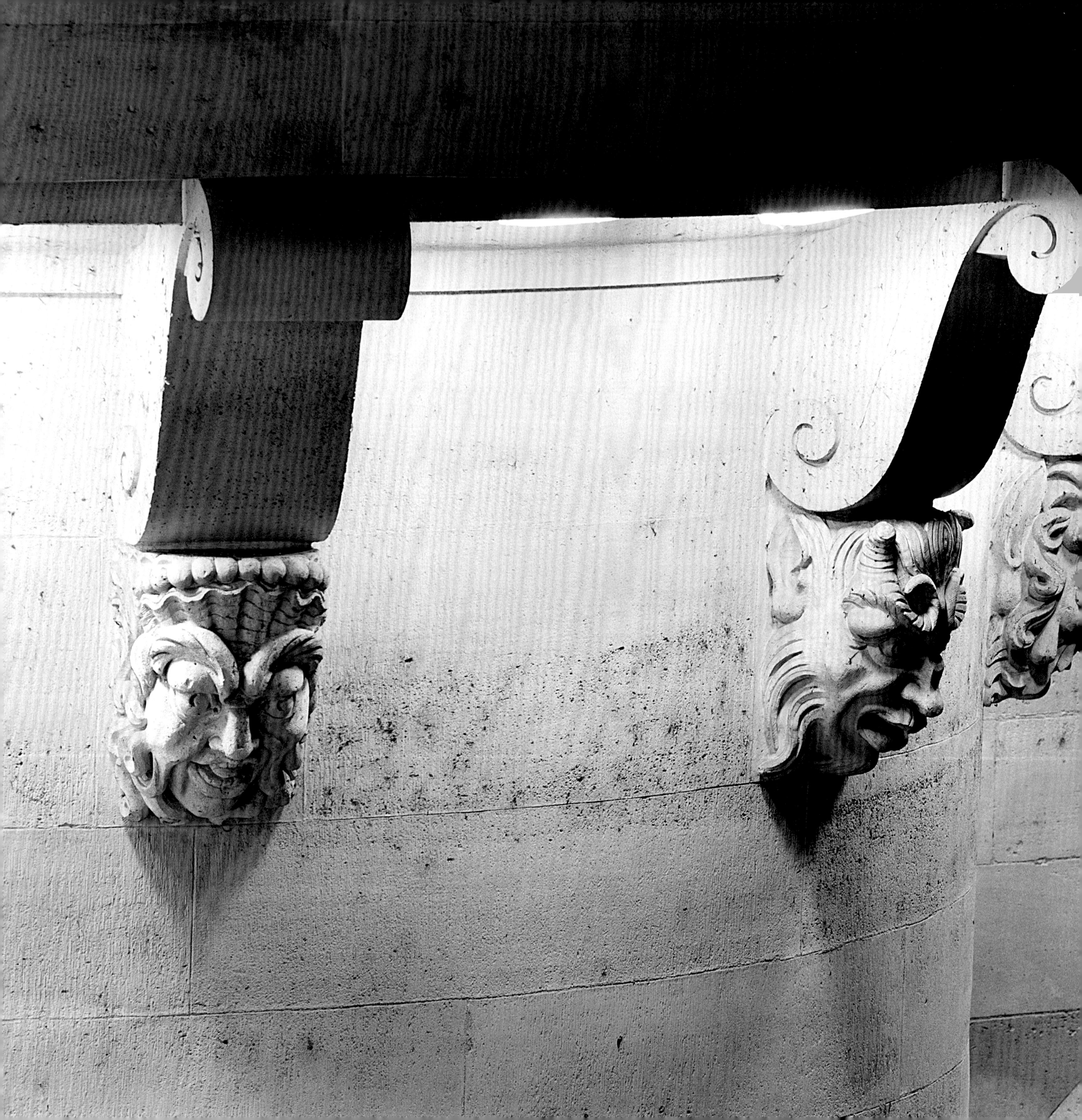

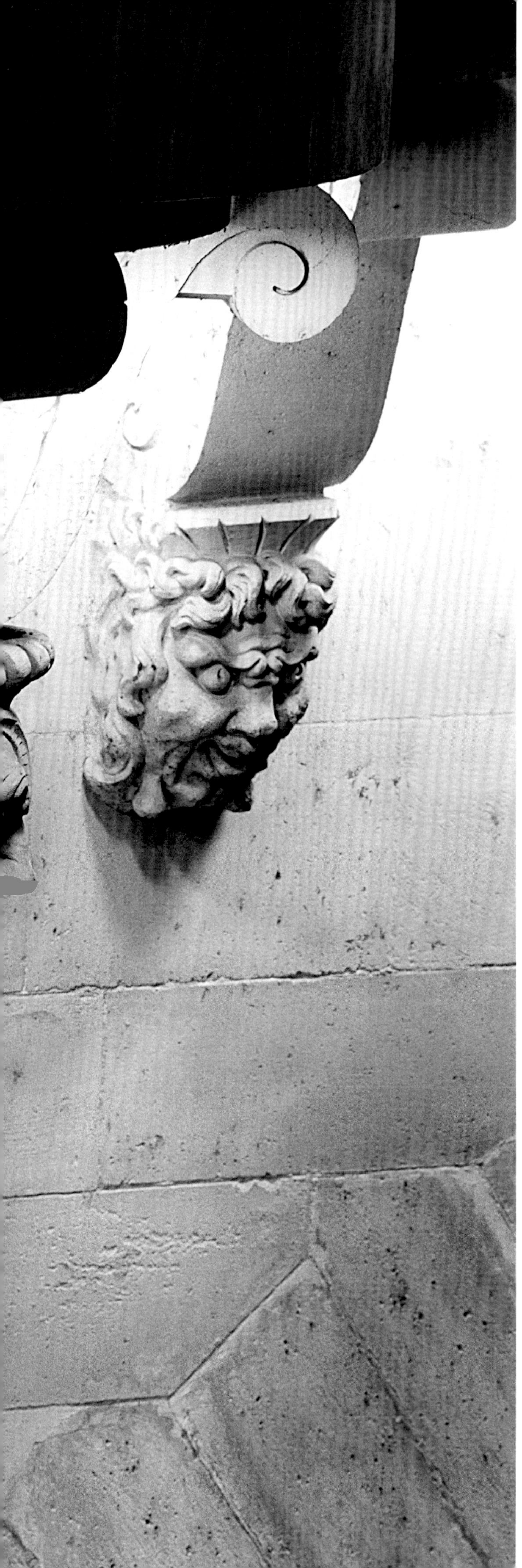

Pont Neuf:
Group of Mascerons.

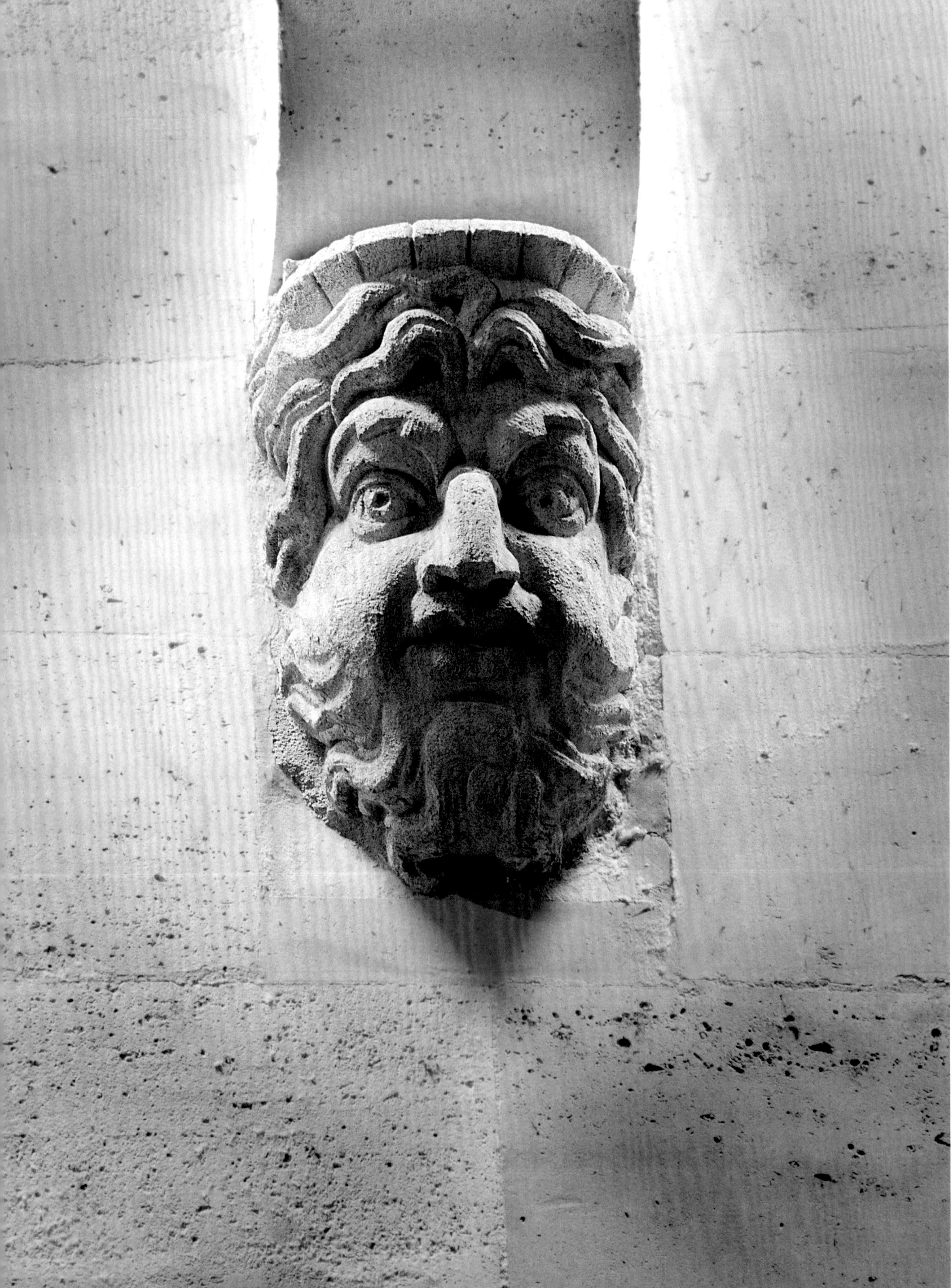

Pont Neuf:
Masceron.

The Seven Bridges from the Louvre to Pont des Invalides

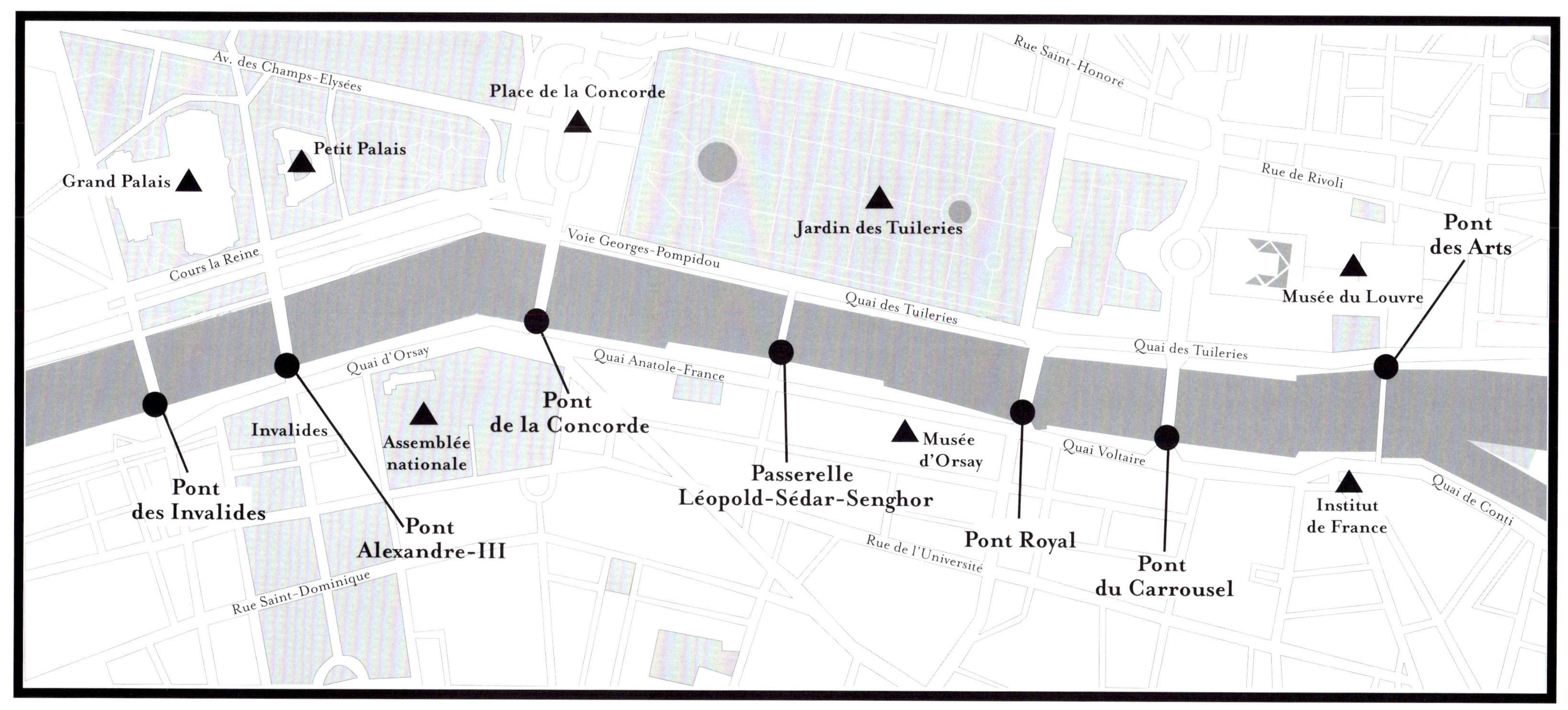

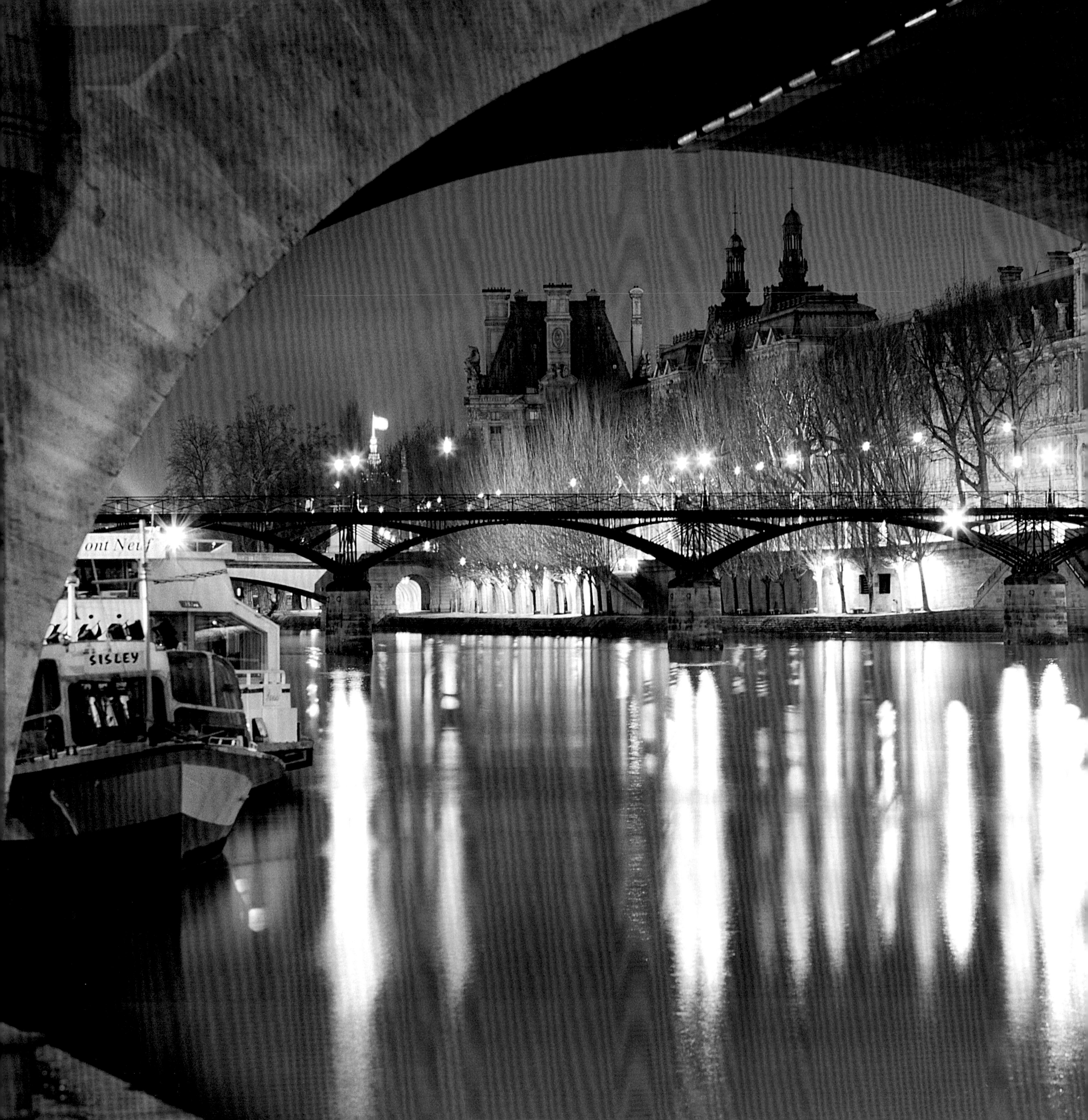
ont Neuf
SISLEY

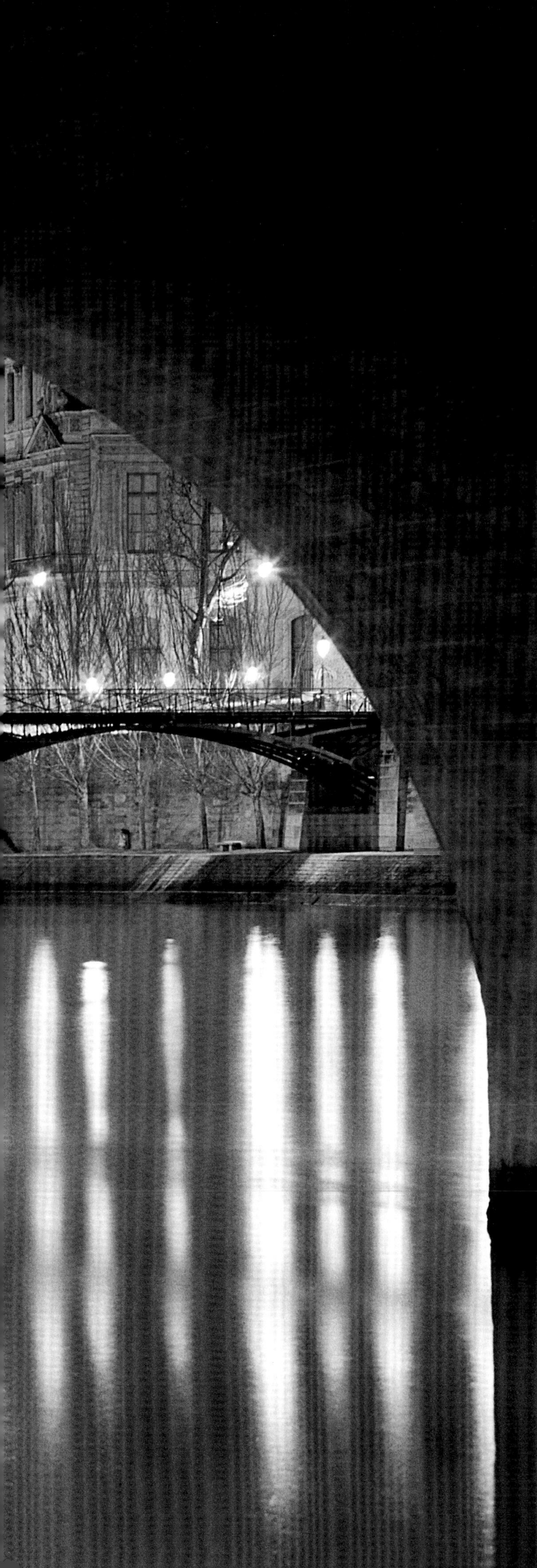

PONT DES ARTS

Built in 1804 under the reign of Napoleon Bonaparte, the Pont des Arts was the first iron bridge in France. Declared a Monument Historique in 1975, it is an elegant example of grace and form, with its metal arches creating a structure of rare lightness.

The Pont des Arts is a passerelle linking two prestigious monuments: the Institut de France on the left bank and the Cour Carrée of the Louvre on the right bank. The Cour Carrée was previously named the Palais des Arts, thus the origin of the name of the Pont des Arts.

Some people call the Pont des Arts the most romantic spot in Paris. The original design concept was a bridge resembling a suspended garden. It is elevated ten steps above the roadways on each side of the river. This elevation gives one a sense of standing on a balcony with a breathtaking view. Downstream, the right bank presents a full-length view of the Louvre. Upstream, the building La Samaritaine displays its original grandeur. Beyond it is the Pont Neuf crossing the Île de la Cité. The park of the Vert Galant, found at the tip of the Île de la Cité, splits the Seine into the two branches that encircle the island. A splendid view of the majestic Institut de France can be seen on the left bank.

Pont des Arts:
From beneath the Pont Neuf on Île de la Cité.

It is the finesse of the structure and the ambiance of the Seine that contribute to the simple beauty of the Pont des Arts.

However, the bridge was not always regarded with such enthusiasm. Napoleon Bonaparte's architects criticized it severely when it was first proposed, and numerous others criticized it following completion. They complained that the new bridge was of insufficient grandiosity to connect two such marvelous monuments. In spite of the criticism the bridge quickly became popular with Parisians. On the day it opened, in 1804, a reported sixty-four thousand people visited the bridge, even though it was a toll bridge. Thereafter the reported usage was eleven thousand per day.

Stone and concrete bridges have a certain resistance to shock, whereas metal bridges like the Pont des Arts are more vulnerable to repeated impacts.

In January 1961 a barge slammed into the bridge and damaged the fifth arch. It was repaired with a temporary replacement. Ten years later another barge, running with a damaged rudder, collided with the bridge, damaging the sixth, seventh, and eighth arches. Repairs were made but the bridge remained frail. In 1976, in one of his reports, the inspector of Ponts et Chaussées (bridges and roads) pointed to the deficiencies of the bridge. The report detailed not only the harm done from the multiple collisions by boats, but also the damage caused by two aerial bombardments during World War I and World War II. Following his report, in 1977 the bridge was closed to pedestrians. The coup de grâce was administered in 1979 by yet another barge that rammed the bridge, causing a 60-meter (197 feet) length of the bridge to collapse.

The Pont des Arts was rebuilt between 1981 and 1984. It is identical to its predecessor, but with seven arches instead of nine, and made from steel instead of cast iron. It was rebuilt despite the opposition of certain historians who pleaded against the reconstruction because they said it would spoil the view of the Louvre. In June 1984 the then mayor of Paris, Jacques Chirac, inaugurated the new bridge.

On a summer evening you can find picnickers, lovers, friends, and groups of all cultures and languages; the music and wine enhance the ambiance from sunset to sunrise. Perhaps this is what the original designers of the bridge had in mind when they envisioned it as a suspended garden.

The Pont des Arts is also one of the bridges overloaded with *cadenas d'amour* (locks of love). It was probably the first of the Paris bridges to be inundated with the locks. A couple writes their names on a padlock and locks it onto the guardrail fence. Then they throw the key into the river as a symbol of their eternal love. One of the humorous quips about the custom is that of the Don Juans who use a combination lock and washable ink.

A recent counting of the locks (February 2014) found in excess of eight hundred locks per lineal meter. Calculating that the bridge is 155 meters (508 feet) long and locks are found on both sides of the bridge, it is probable that the Pont des Arts plays host to between 250,000 and 500,000 locks. According to the newspaper *Le Figaro*, the weight of the locks is 300 kilos per lineal meter. That equals 93,000 kilos (205,207 pounds), a considerable weight for the bridge to bear. The City of Paris has tested various methods of solving the problem, most probably a solution will someday be found, and the locks will disappear from the bridge.

Due to its beautiful and recognizable visage, the bridge has been featured in numerous films, television shows, and other media all over the world.

It very well may be the most romantic spot in Paris.

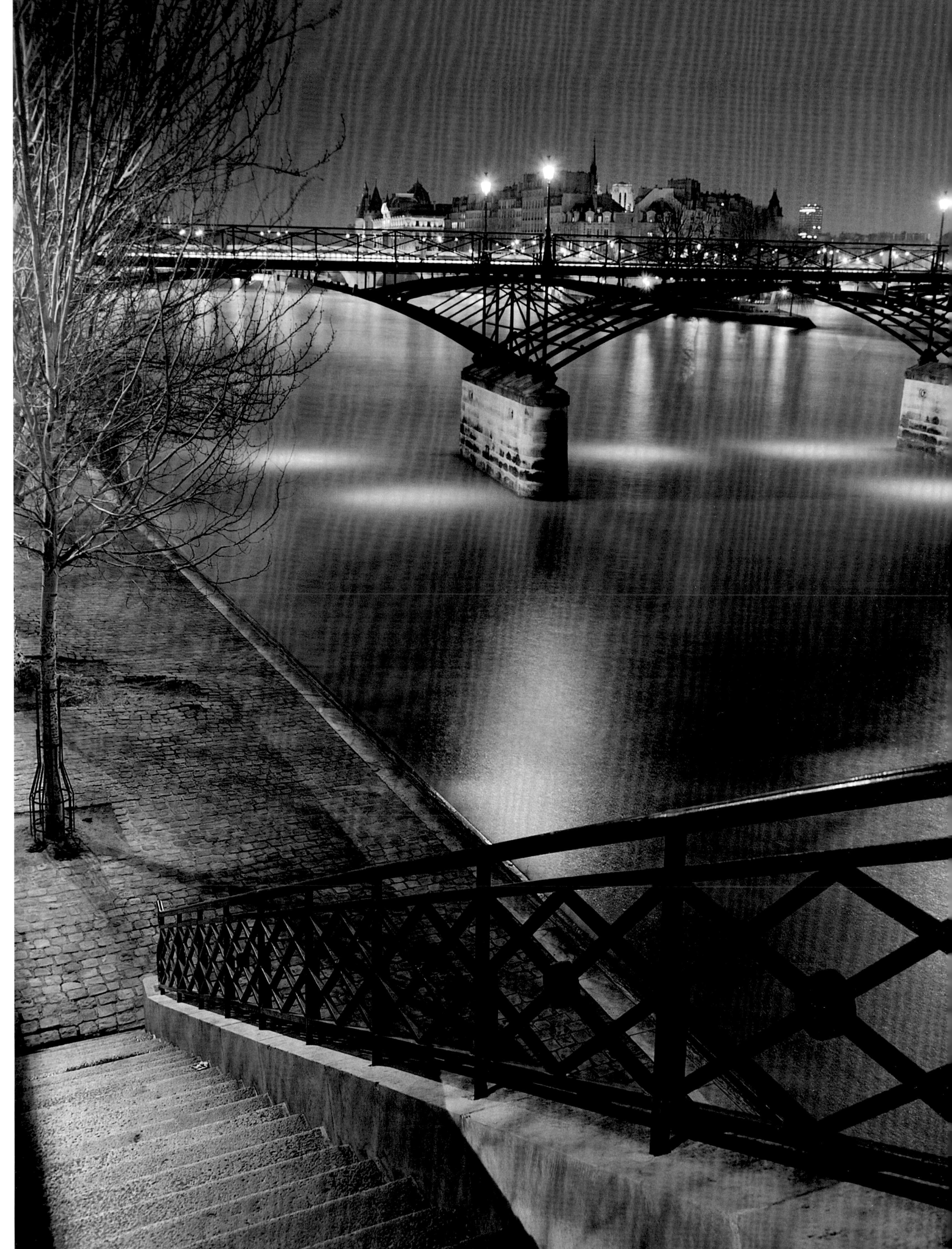

Pont des Arts:
Descent to the quai
downstream.

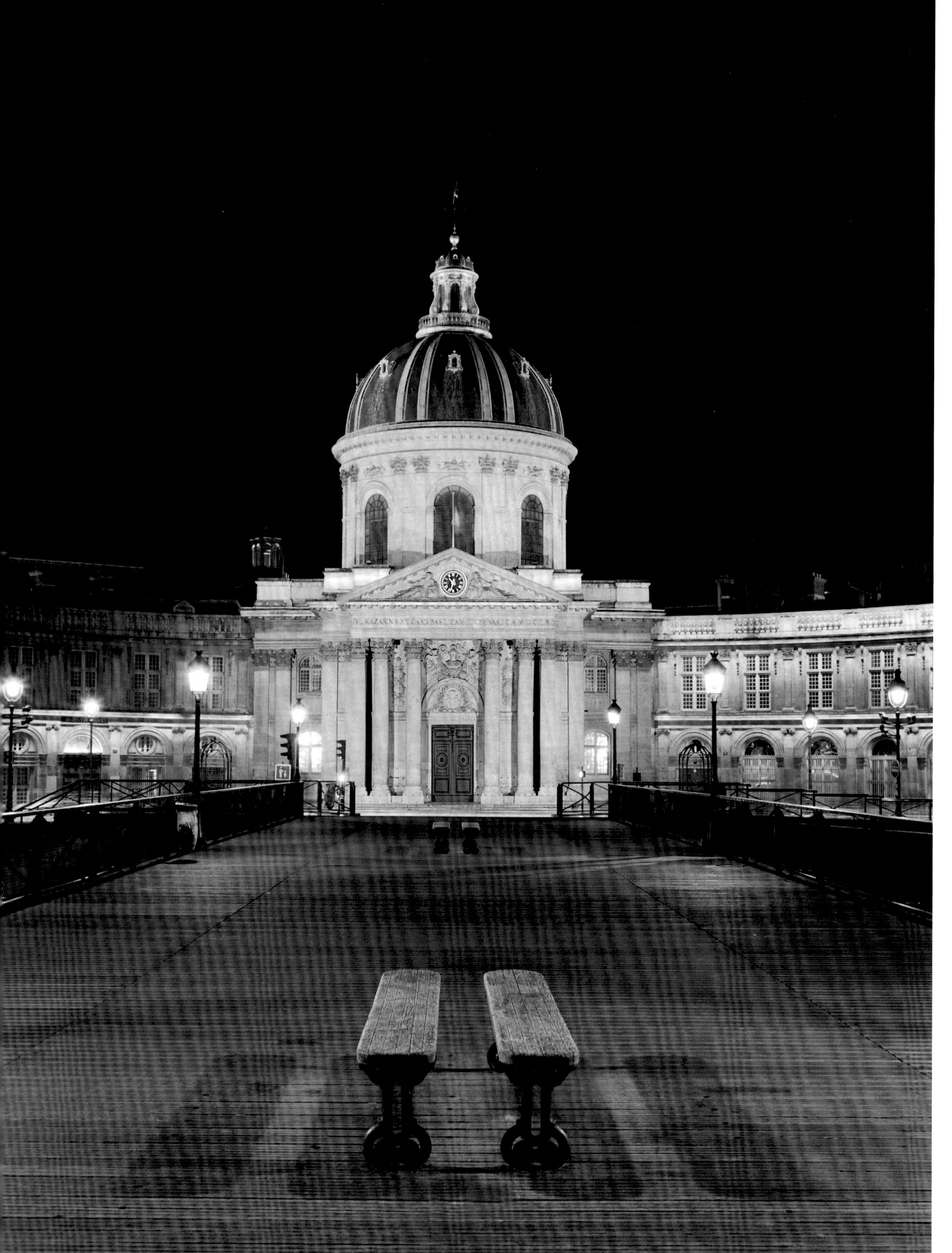

Pont des Arts:
Institut de France on the
left bank.

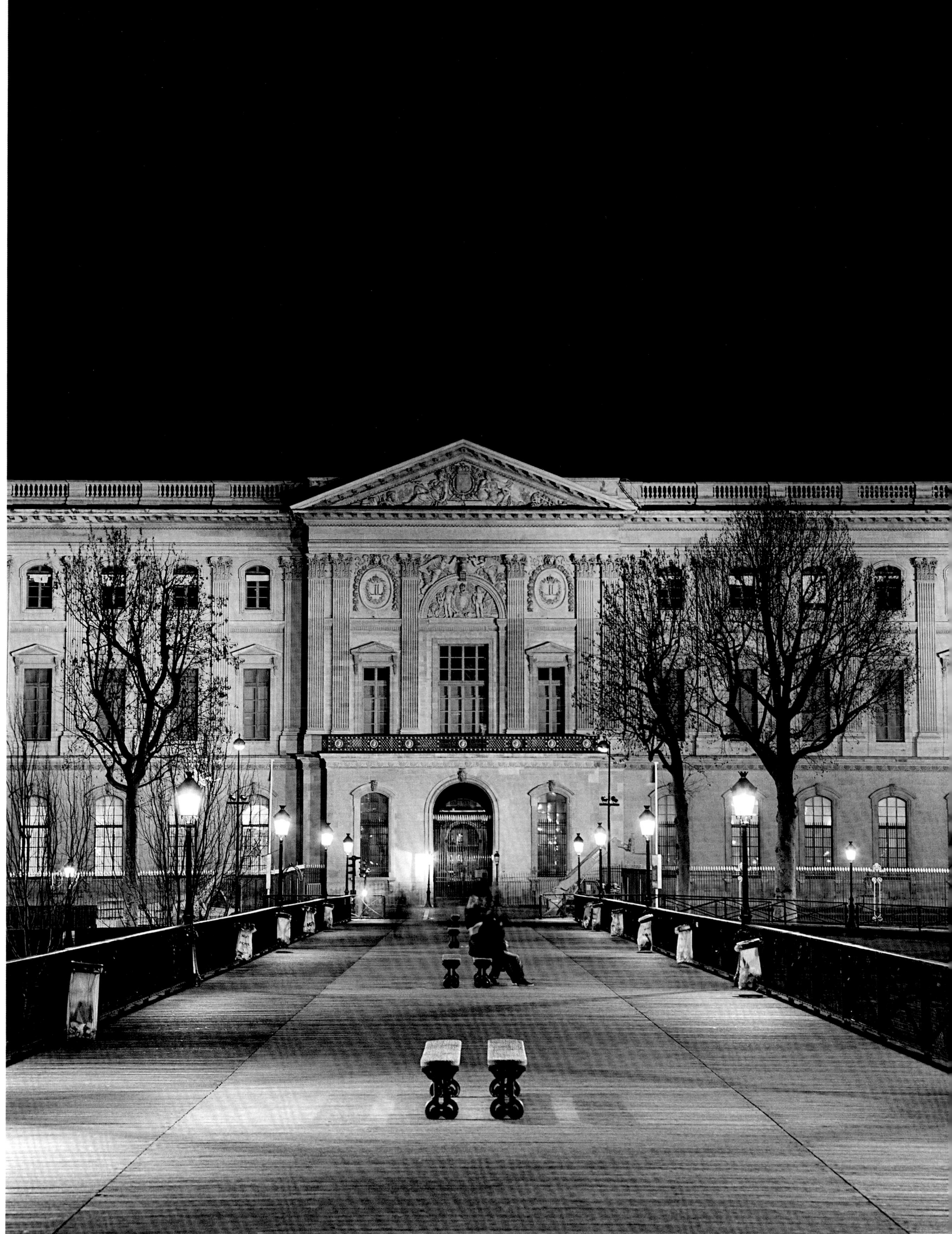

Pont des Arts:
The Louvre toward the
Cour Carée.

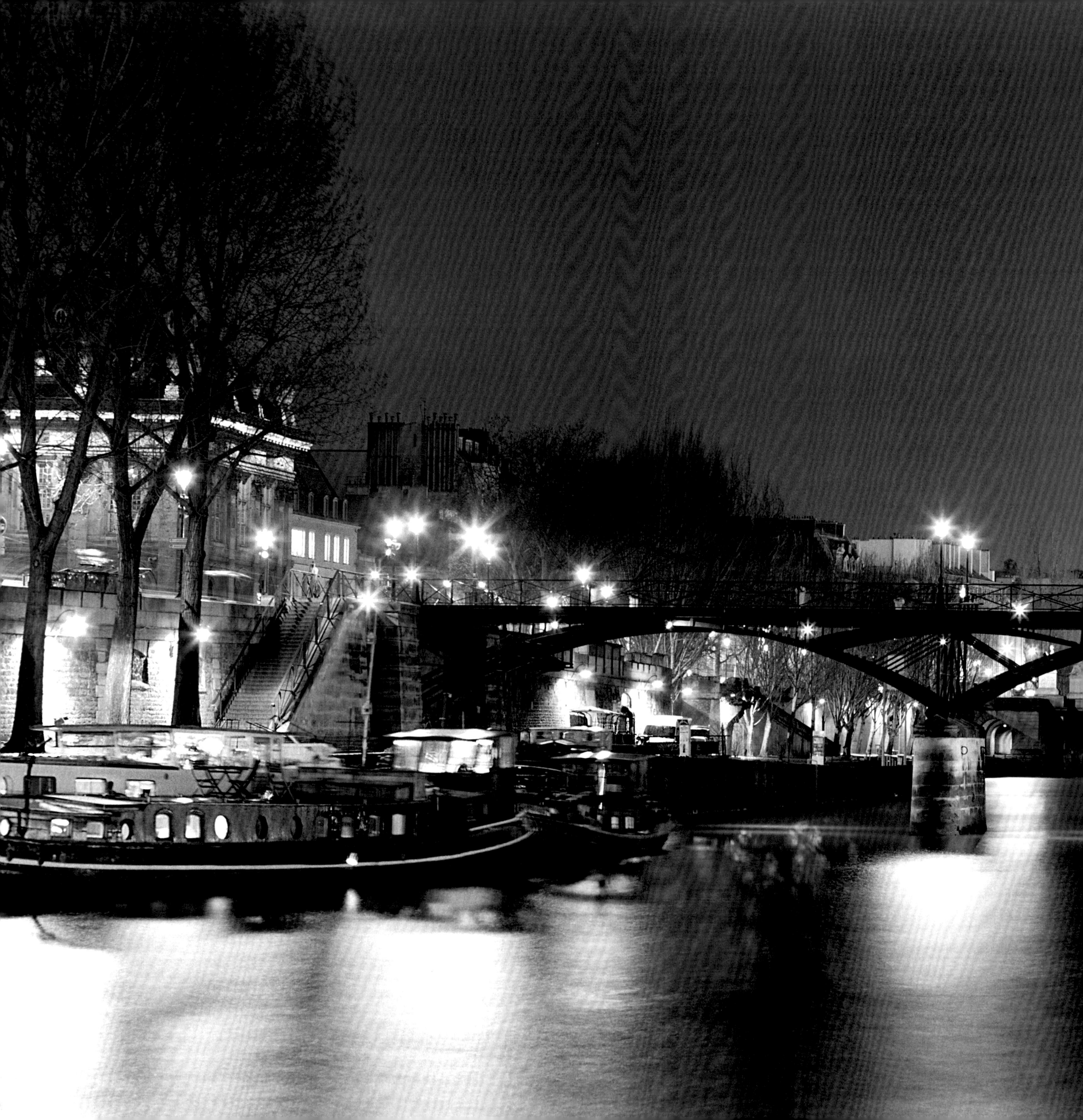

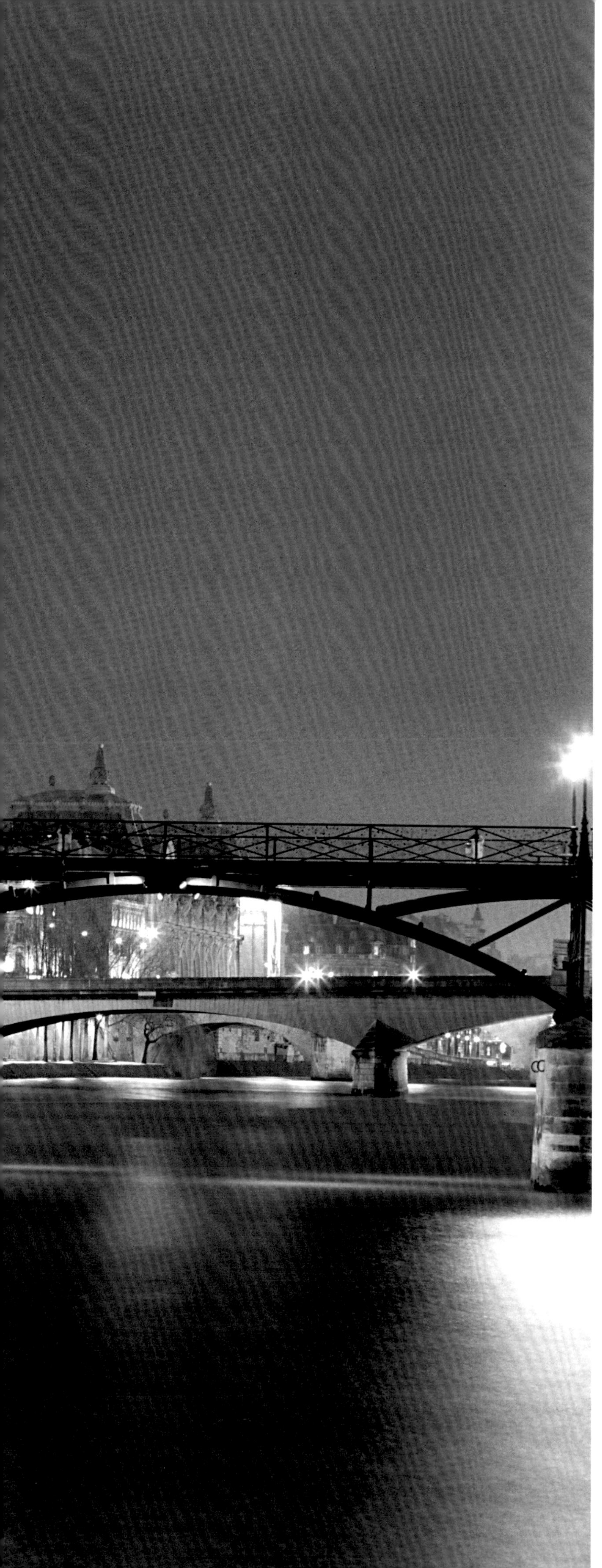

Pont des Arts:
Downstream from the Vert Galant.

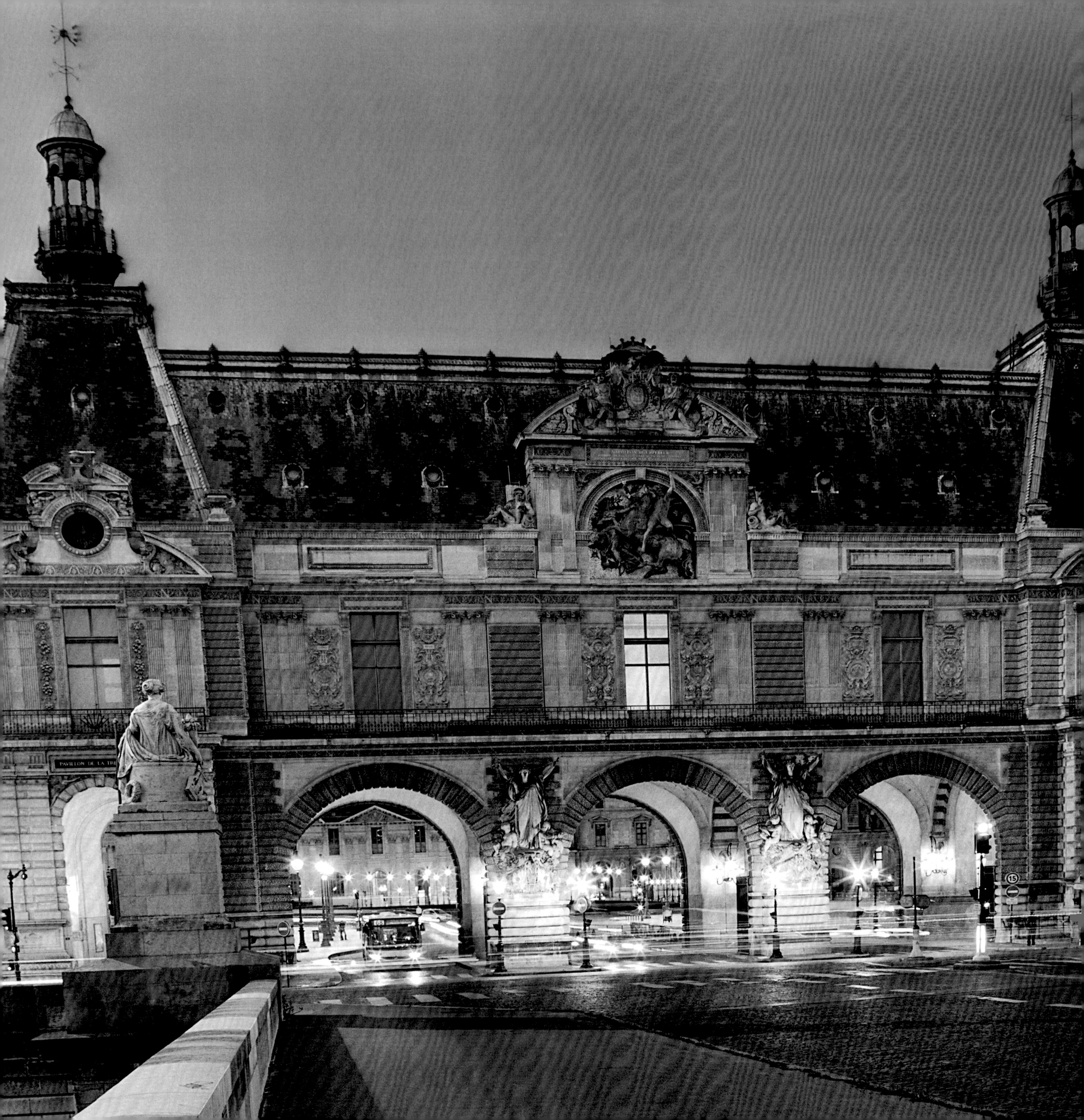

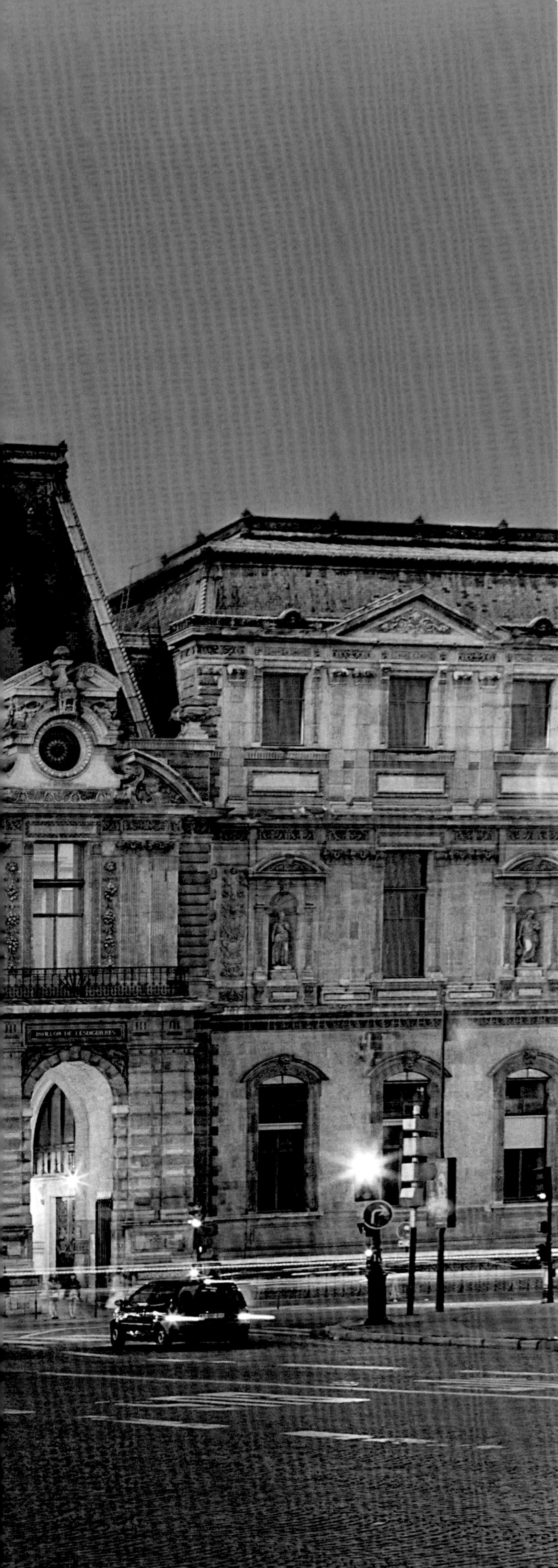

PONT DU CARROUSEL

The modern day Pont du Carrousel is located a few dozen meters downstream from the site of the original bridge. The move allowed the new bridge to create a direct pathway from the left bank to the Place du Carrousel inside the Louvre. Les Guichets du Palais du Louvre, the three identical arched tunnels made of stone and adorned with sculptures, are located at the end of the bridge and provide access to what is probably the most attractive and picturesque entrance to the Louvre.

The first bridge was built during the time of King Louis-Philippe (1830–1848), who named it Pont du Carrousel. Two designs were in competition for the work; one was for a suspension bridge, while the other was for a cast iron bridge. The suspension bridge would have required towers and cables, which were considered unacceptable additions to Parisian scenery. The low profile, cast iron design was chosen; work began in November 1831 and was completed in October 1834.

Along with cast iron, the structure incorporated timber for the roadway. On both sides of the bridge were cast iron, circular ring

Pont du Caroussel:
Louvre entry at the
Guichets du Louvre.

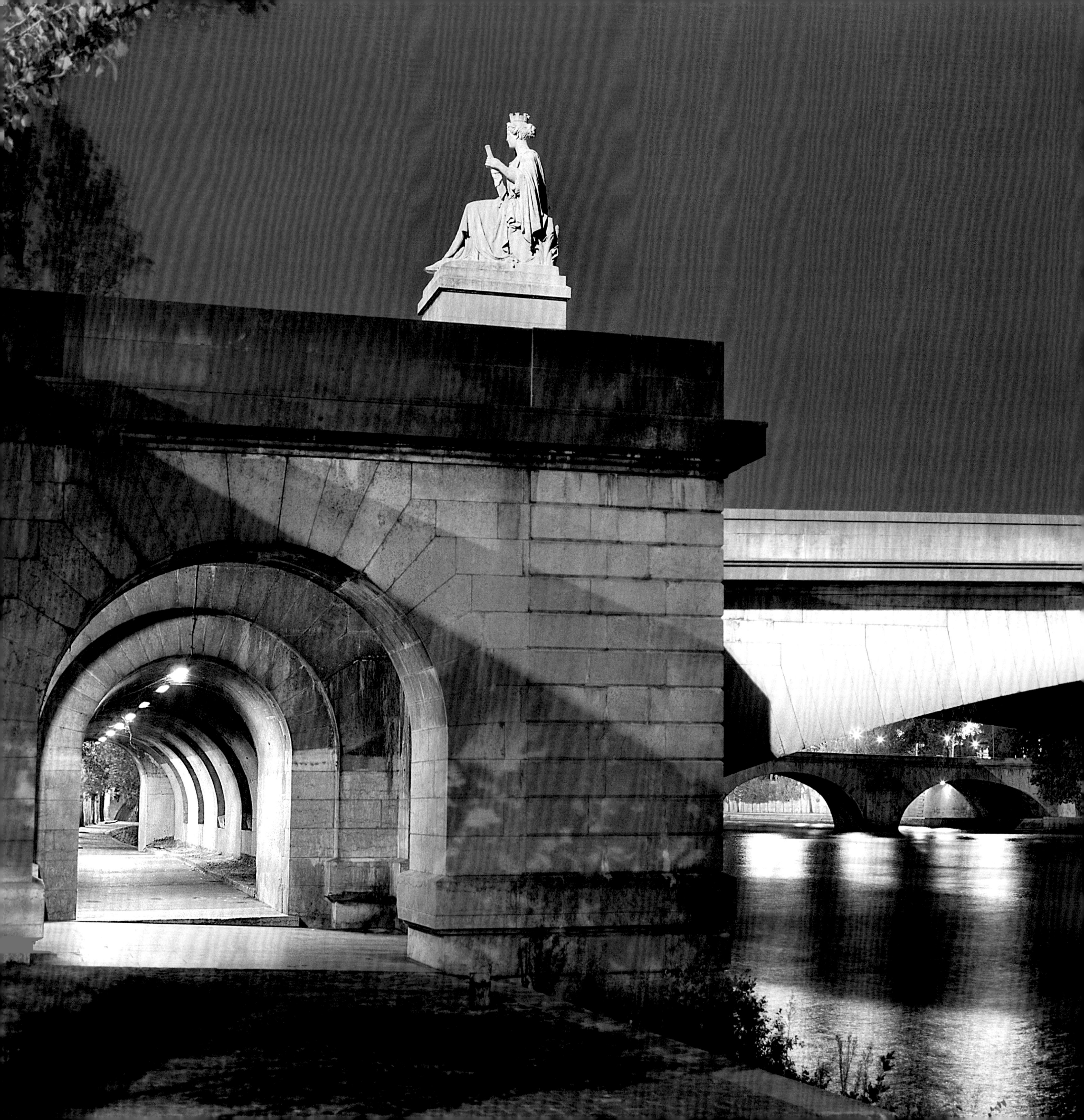

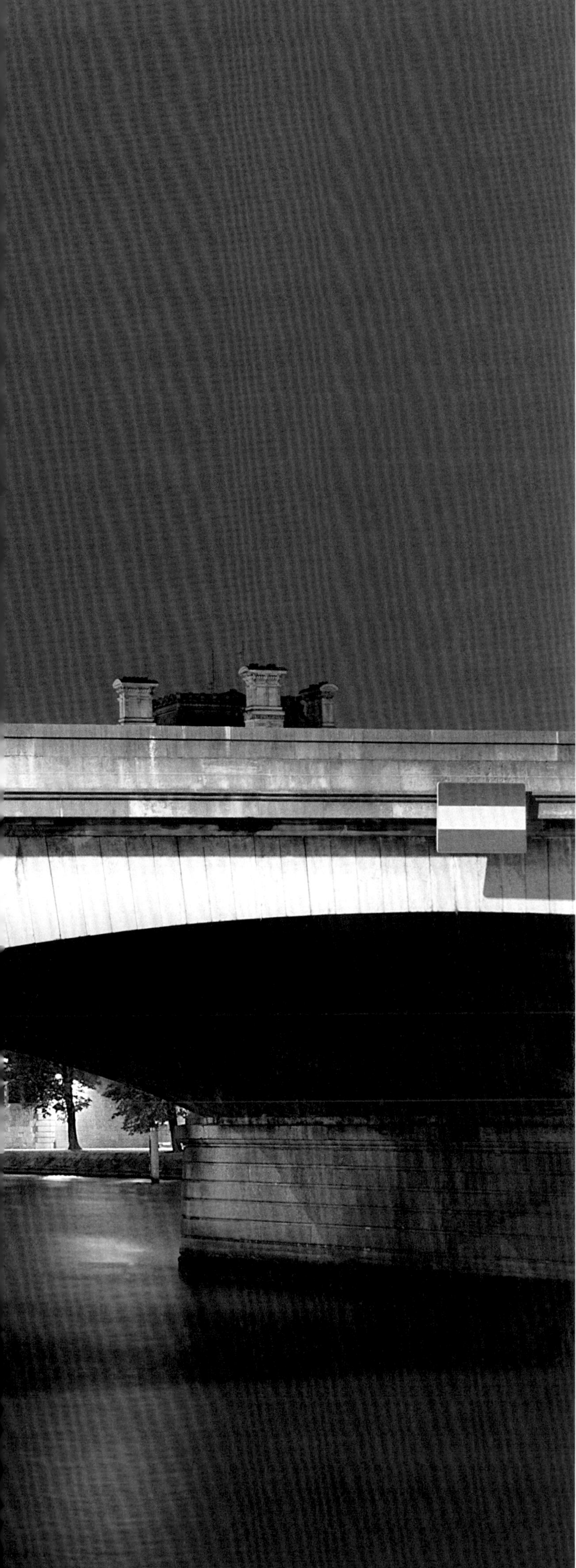

supports that were jokingly called *ronds de serviette* (napkin rings). In 1846, the bridge was adorned with four large and impressive female statues. The works of stone were created in a classical style by French sculptor Louis Petitot (1794–1862). These allegorical figures, located at the four corners of the bridge, are named *L'Industrie, L'Abondance, La Ville de Paris,* and *La Seine* (Industry, Abundance, The City of Paris, and The Seine).

Pont du Carrousel was originally a toll bridge. In 1833 the concessionaire was given a contract for a term of thirty-four years and ten months. The revolution of 1848 interrupted the toll for a short time, but it was reestablished shortly thereafter, finally being abolished in 1850 after the city bought the bridge from the concessionaire.

As time passed, the volume of traffic increased, as did the weight of the goods being carried. It became clear the bridge was too narrow and the space underneath insufficient for navigation. Adding to these problems, the bridge bounced and vibrated alarmingly. In 1930 it was decided that a new bridge would be built and that the site would be moved downstream to align with the entrance to the Louvre. Construction began in 1935 and finished in 1939. The new bridge was constructed of reinforced concrete and, like its predecessor, has three arches. The four Petitot sculptures were moved to their corresponding locations on the new bridge, and underwent restoration in 2006 and 2007.

On May 1, 1995, during the annual Joan of Arc parade (organized by the political party, Front National), a homicide was committed at the Pont du Carrousel. Right-wing extremists threw a young Moroccan named Brahim Bouarram into the swollen Seine. The married, twenty-nine-year-old father of two could not swim, and drowned.

Two days later, the outgoing President, François Mitterrand, in one of the last acts of his presidency, paid homage to the young Moroccan. He observed a minute's silence on the riverbank and then tossed a bouquet of lily-of-the-valley flowers—the symbol of May Day—into the Seine. Following his gesture, some twelve thousand people held a demonstration in memory of Brahim Bouarram, and against racial hatred.

In 2003, Paris Mayor Bertrand Delanoë placed a plaque on the Pont du Carrousel in memory of Bouarram and, as the mayor explained, in memory of all who have suffered from racism. It reads *Á la Memoire de Brahim Bouarram 1965–1995 Victime du Racisme Assasiné à ces Lieux le 1er Mai 1995* (In memory of Brahim Bouarram 1965–1995 Victim of Racism Assassinated at this Location the First of May 1995).

Pont du Caroussel:
Sculpture La Ville de Paris by Louis Petitot
(1794–1862) sits atop the bridge.

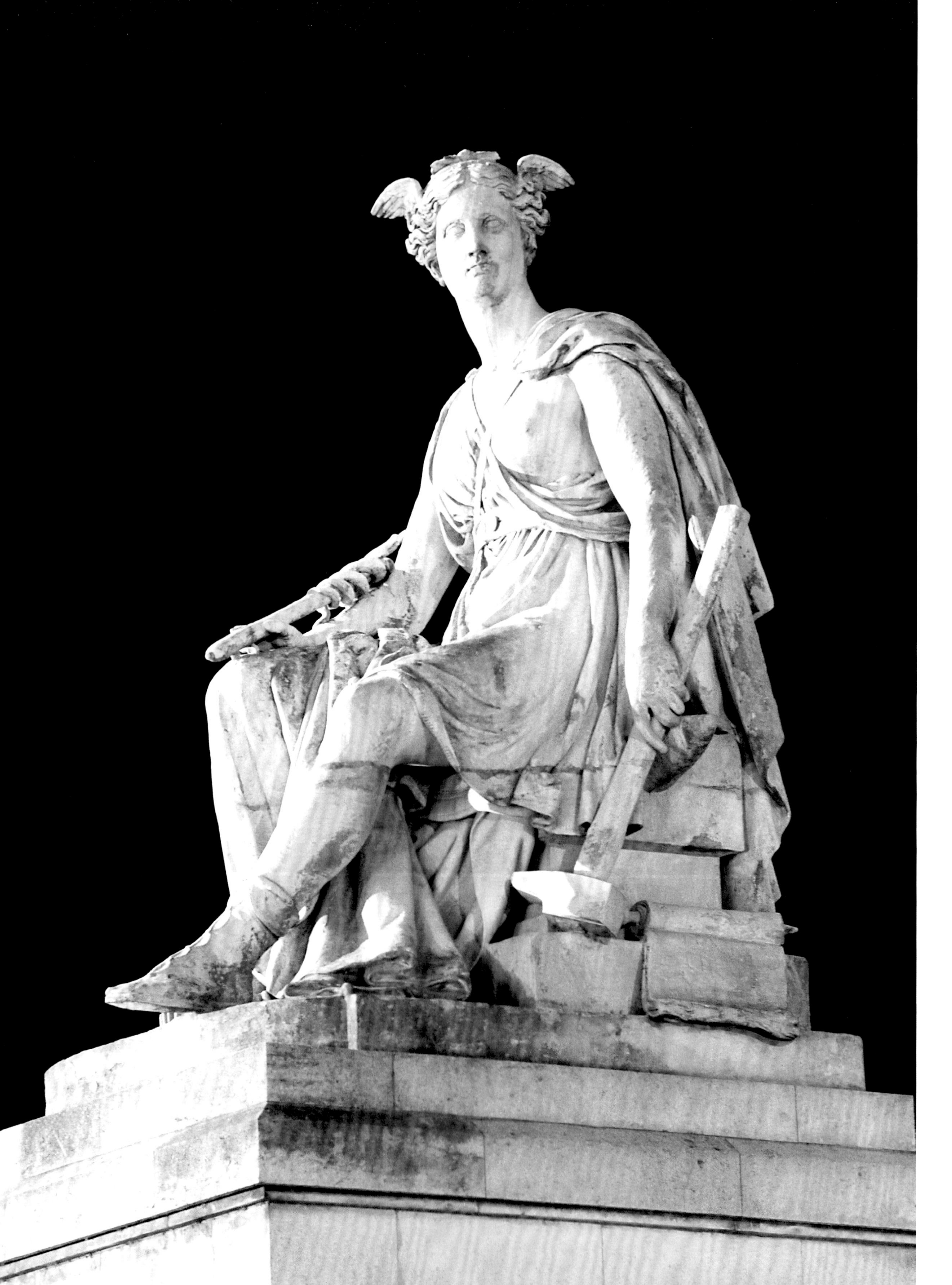

Pont du Caroussel:
Sculpture L'Industrie by
Louis Petitot (1794–1862).

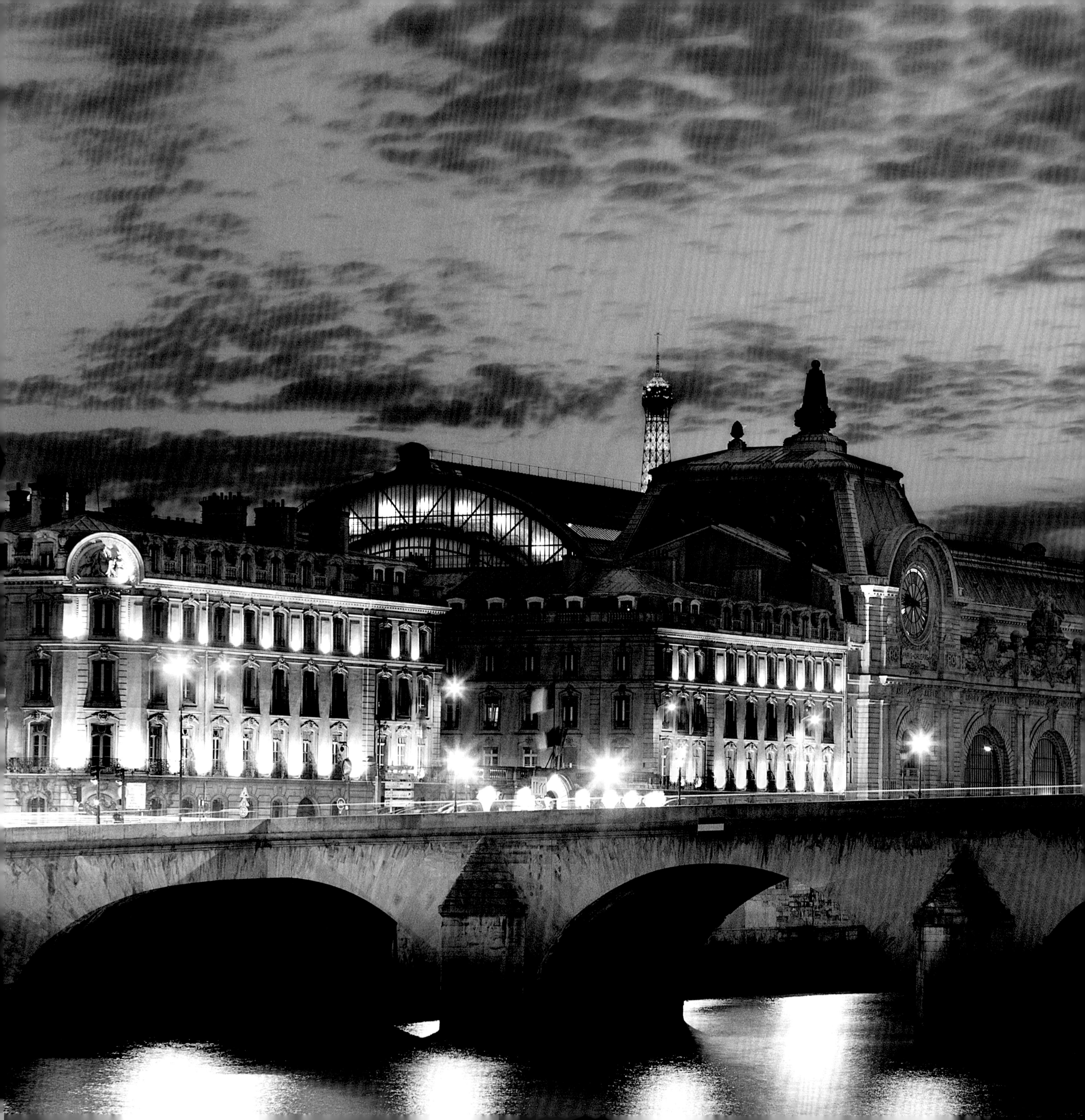

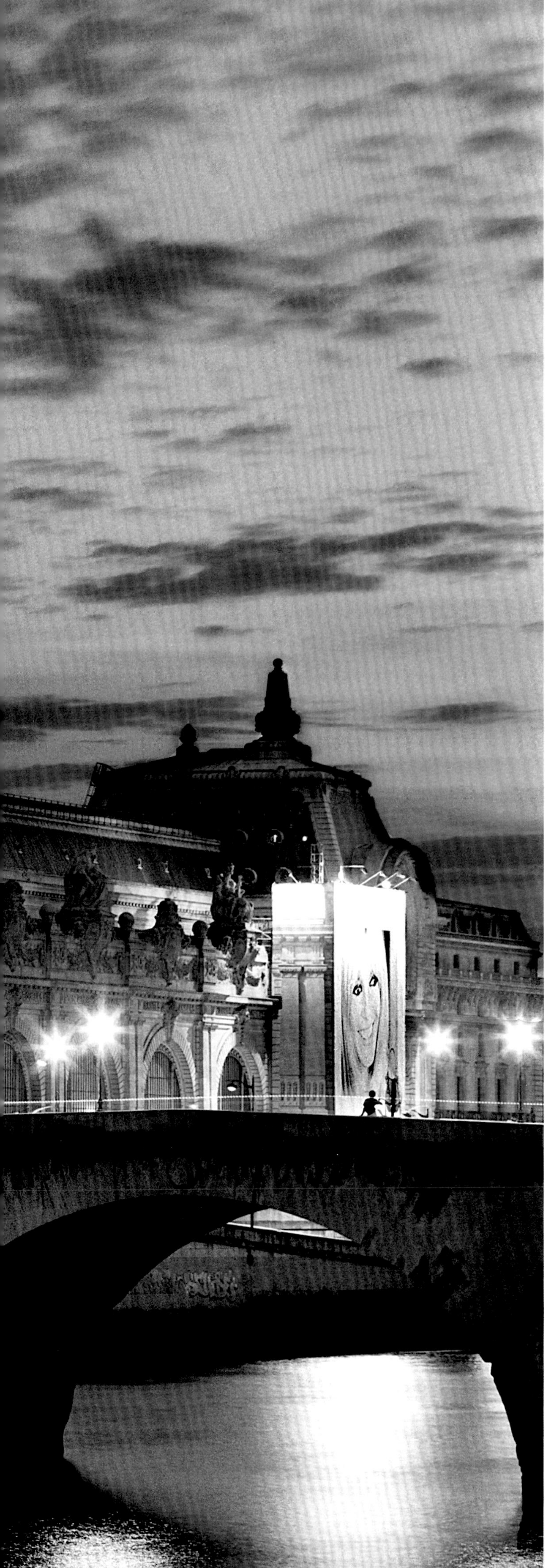

PONT ROYAL

Along with the Pont Neuf and the Pont Marie, the Pont Royal—built in 1689—is one of the three oldest Paris bridges.

The Pont Royal links the Musée d'Orsay and the rue du Bac on the left bank with the Pavillon de Flore, a section of the Palais du Louvre, on the right bank. Before there was a bridge here, the crossing was made by ferry boat—*bac* in French—hence the name rue du Bac. The history of the ferry can be traced back to 1550 and letters patent granted by Henri II for a ferry crossing at this site.

In 1632 a wooden toll bridge was built to supplement the ferry. Financed by a man named Barbier, the bridge was named Pont de Barbier. It was later named Pont Sainte-Anne and then Pont Rouge. Guardhouses were built on both sides for the collection of tolls. The historians of that era recorded the discontent with the toll, which was considered abusive. They chronicled the story of the pedestrian who, having disagreed with the toll, drew his sword and killed the toll collector.

The wooden bridge with its fifteen arches was the victim of continual mishaps. It was swept away by flood in 1649 and rebuilt in 1651. It was burned down in 1654. Carried away by flood again in 1656, it was rebuilt in 1660. It was finally demolished by ice and flood in February 1684.

Pont Royal:
The Musée d'Orsay beyond the bridge.

In 1685 the cornerstone was laid for a new stone bridge with five arches. Finished in 1689, it is one of the plainest and least adorned of the older Paris bridges. It is this bridge that has endured to the present day. It was constructed of *pierre de taille*, an easily worked, fine-grained stone material, usually a sandstone or granular limestone, often called freestone in English.

The famous architect Jules Hardouin-Mansart, under the patronage of King Louis XIV, headed up the project. The king fully funded the work and named the bridge Pont Royal.

Great festivals and fairs were held at the new Pont Royal. On January 24, 1730, in celebration of the birth of Louis, Dauphin of France, Paris experienced the greatest display of fireworks ever seen. In August 1739 Princess Louise-Élisabeth of France, daughter of Louis XV, was married to Philip of Spain, Duke of Parma. The celebration attracted a reported five hundred thousand people to the festivities held on the Pont Royal and on the banks of the river.

In 1792, during the French Revolution, the bridge's name was changed to Pont National; during the First French Empire (1804–1814), Napoleon Bonaparte renamed it Pont des Tuileries. It kept this name until the Restoration in 1814 when Louis XVIII changed it back to Pont Royal.

Following the Revolution of 1830, Louis-Philippe was installed as king. Six times during his reign (1830–1848) he was the target of assassination attempts. They all failed. Two of the six occurred at the Pont Royal.

In November 1832, as the King was crossing the Pont Royal on his way to the Palais Bourbon, a would-be assassin fired at him. In the following melee the shooter escaped into the crowd. Later that evening a student activist was arrested but subsequently acquitted for lack of proof.

Two days after Christmas in 1836, a young man named Meunier fired a pistol at the royal cortege as it crossed the Pont Royal. The king's three sons were slightly wounded by flying debris; the king was unharmed. The twenty-two-year-old terrorist was captured and sentenced to death, but the king, in a politically astute maneuver, commuted his sentence and exiled him to America. And it is said that the king gave Meunier a small stipend to ease his transition to exile.

Until the construction of the Pont de la Concorde in 1788, there were no bridges downstream of the Pont Royal.

Since 1689 the bridge has had very little modification, with the exception of the reduction of its humped slope in 1852 and its numerous name changes. It was classified a Monument Historique in 1939. Today it accommodates one-way traffic running from the left bank to the right bank. ❧

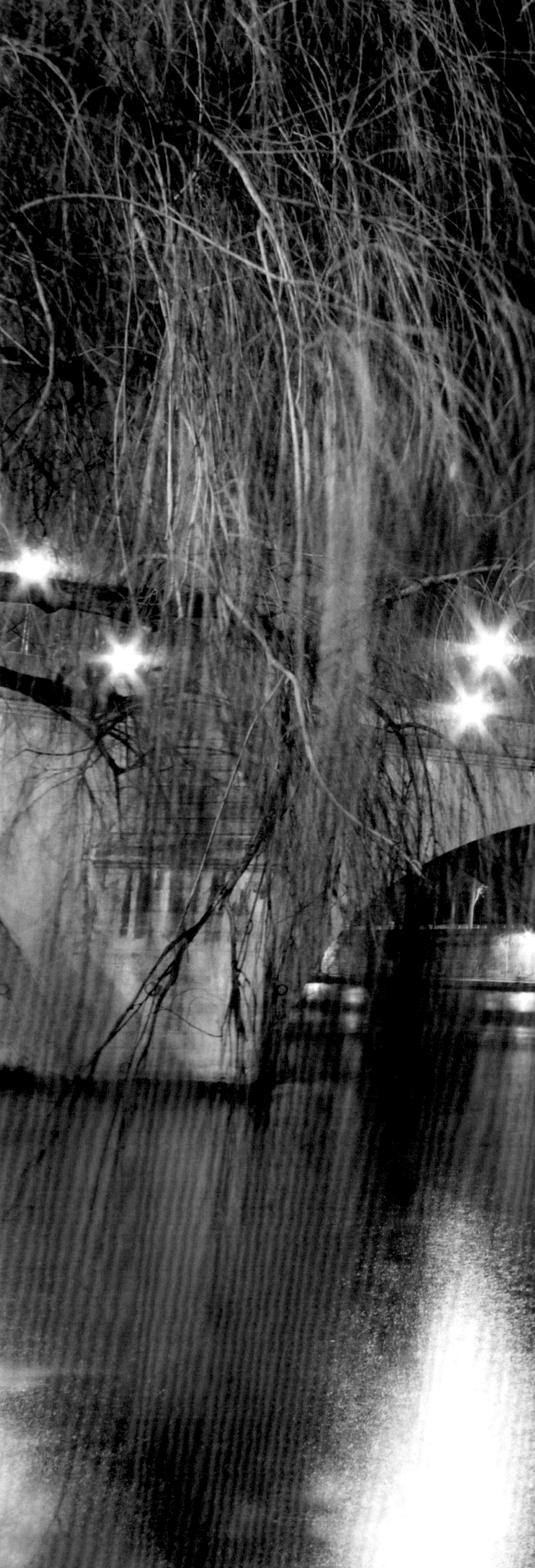

Pont Royal:
The Pavillon de Flore of the Louvre.

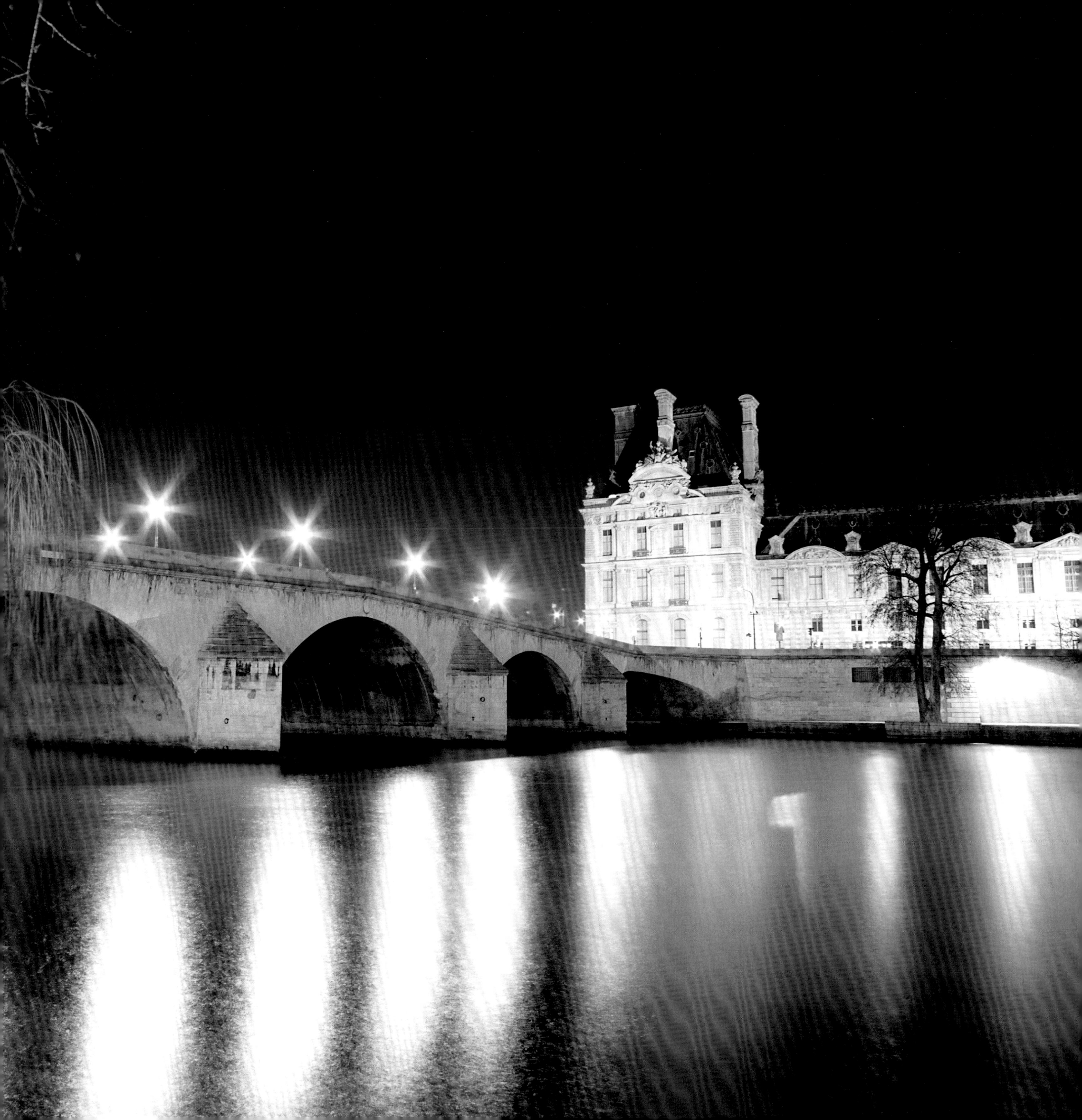

PASSERELLE LÉOPOLD-SÉDAR-SENGHOR

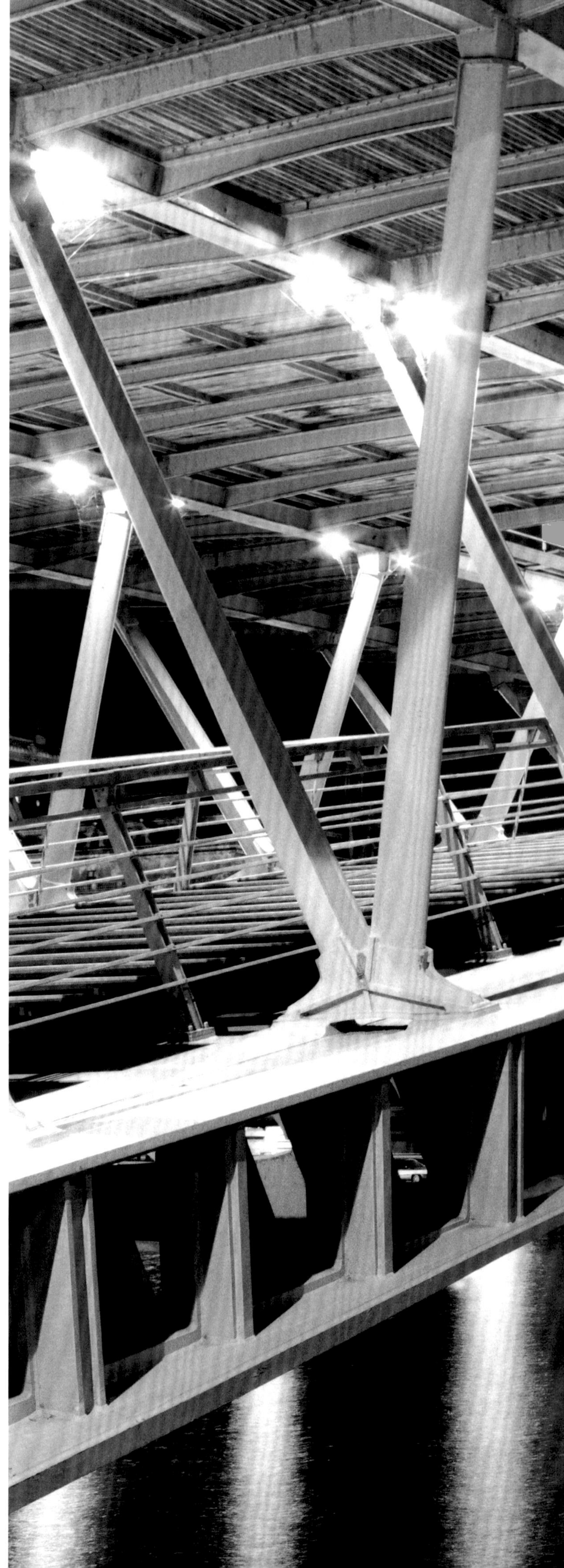

Passerelle Léopold-Sédar-Senghor:
Spanning the Seine without
support legs in the river.

The current Passerelle Léopold-Sédar-Senghor, originally named Passerelle Solferino, was inaugurated December 15, 1999. It was closed two days later and remained closed for the next ten months, finally reopening on November 12, 2000.

The reason for the closure was a disagreement between the City of Paris and the French government. The government paid for the design and construction of the bridge and the city was to be responsible for accepting and maintaining the bridge.

On the day of the inauguration, with some four hundred guests in attendance, the bridge began to sway and vibrate. Adding to that problem,

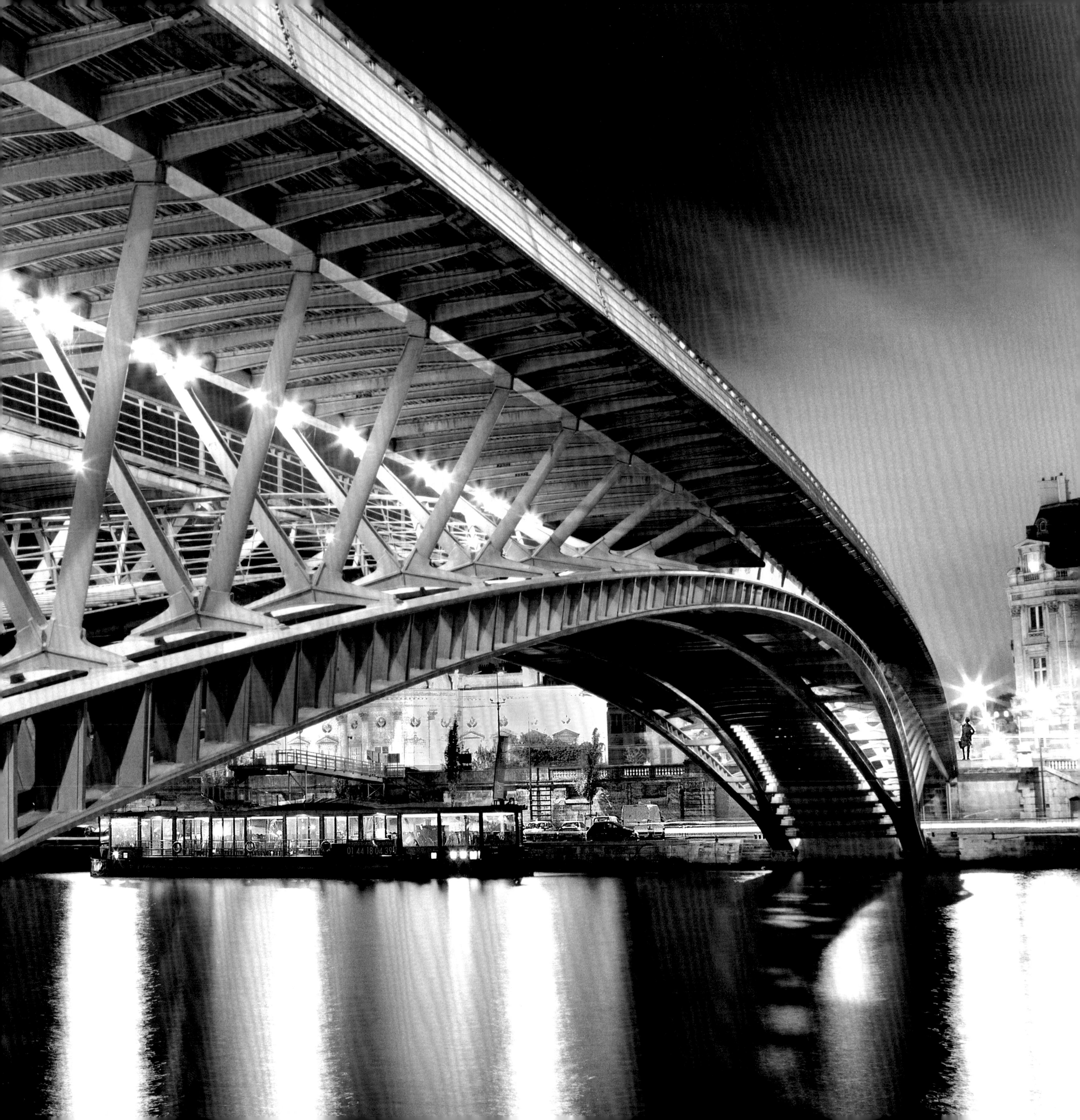

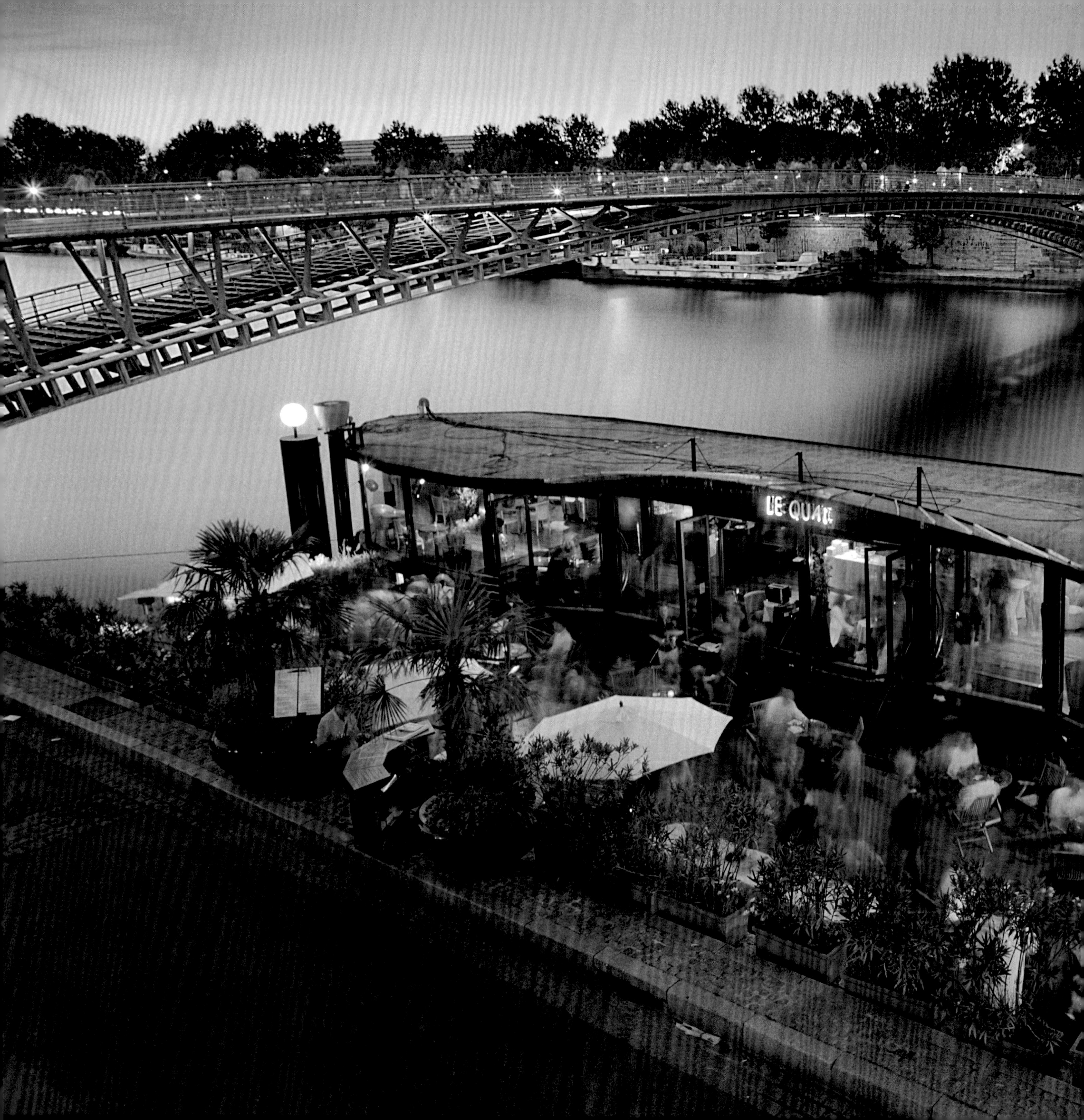
LE QUAI

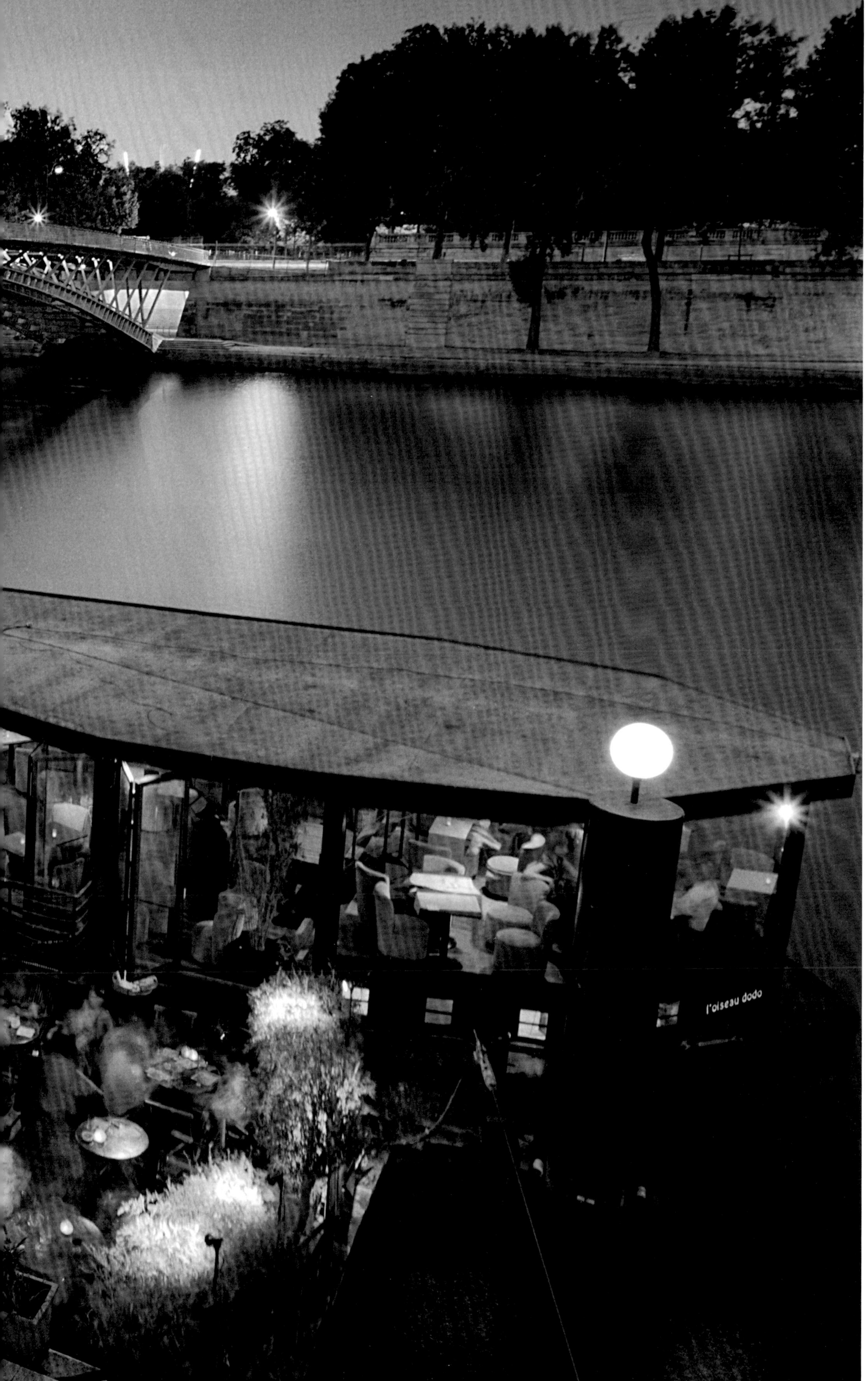

the special wood used for the decking—Ipé from Brazil—was found to be quite slippery when wet. As a result, the city refused to accept the bridge and its attendant liability. Compounding these technical problems was a political problem. The elected officials of the government and the city were from different and opposing political parties. As often happens, the two parties were in disagreement. Thus the bridge was closed two days after it opened.

The design, by architect Marc Mimram, had already won praise for its beauty and originality. Mimram was awarded the prestigious prize for excellence in architecture, the *Prix de l'Équerre d'argent* (the silver T-square prize), for his innovative design. The bridge is a lightweight, single arch, long-span structure. It crosses the Seine with no intermediate supports in the water. On each side of the river the bridge provides access from the riverside at the lower level and from the roadways located at the upper levels. All four of these entryways converge at the top center of the bridge.

"Tuned mass dampers," also known as harmonic absorbers, were installed to solve the sway and vibration problems. Anti-slip treatment was put in place to solve the deck problem.

The original Pont de Solferino, inaugurated by Napoleon III in 1861, stood until it was taken down in 1961. The temporary steel footbridge that replaced it lasted until 1992. The name Solferino comes from the 1859 battle of Solferino in Northern Italy where Napoleon III defeated the Austrian Army under Franz Joseph I.

Passerelle Léopold-Sédar-Senghor:
Restaurant le Quai.

On October 9, 2006, the current bridge was renamed Léopold-Sédar-Senghor to honor Léopold-Sédar-Senghor, a Senegalese poet, politician, and cultural theorist who for two decades served as the first president of Senegal. Senghor was the first African elected as a member of the Académie Française. He described himself as a poet who tumbled into politics.

There doesn't seem to be any significant history surrounding the bridge until one sunny Sunday afternoon on July 23, 1944. At 3 PM on that date a young woman named Madeleine Riffaud, nineteen years old at the time, shot a Nazi officer to death as he was walking on the Pont de Solferino. Riffaud's act was in revenge for the slaying of a friend. Her action was also a sign of the rising fever of resistance taking hold within the underground and on the streets of Paris. She was arrested, tortured, and sentenced to death. However, she was later freed in a prisoner exchange and went on to become a well-known and highly regarded journalist.

At the upper entrance on the left bank of the passerelle stands a 3 meter (10 feet) bronze statue of Thomas Jefferson, the third President of the United States, who also served as the U.S. minister to France from 1785 to 1789. Created by sculptor Jean Cardot, it was unveiled on July 4, 2006, the 230th anniversary of American independence.

There is a magnificent view from the center of the bridge: upstream are the Pavillon de Flore, the Pont Royal, the spires of Notre Dame, the Musée d'Orsay, and the Musée National de la Légion d'honneur. Downstream are the Eiffel Tower, the Assemblée Nationale, the Pont de la Concorde, the golden horses of the Pont Alexandre III, the glass roof of the Grand Palais, and finally the Place de la Concorde. And at the foot of the bridge the barge-restaurant named Le Quai is found.

Unfortunately, the Passerelle Léopold-Sédar-Senghor, like the Pont des Arts and the Pont de l'Archevêché, has fallen victim to the *cadenas d'amour* (love locks) that have proliferated since 2008.

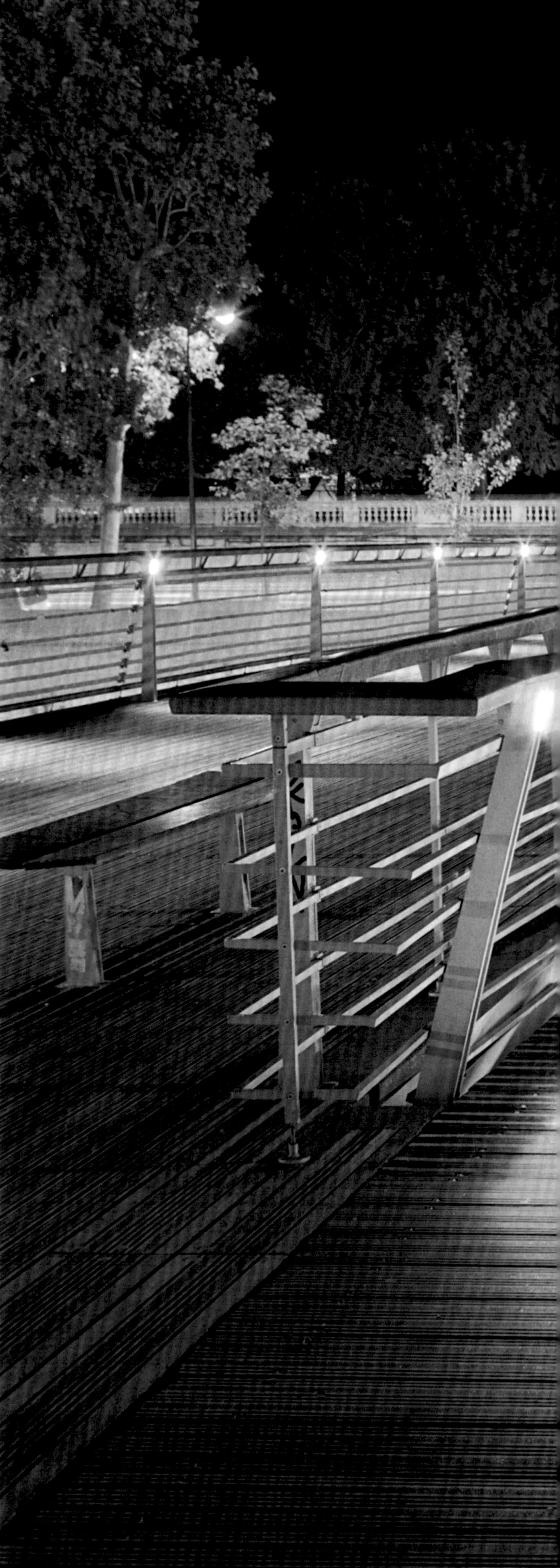

Passerelle Leopold-Sédar-Senghor:
Topside on the bridge.

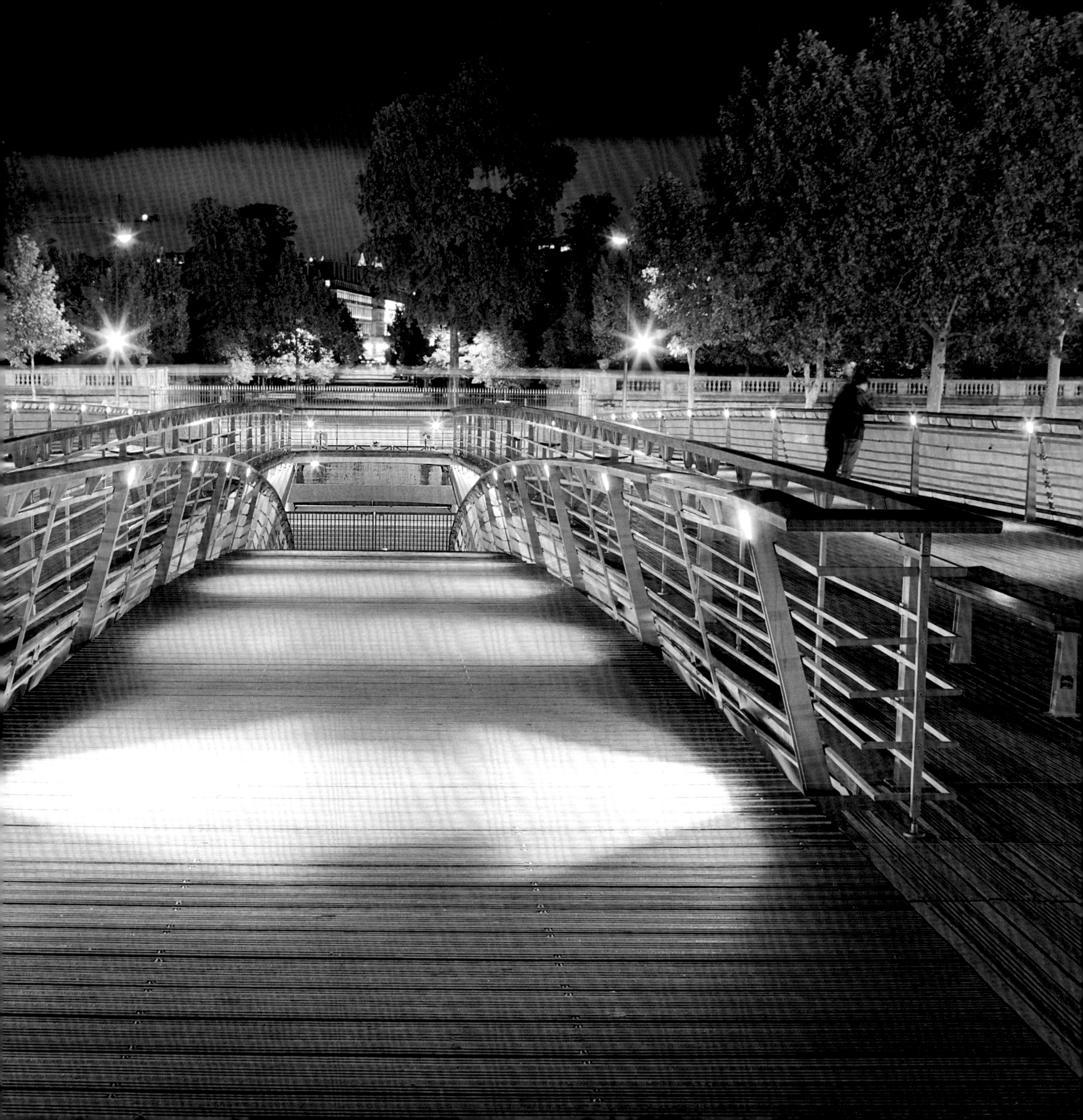

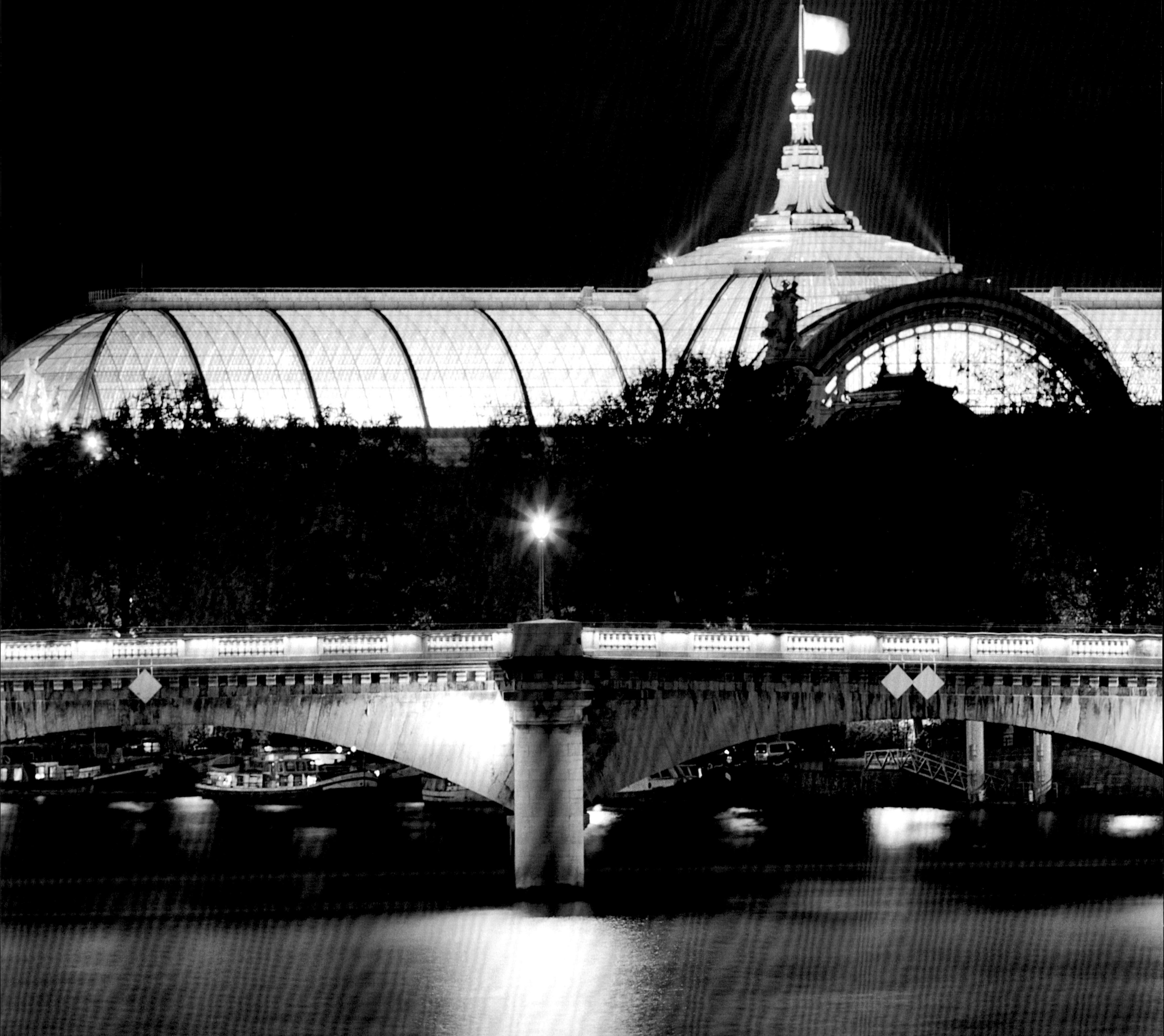

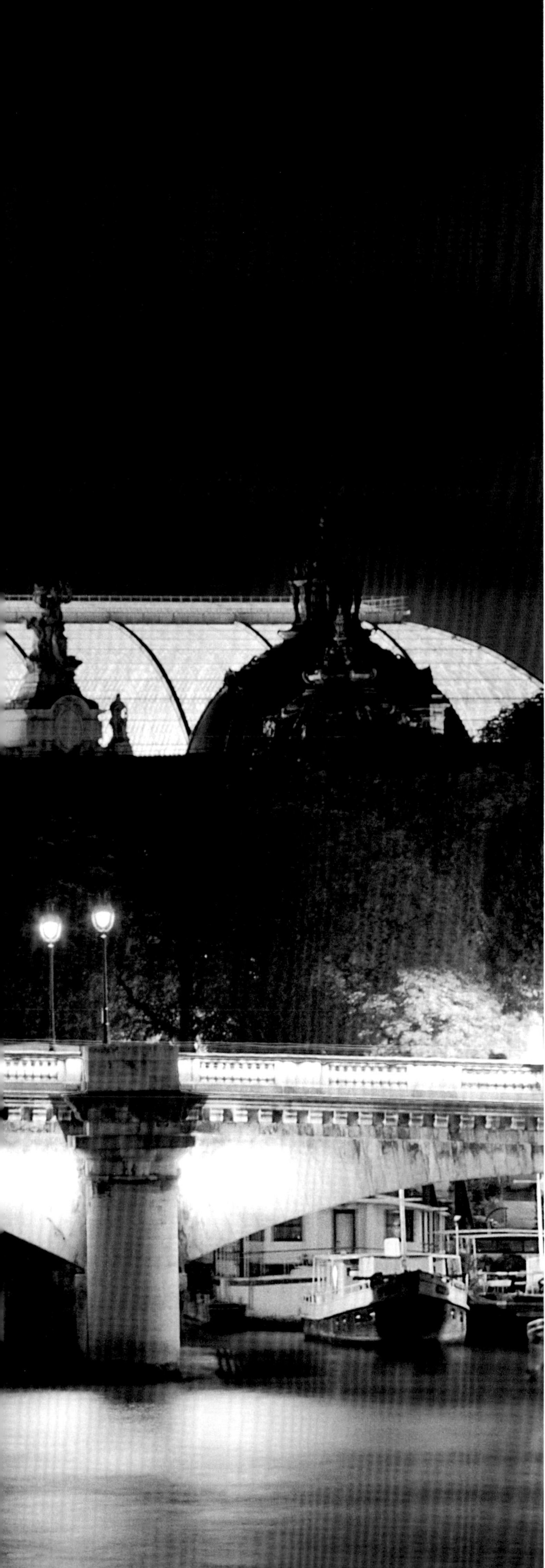

Pont de la Concorde

The Pont de la Concorde is the busiest of the thirty-five Paris bridges, with more vehicles using this bridge than any of the others. It links two of the most notable sites in the city, the Place de la Concorde and the Palais Bourbon (location of the Assemblée Nationale, home of the French Parliament's lower house).

A straight line runs from the Palais Bourbon, across the Pont de la Concorde and the Place de la Concorde to the Church of the Madeleine, a distance of approximately one mile. The view from one end to the other is impressive.

The bridge was built during the French Révolution in 1789, one of the most turbulent times in the history of France. A new bridge to alleviate the congestion of traffic upstream on the Pont Royal had long been needed. It was also necessary in order to connect the growing districts of the Faubourg Saint-Honoré on the right bank to Saint-Germain on the left. A bridge had been planned since 1755 and finally, in 1787, King Louis XVI commissioned his architect Jean-Rodolphe Perronet to begin work on the bridge to be named Pont Louis XVI.

Less than two years later, the storming of the Bastille took place on July 14, 1789; it was the opening stage of the Revolution. A medieval

Pont de la Concorde:
The Grand Palais downstream from the bridge.

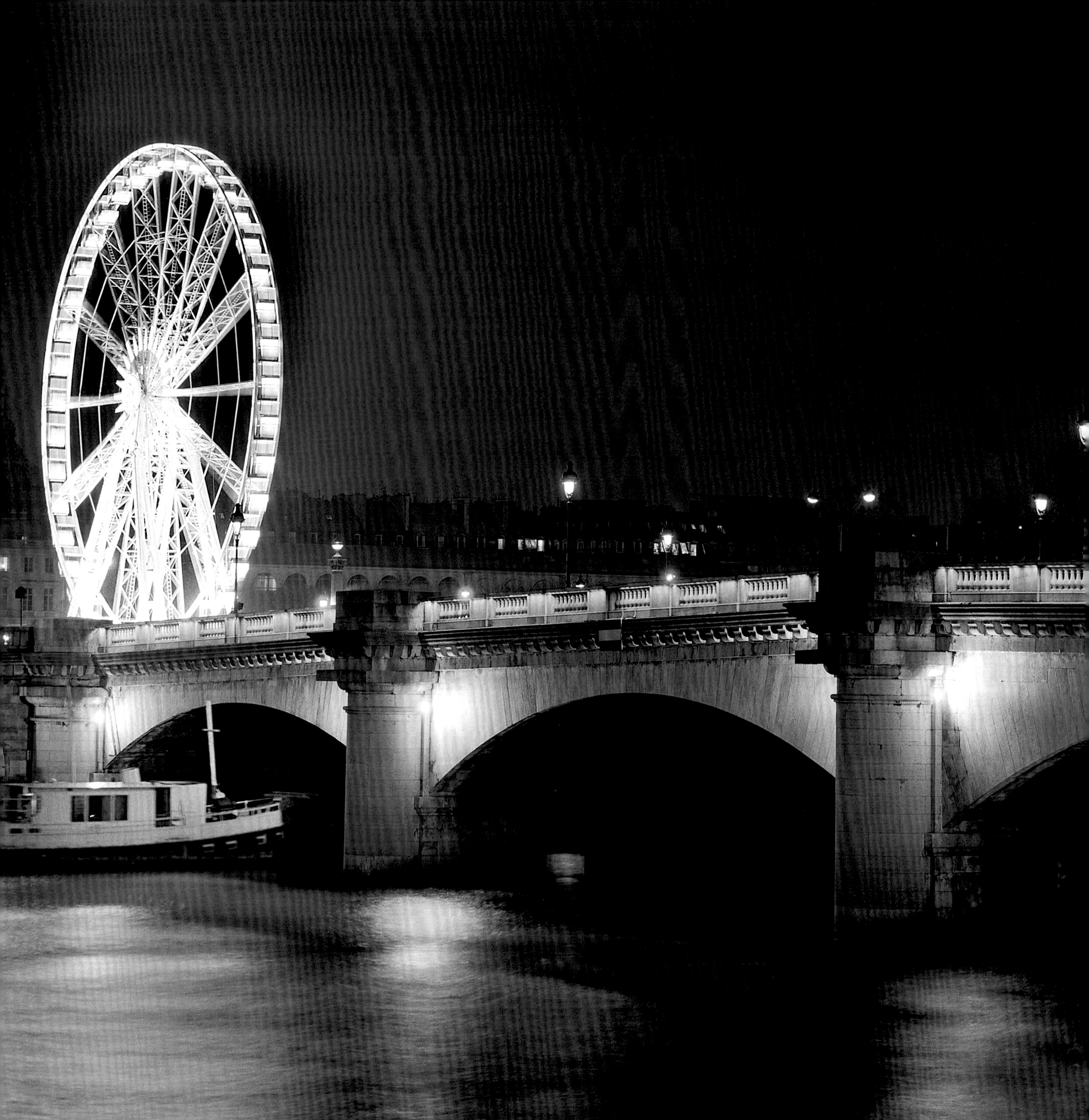

fortress and prison, the Bastille had long been a despised symbol of royal authority. Its destruction left mounds of rubble and stones in its wake. Although the construction of the new bridge was well underway, the majority of the stone needed to finish the project had not yet been procured. The wreckage of the Bastille provided the needed stone along with the opportunity for the new republic to build one of its first monuments.

In spite of these events, work on the bridge continued with as many as 1,200 workers employed. The bridge finally opened in 1791. In 1792 the name was changed from Pont Louis XVI to Pont de la Révolution. And Place de la Concorde, which at that time had been named Place Louis XV, was changed to Place de la Révolution.

Shortly thereafter, on January 21, 1793, Louis XVI was executed by guillotine at the Place de la Révolution. Marie Antoinette was also executed by guillotine, eight months later, at the same site. That guillotine was most active in the summer of 1794, when in a single month more than 1,300 people were beheaded. In 1795, as the turbulence of the Revolution ebbed, the Place de la Révolution was renamed Place de la Concorde.

The Pont de la Concorde has been witness to many historical moments. One such moment was December 15, 1840, when the ashes of Napoleon Bonaparte were returned to France from the island of St. Helena, where he had died in exile. It was reported that many hundreds of thousands of Parisians turned out to view the casket as it passed. The route of the cortege crossed the Pont de la Concorde on its way to Hôtel des Invalides where his ashes were entombed.

Another occurred on the night of February 6, 1934, when a mob went on a rampage against the government. The mob, intent on attacking the National Assembly across the river, converged on the Place de la Concorde. The police managed to defend their position at the bridge, preventing the mob from crossing. Several rioters were armed, and the police fired on the crowd. The riot continued until 2:30 AM. At the end of it, sixteen people had been killed and around two thousand injured.

Some modification has been made to the bridge. In 1930 the bridge was widened from 15 to 35 meters to accommodate the growing volume of traffic. The work was performed on both the upstream and downstream sides, but the original design was diligently maintained.

Originally built without excessive decoration, the only adornments found on the bridge today are the lamps for night lighting.

Every year since 1993, from the middle of November to the middle of February, the Grande Roue is erected next to the bridge at the Place de la Concorde. The Grande Roue is a giant Ferris wheel 65 meters (213 feet) high that every winter provides stunning panoramic views of the city and its holiday illuminations.

Pont de la Concorde:
The Grande Roue (Ferris Wheel)
at the Place de la Concorde.

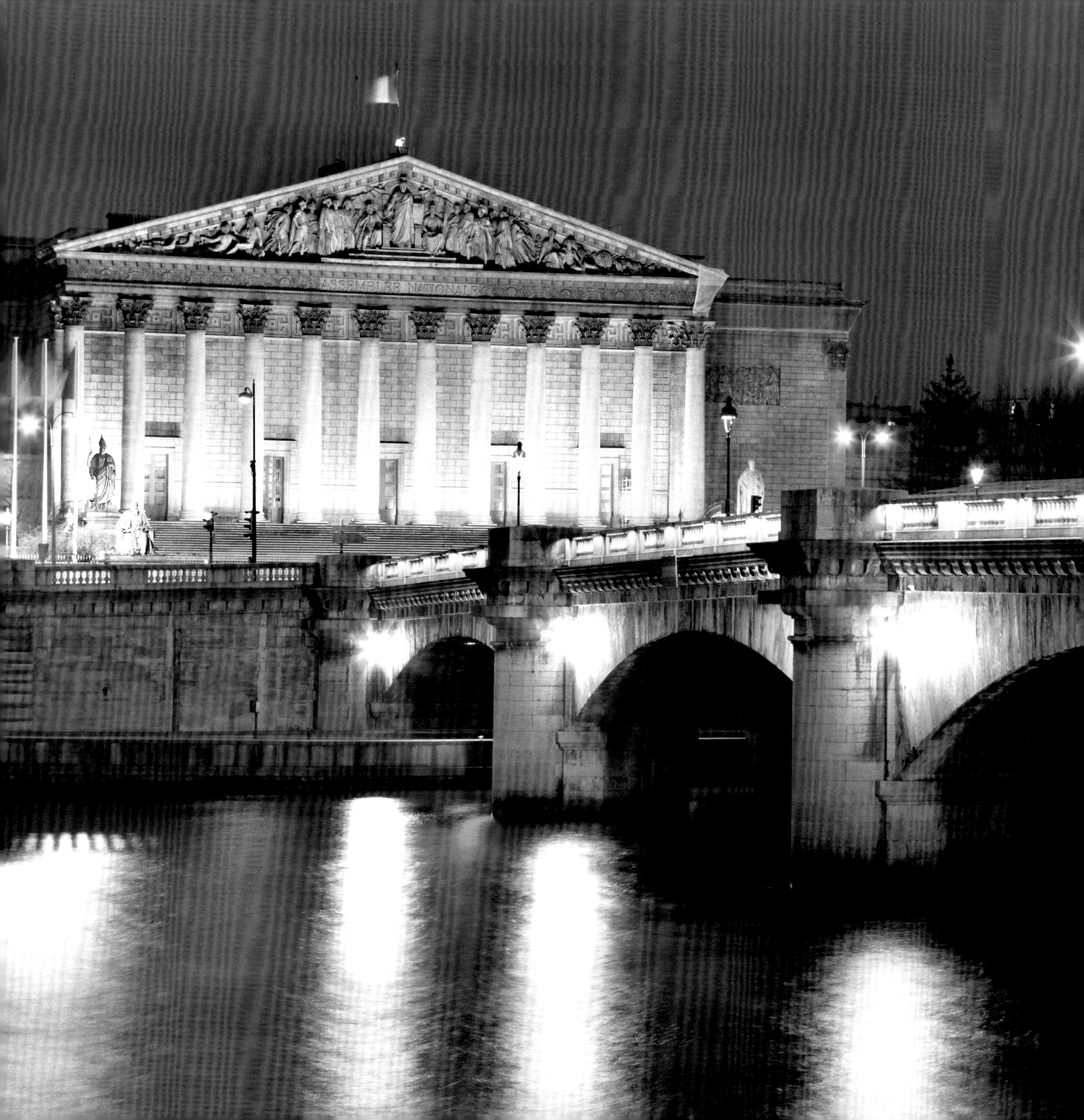

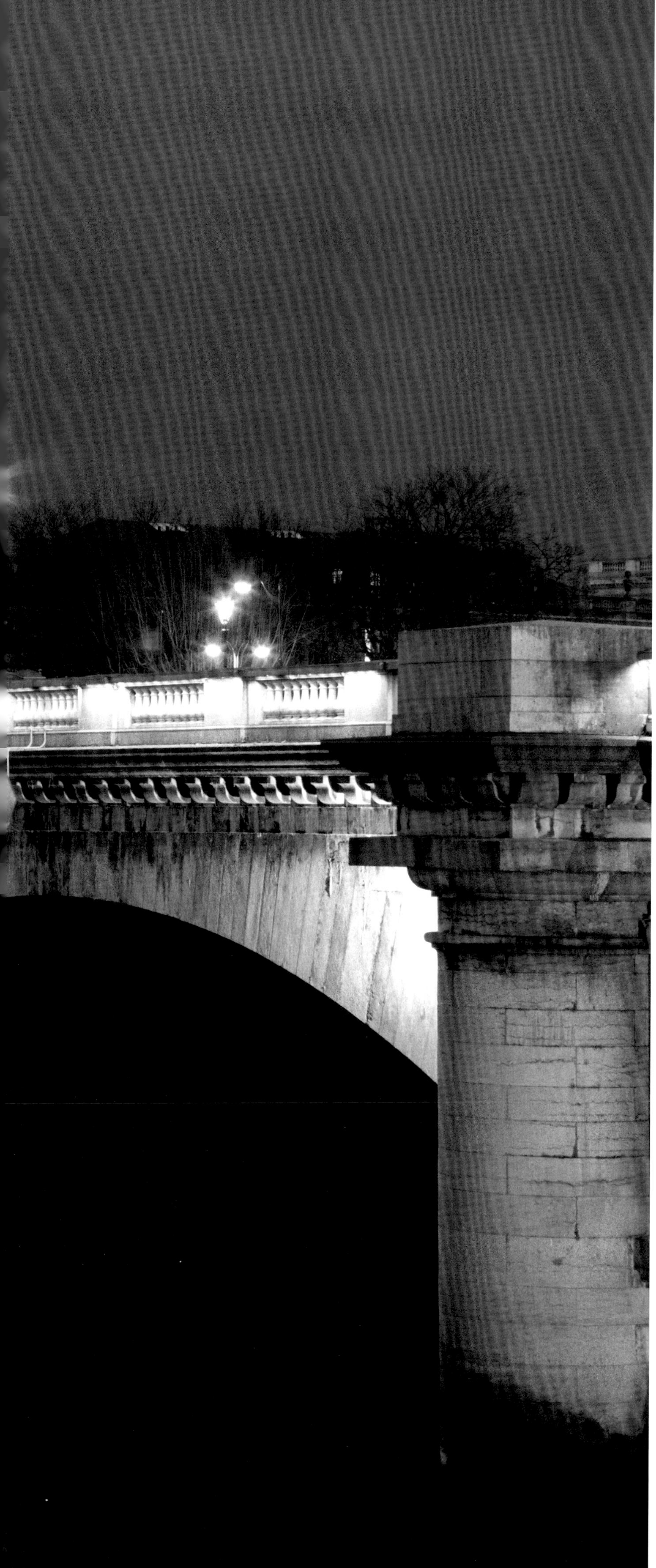

Pont de la Concorde:
The Assemblée Nationale.

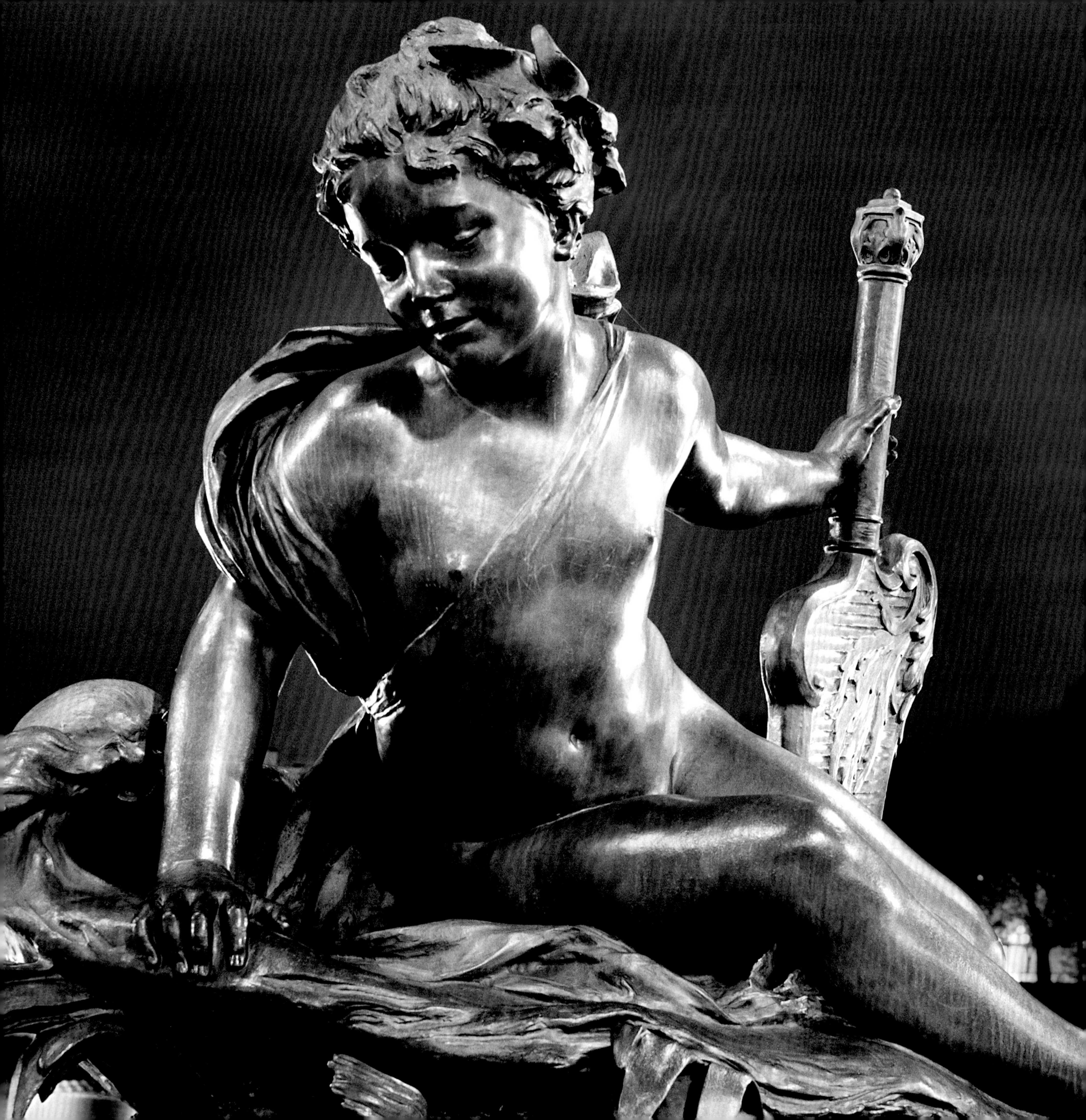

PONT ALEXANDRE III

The Pont Alexandre III is without a doubt the most elegant bridge in Paris. It is certainly the city's most opulently decorated bridge and is as grand as it is elegant.

Compared with some of the other bridges, the Pont Alexandre III has had a relatively short history. In 1811 and 1824 two separate attempts were made to build a bridge at this site. Although construction began on both, neither was finished.

In 1896 France developed a politically convenient friendship with Russia to serve as a counterweight to the growing might of Germany. On October 7, President Félix Faure and Tsar Nicolas II laid the first stone for the new bridge, to be built in honor of the tsar's father, Alexandre III, thus sealing the new alliance between the two countries.

The bridge was planned for the upcoming Universal Exposition of 1900. The objective was to create a spectacular showpiece, as the Eiffel Tower was for the 1889 exposition. The Pont Alexandre III was finished and inaugurated at the start of the exposition in April 1900.

Pont Alexandre III:
Sculpture "Néréide" André
Massoule (1851–1901).

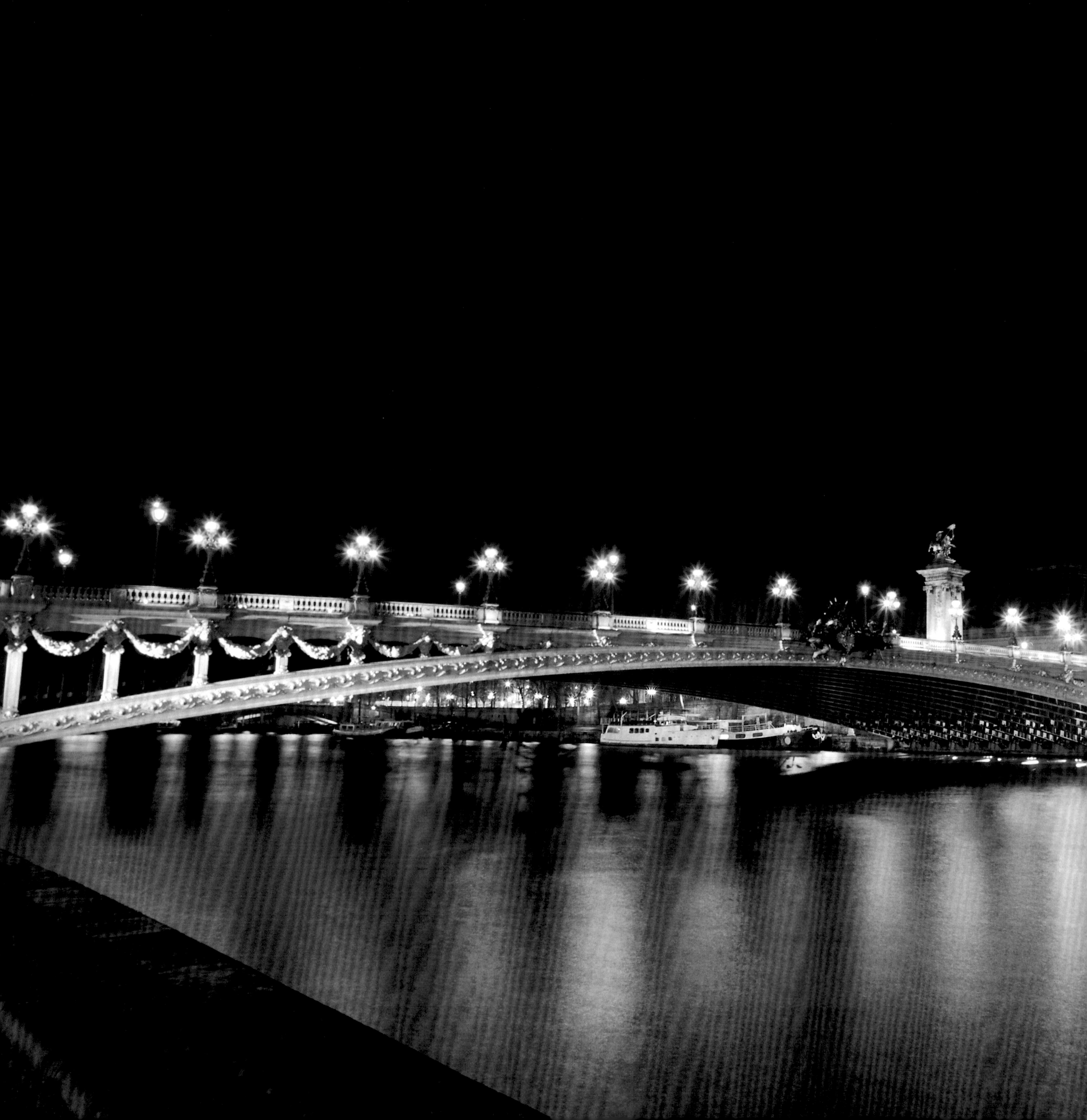

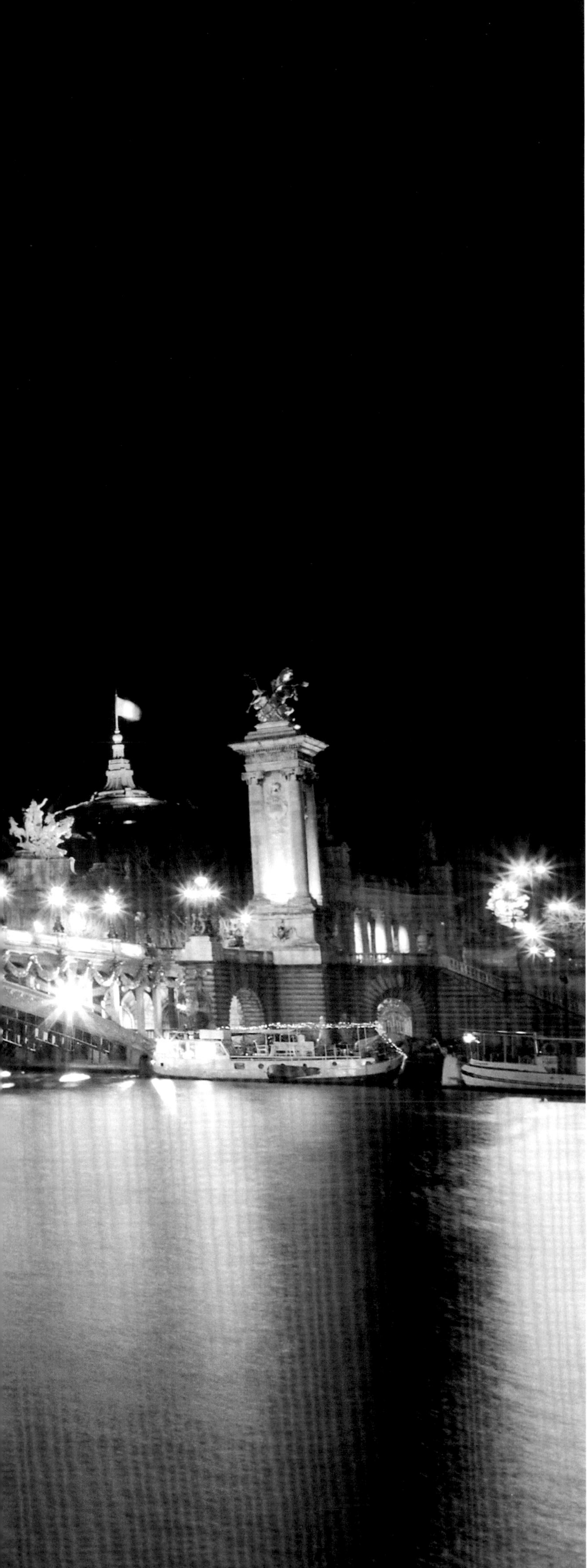

Also for the exposition, the Grand Palais and the Petit Palais were constructed adjacent to the bridge on the right bank. A wide new avenue, named Alexandre III—later renamed Avenue Winston Churchill—was to run between them, linking the new bridge with the Champs-Élysées. On the left bank the bridge connects to the esplanade and the entrance to the Hôtel des Invalides, founded by Louis XIV in 1670 as a home and hospital for aged and ailing soldiers.

The Pont Alexandre III was designed to comply with certain constraints. Since the new avenue was built to enhance the view of the Hôtel des Invalides, it could not infringe upon that view. It could not overshadow the two large edifices of the Grand Palais and Petit Palais. It had to be wide enough to be harmonious with the new avenue. Thus, with its 40-meter (130 feet) width (including broad sidewalks) it became the widest of all the bridges. It was built on a slight bias instead of perpendicular to the river to allow the ends to nestle more comfortably into the avenue and structures on both sides. To keep a low profile, the bridge has a very shallow arch.

A splendid new vista, 1.2 kilometers (¾ mile) long, was created from the Hôtel des Invalides across the Pont Alexandre III to the Place Georges Clemenceau on the Champs-Élysées. More than fifty million visitors to the exposition between April and November 1900 enjoyed the view.

More than fifty works of art created by seventeen different artists are found on the bridge.

The first works that come into view are the four immense columns, each 17 meters (56 feet) high. A statue of the winged horse Pegasus, sculpted in a brilliant gold, is atop each of the columns. The two columns on the right bank personify peace: the Arts on the upstream side and Agriculture on the downstream side. On the left bank they symbolize glory and conflict: upstream is Combat and downstream is War.

A seated statue is at the foot of each column. They represent four periods of French history, with the France of Charlemagne and Contemporary France on the right bank and the France of the Renaissance and of Louis XIV on the left bank.

Four handsome stone lions, two on the left bank and two on the right, guard the entrances to the bridge.

In the middle of the bridge are hammered copper sculptures depicting nymphs holding a coat of arms. On the downstream side nymphs of the Seine hold the coat of arms of Paris, and on the upstream side nymphs of the river Neva hold the coat of arms of Imperial Russia.

Sculptures of children in a marine motif are found on the balustrades on each side of the bridge. They are *L'enfant au crabe* (child with a crab), *La Fillette à la coquille* (girl with a shell), *L'Enfant au poisson* (child of the fish), and *La Néréide* (nymph of the sea).

Pont Alexandre III:
View from upstream.

The Pont Alexandre III is lit by thirty-two unique candelabras, twenty-eight of which have three elegant glass globes; the larger ones, on the four corners of the bridge, each have five glass globes and three cherubs dancing at their base.

Features such as cupids, starfish, sea urchins, shells, and mascarons can also be found among the works of art.

The bridge was classified as a Monument Historique in April 1975.

In 1991 the bridge was completely refurbished without any change to its original design, and its faded color was restored to the original gray.

No other bridge in France offers the quality and quantity of art that is found on the Pont Alexandre III.

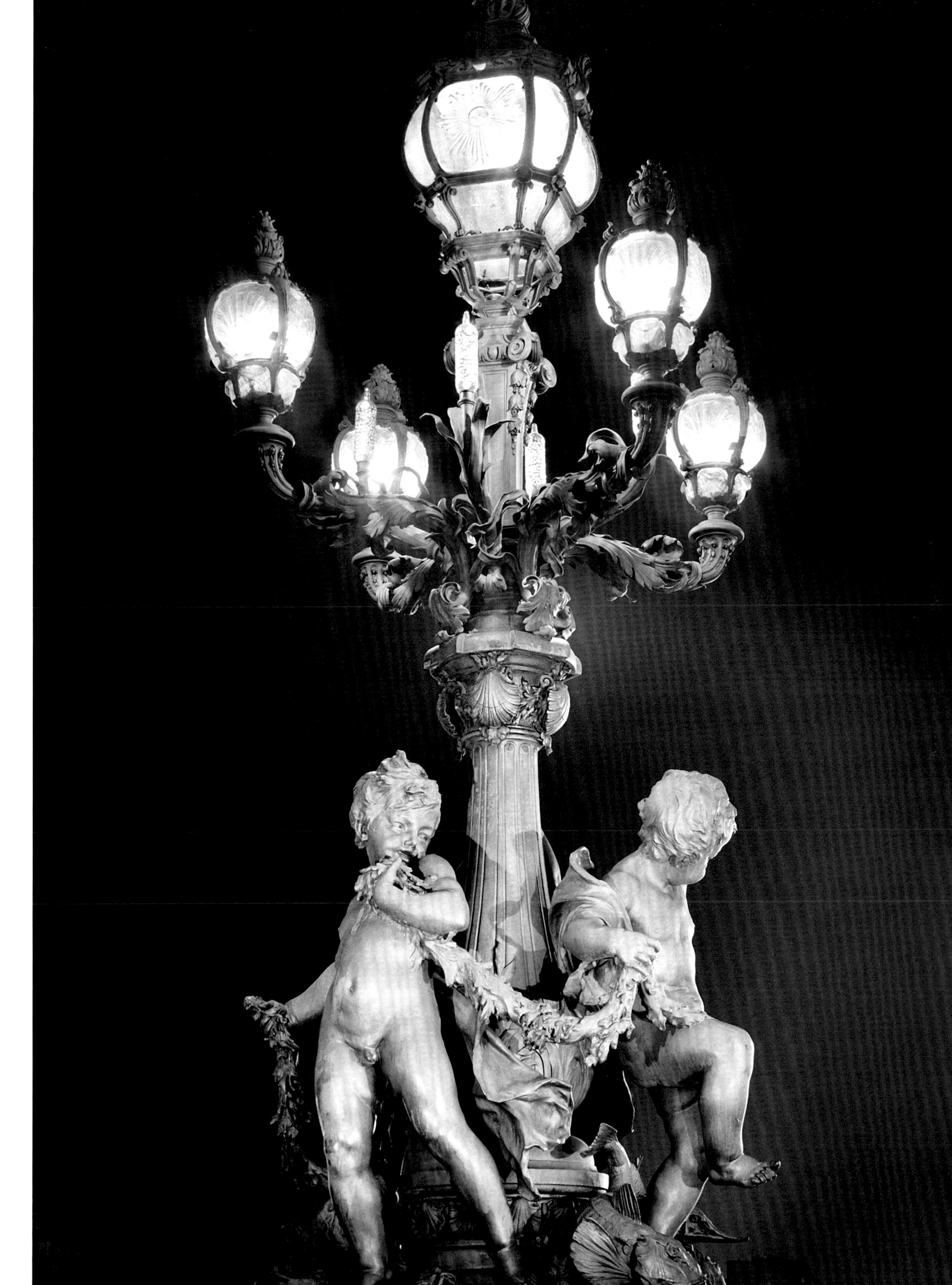

Pont Alexandre III:
"Les amours" supporting four
lamp post lights on four corners
of the bridge. Henri Désiré
Gauquié (1858–1927).

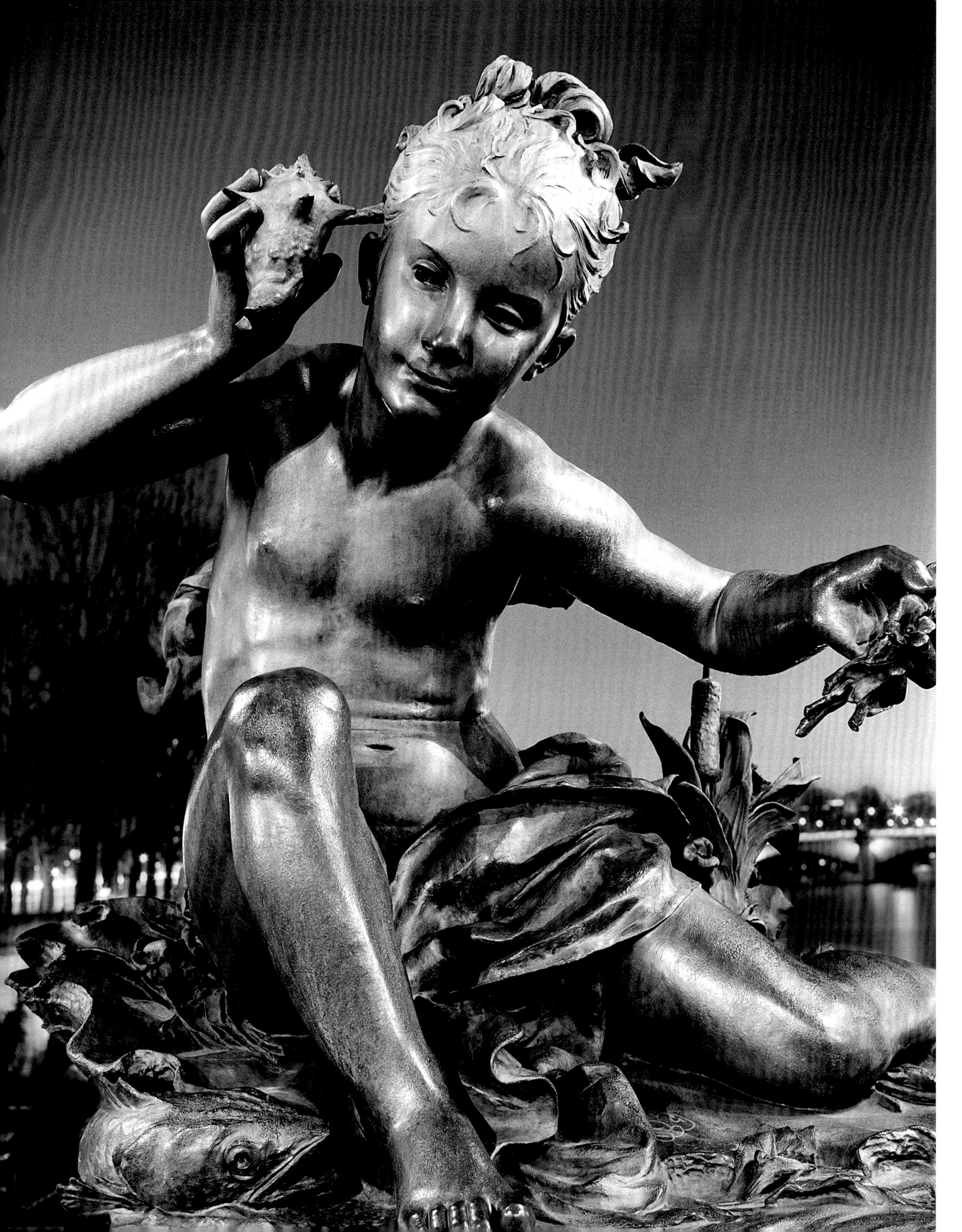

Pont Alexandre III:
Sculpture "La fillette à la coquille" Léopold Morice (1846–1920).

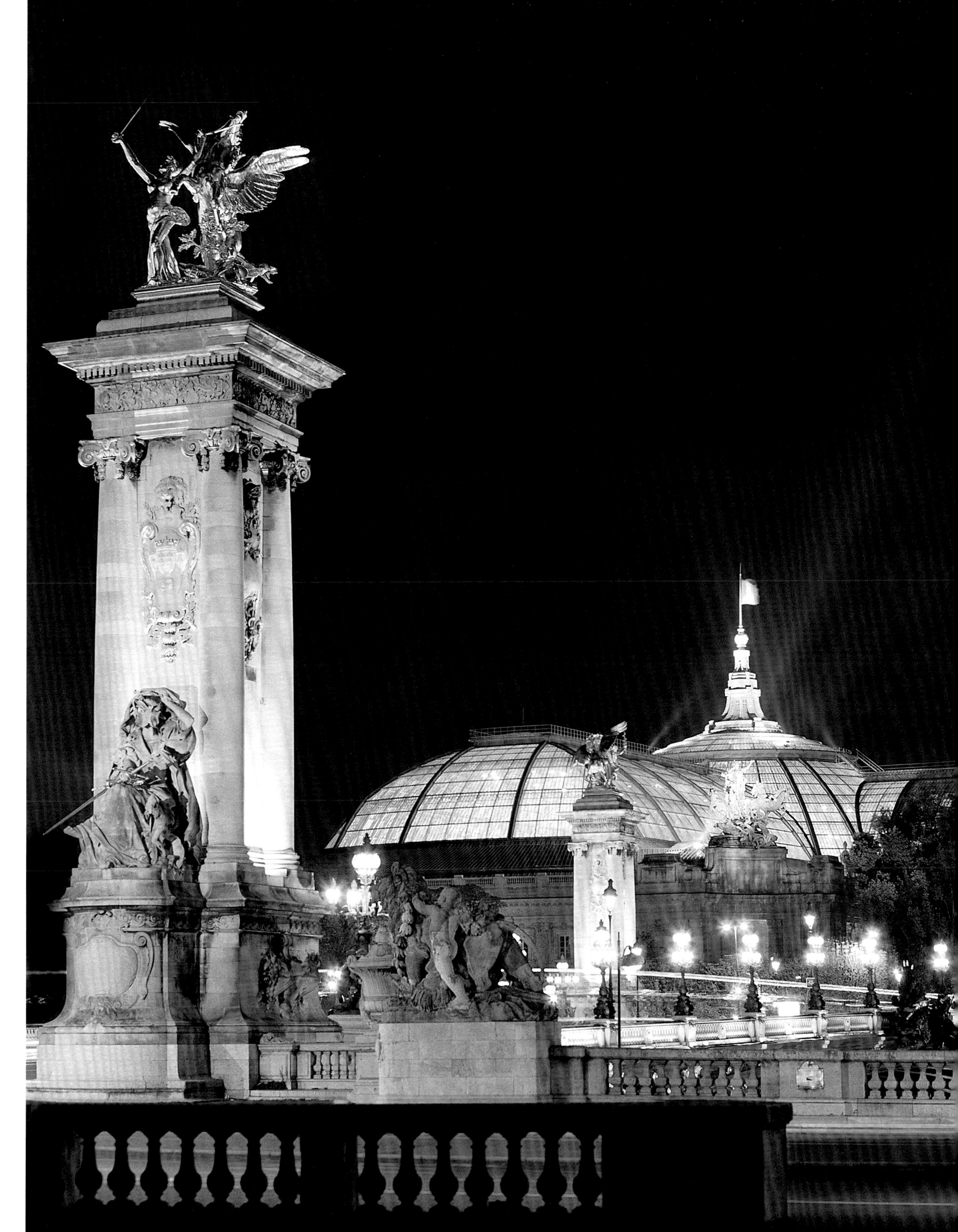

Pont Alexandre III:
Sculpture atop the pillar "La Renommée de la Guerre" by Clément Steiner (1853–1899).

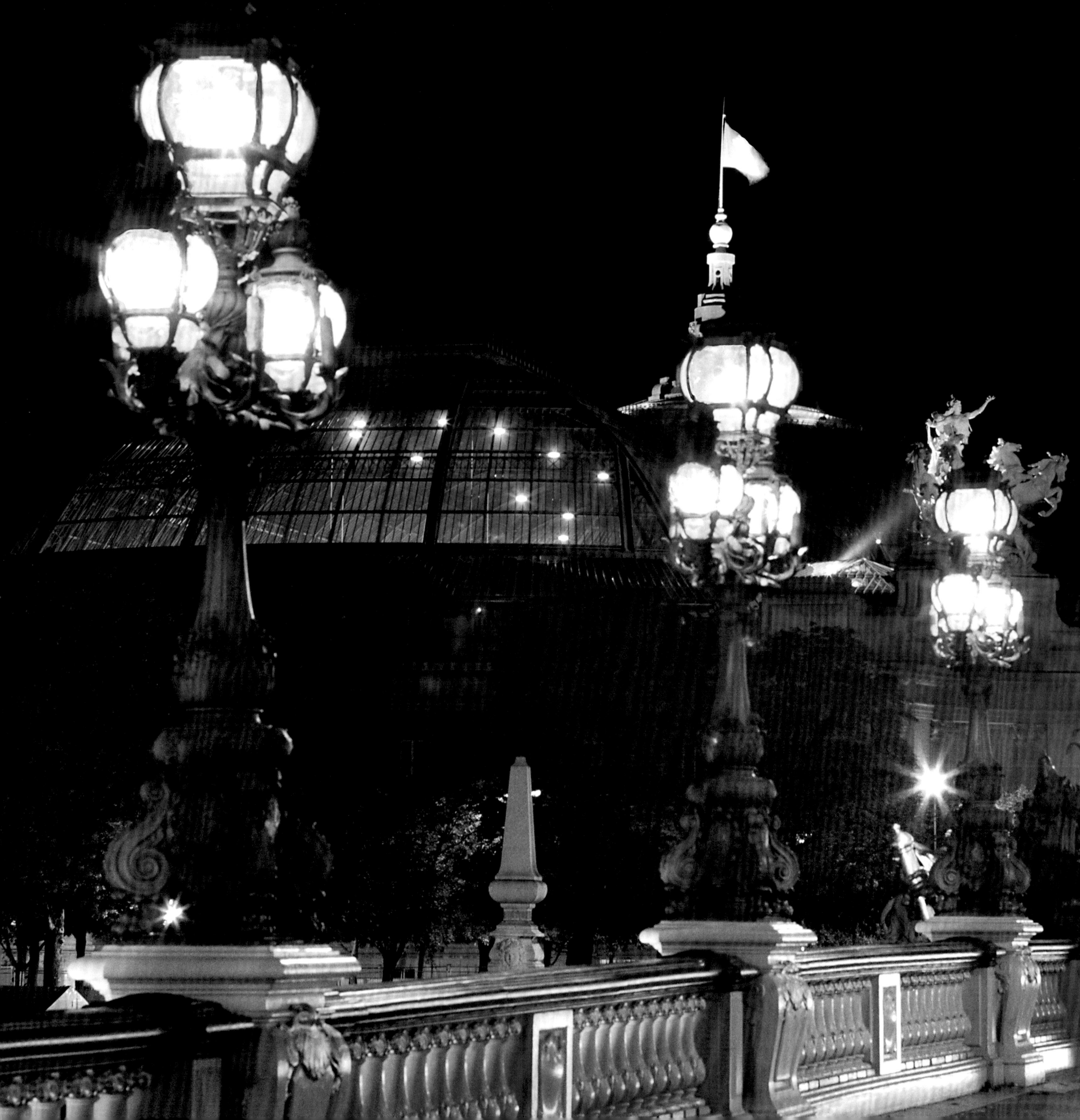

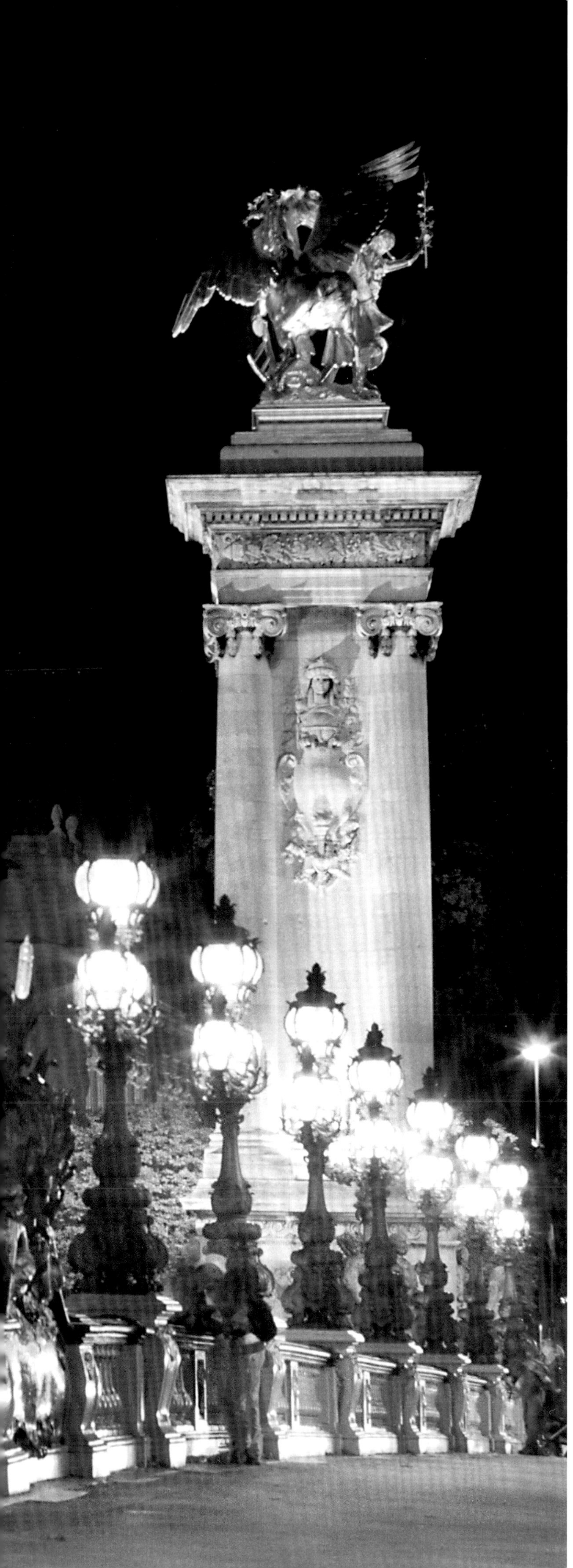

Pont Alexandre III:
Decorative lighting on the bridge.

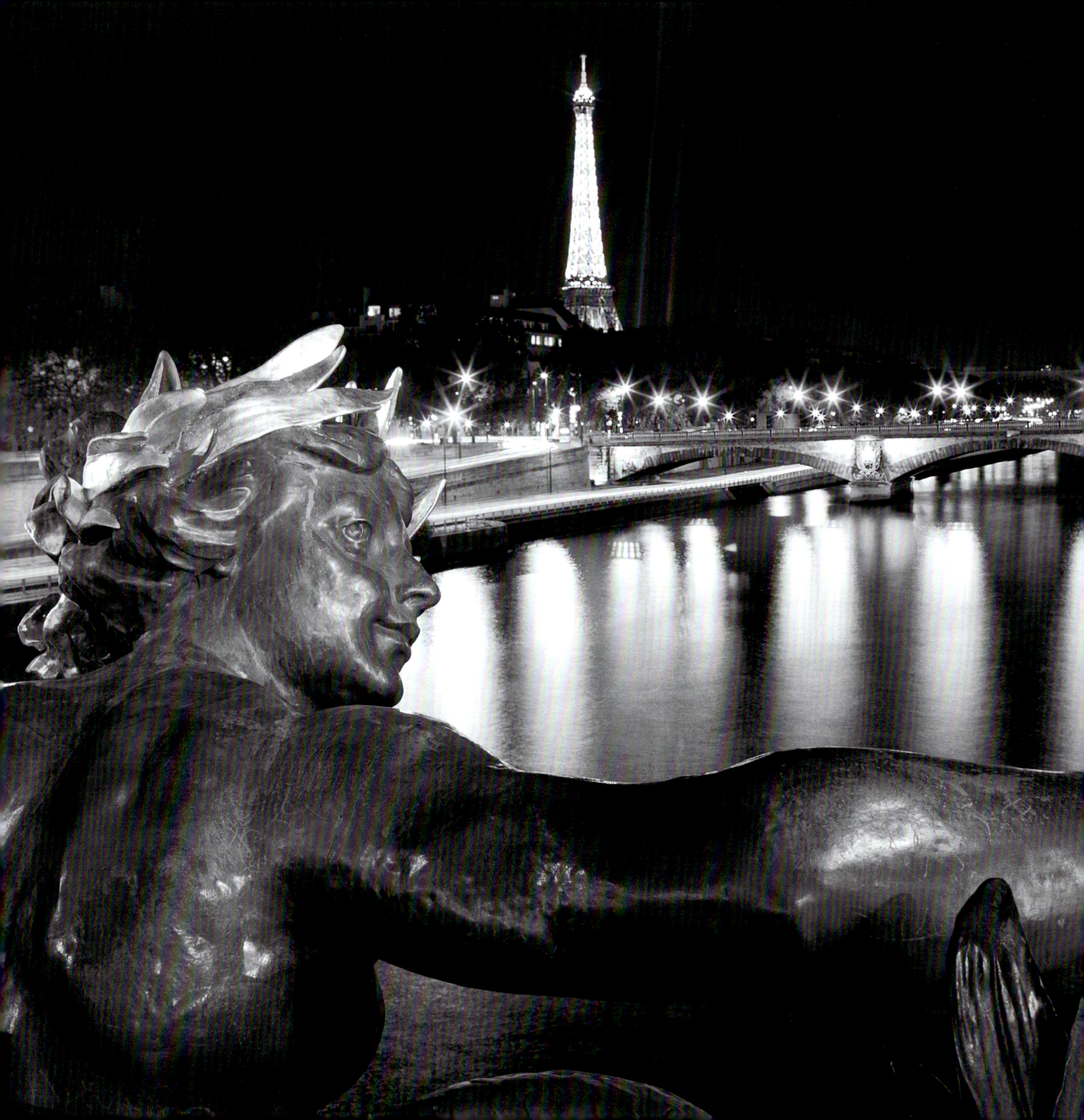

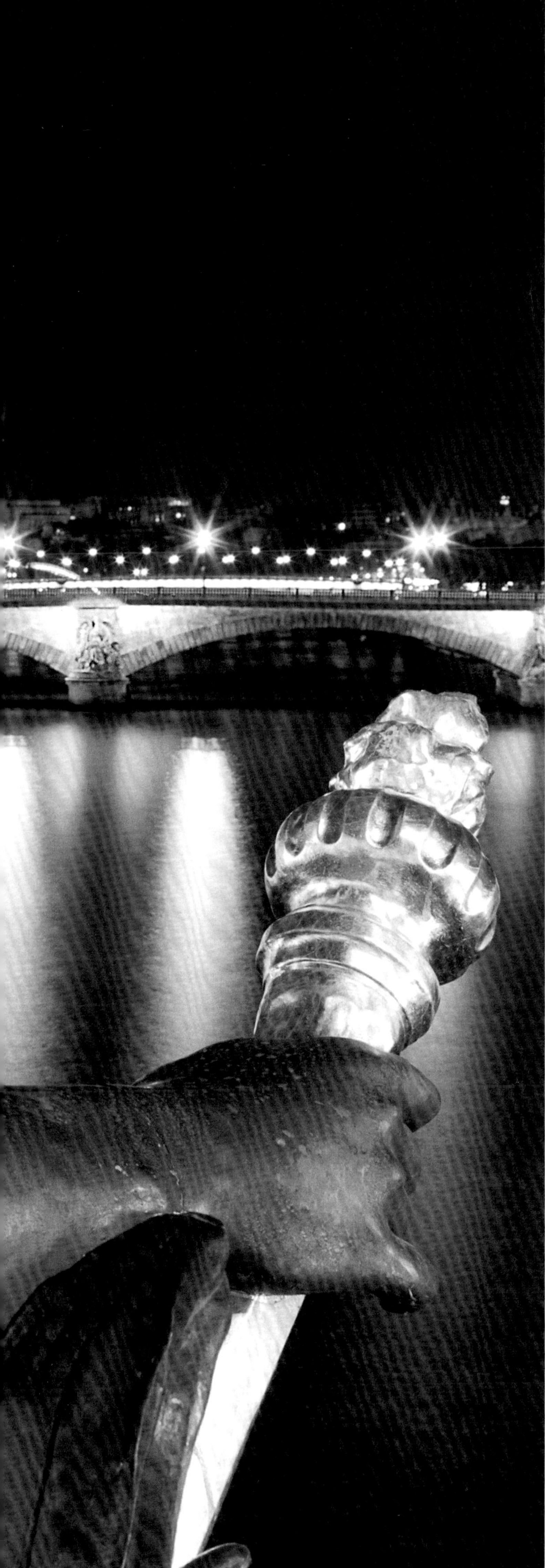

PONT DES INVALIDES

The Pont des Invalides was supposed to be an important component of the 1855 International Exposition in Paris.

Construction began on October 25, 1854. The contractor had agreed to finish the new bridge by May 1855 to coincide with the opening day of the exposition. To great consternation, the bridge was not ready on time, and in fact was not finished until one year later, in May 1856, after the exposition had closed.

The bridges prior to the 1856 bridge were also beset with problems. The first bridge was designed by well-known engineer Claude Navier, who taught at the École Nationale des Ponts et Chaussées and wrote textbooks on bridge building. His plan for the first Pont des Invalides, a single-span suspension bridge that would cross without support in the Seine, was ratified by royal order in 1824. Named the Pont des Invalides, it was built adjacent to the Hôtel des Invalides.

A few weeks before that bridge was supposed to open, one of the suspension chains broke; at the same time a broken water pipe caused one

Pont des Invalides:
View from Pont Alexandre III with the sculpture "Nymphes de la Seine" by Georges Récipon (1860–1920).

of the buttresses to crack. The towers that supported the weight of the deck began to tilt. In 1827 the Municipal Council of Paris decided to order the bridge demolished and the project abandoned.

That was the last Pont des Invalides at this location. Protests against the location came from groups wishing to preserve the unencumbered view of the Hôtel des Invalides. As a result the site was moved farther downstream. However, seventy years later the Pont Alexandre III would be built on this site.

The next bridge, built in 1829, was again a suspension bridge, this time with five arches. It connected what is now Avenue Franklin D. Roosevelt with the Boulevard de la Tour-Maubourg. By 1850 stress cracks began to appear, and as a result parking on the bridge was banned and vehicles pulled by two or more horses prohibited. This bridge was replaced by the 1856 bridge that was late for the International Exposition.

The 1856 bridge, composed of four stone arches, utilized the existing abutments and piers from the previous bridge; only the central pier was new. Despite restoration work on some of the arches in 1876, the bridge sagged 30 centimeters (12 inches), and a complete restoration was begun in 1879. A temporary passerelle was erected upstream to serve in the interim. In January 1880 ice destroyed the passerelle; its remnants were carried downstream and destroyed most of the restoration work on the bridge. Nevertheless the restoration was complete by the end of 1880.

The restoration work proved effective and very little additional work has been needed since then, with the exception of the widening of the bridge in 1956.

The center pier is crowned with sculptures in allegorical themes of victory, upstream representing victory on land and downstream victory at sea. On each of the other piers sits a sculpted head of Medusa surrounded by military emblems.

THE EIGHT BRIDGES DOWNSTREAM

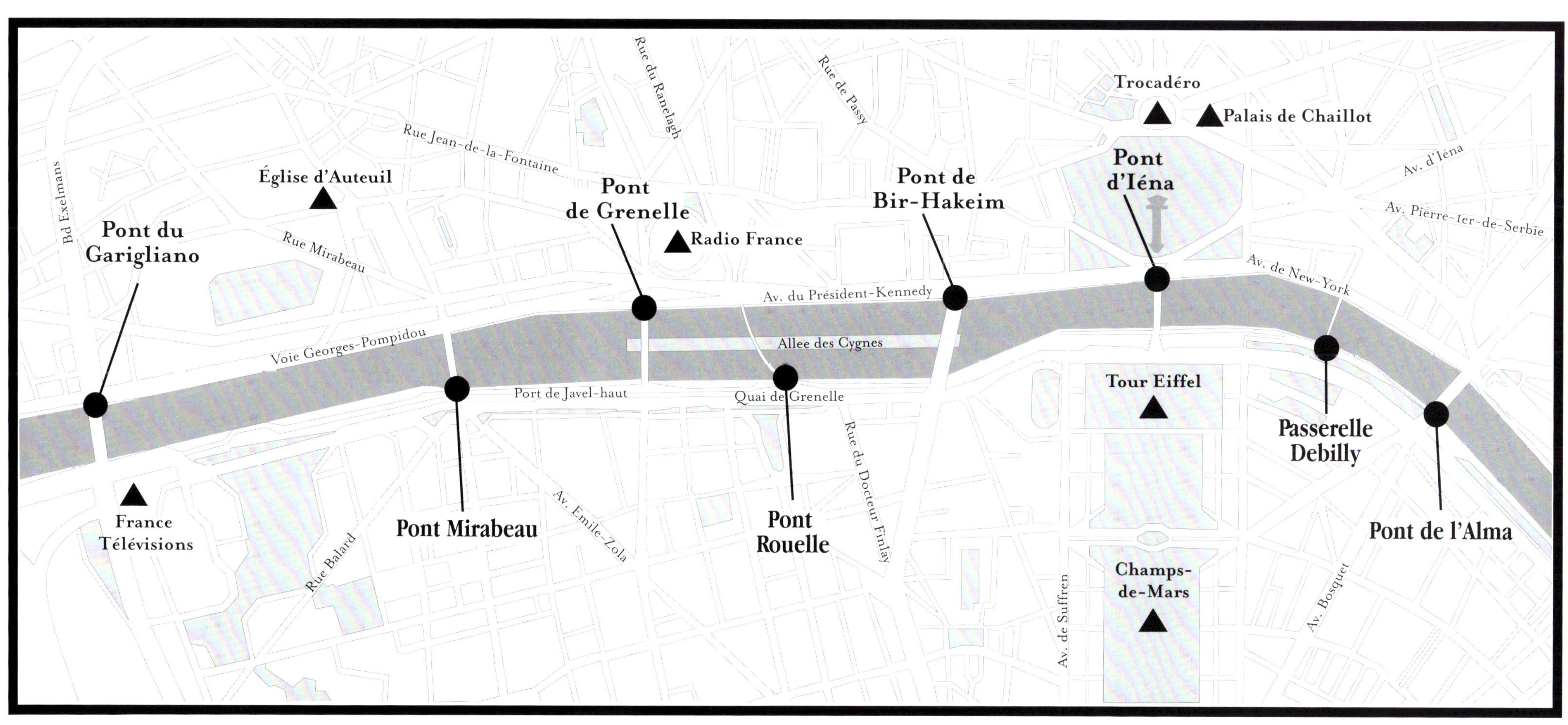

PONT DE L'ALMA

On April 2, 1856, Napoleon III inaugurated the Pont de l'Alma, named to commemorate his victory in the Crimea during the Crimean War. Alma was a battle where the Franco-British alliance achieved victory over the Russian army in 1854.

A stone and masonry bridge of three arches, it was decorated with statues of four soldiers representing various elements of the battle. Each 6-meter-tall statue was erected on a pedestal at the base of each arch. On the downstream side was *un Artilleur* (an artillery man) and *un Chasseur à pied* (a foot soldier), created by the sculptor Auguste Arnaud, and upstream a *Grenadier* and a *Zouave*, created by sculptor Georges Diebolt.

The Zouaves were a tribe of Berbers from the mountains of Algeria. In 1852, the French Army included three regiments of Zouaves. Their chief distinguishing characteristic was the Zouave uniform, which included short, open-fronted jackets, baggy trousers, and, often, sashes and oriental headgear. Napoleon III honored them because the Zouaves had distinguished themselves particularly well in the fighting at Alma.

Pont de l'Alma:
Looking downstream past the
Bateaux Mouches tour boats.

BATEAUX-MOUCHES

Although it was not the original intention, the statues of the four soldiers became indicators of the severity of floods. The famous flood of 1910 was the worst in modern Paris history. During that flood the water level rose to the neck of the Zouave, more than six 6 meters (20 feet) above normal water level.

The bridge was meant to be an important part of the 1855 Universal Exposition in Paris. However, like its neighbor the Pont des Invalides, it was delayed and neither bridge opened in time for the exposition.

By the early 1960s the bridge had sagged and become too narrow for the increased road traffic; it was time for a new bridge. Construction began in 1970, and was completed in June 1974. Nothing was retained from the prior bridge except the statue of the Zouave. The current bridge is a steel girder construction, resting on one pier in the water. This is where the beloved Zouave has been installed: on the upstream side.

In his location on the new bridge the Zouave is placed a bit higher than he was previously. Nevertheless, the Parisians still have the old saying that when the Zouave has *les pieds dans l'eau* (his feet in the water) it indicates a flood.

Located just upstream from the bridge is the Port de la Conférence where the renowned Bateaux-Mouches sightseeing and dinner boats are moored.

On the right bank the bridge connects with a tunnel that passes underneath the roadway above. It was in this tunnel, in August 1997, that the car carrying Diana, Princess of Wales, crashed. She was killed along with her companion Dodi Fayed and driver Henri Paul.

Above the tunnel, at street level on the downstream side, is a sculpture of a large golden torch. It is an exact replica of the torch held by the Statue of Liberty in New York Harbor. The torch was a gift from the *International Herald Tribune* in 1987, commemorating the Franco-American friendship. After the crash, this torch spontaneously became a shrine for fans of Lady Diana. Cards, letters, and flowers were found deposited there in her memory.

Unique to the Pont de l'Alma, and not evident during the daytime, are the unusual light fixtures. By day they look rather mundane and modern, but by night they take on a different personality. They seem to come alive, metamorphosing into striking extraterrestrial forms: the lamp heads take the form of Martian invaders with the bulbs as the eyes of the aliens.

Pont de l'Alma:
The eyes of the martians,
lights on the bridge.

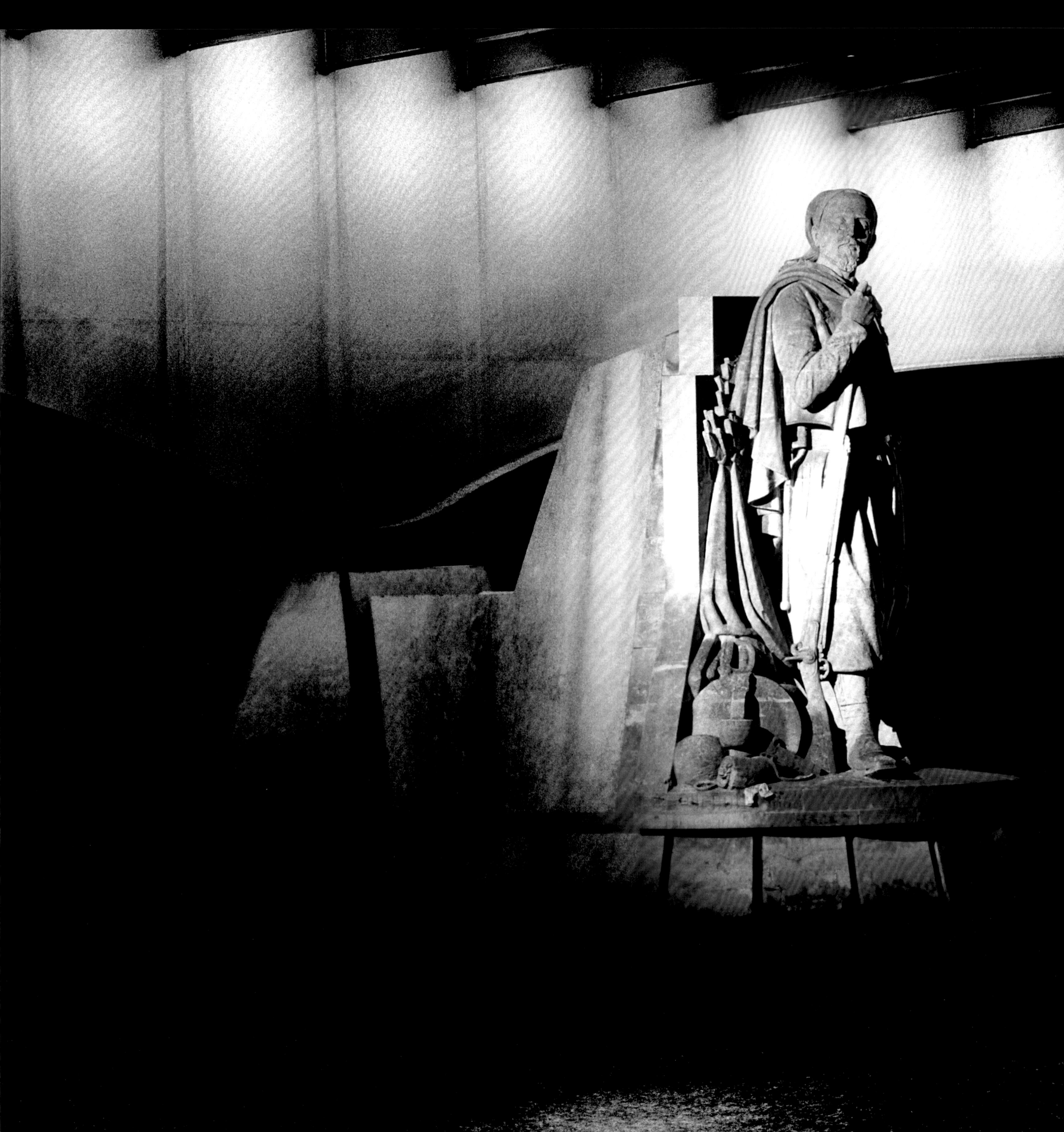

Pont de l'Alma:
The Zoave.

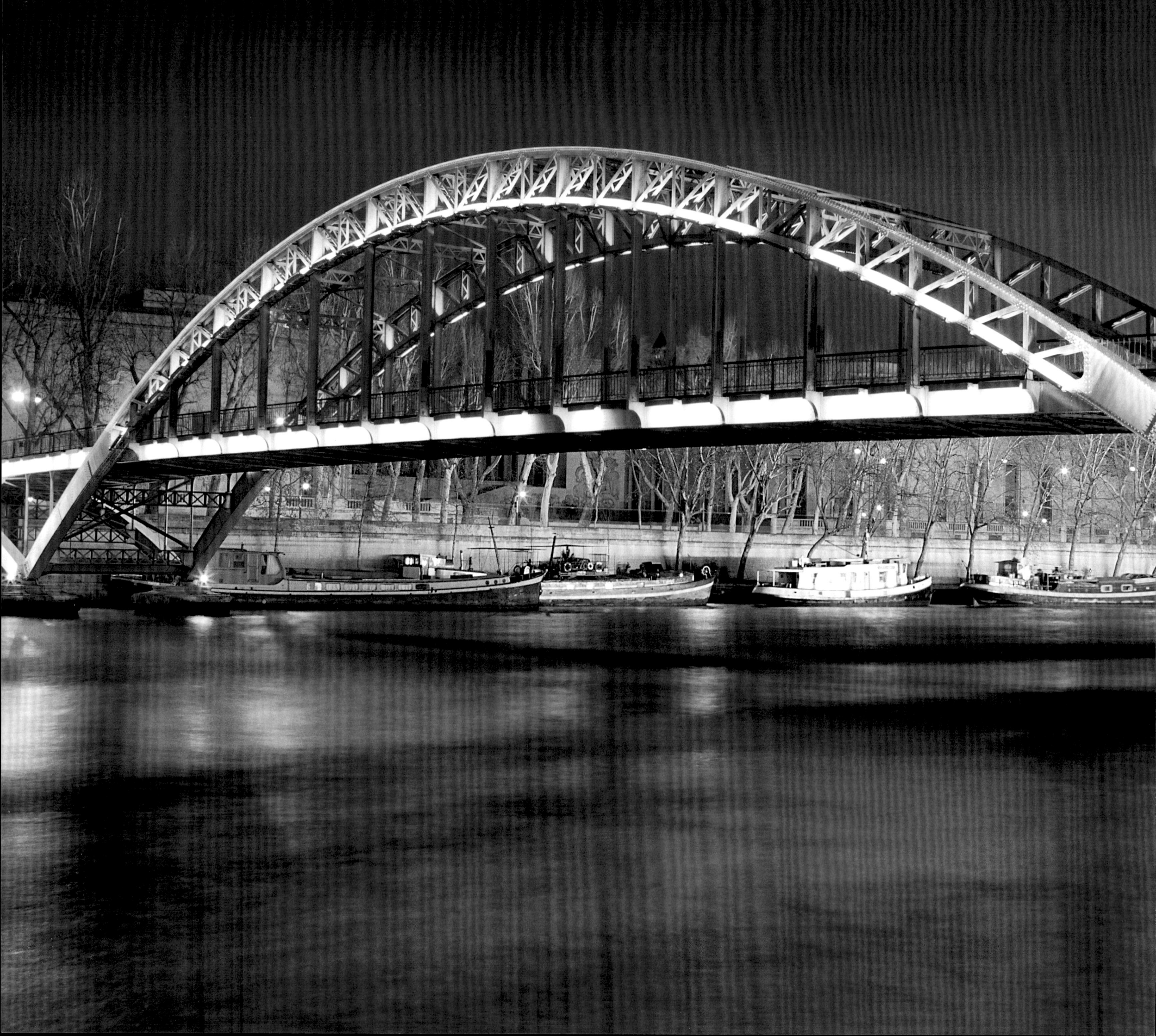

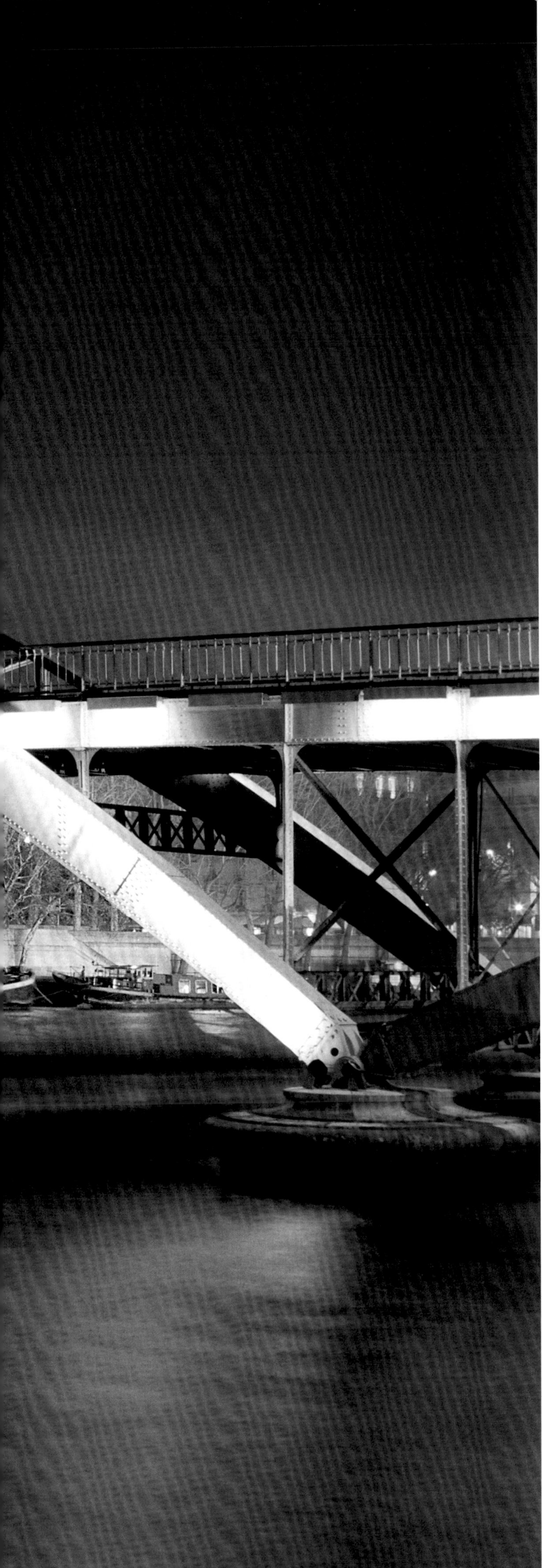

PASSERELLE DEBILLY

The Passerelle Debilly accommodates only pedestrian and bicycle traffic. It is one of the four footbridges among the thirty-five Paris bridges. The others are Passerelle Simone de Beauvoir, Pont des Arts, and Passerelle Léopold-Sédar-Senghor.

Passerelle Debilly was originally built as a temporary structure for the 1900 International Exposition. Most structures made for international expositions do not survive, but a few do, most notably the Eiffel Tower, as well as the Grand Palais and the Petit Palais, which are adjacent to the Pont Alexandre III. The Passerelle Debilly is a member of this group of survivors. It survived in part because it was useful and well built.

The bridge opened on April 13, 1900, one day before the opening of the Exposition. It was originally known as the Passerelle de l'Exposition Militaire and then named the Passerelle de Magdebourg. In 1906 it was named Passerelle Debilly in honor of General Jean-Louis Debilly, a first empire general who was killed in 1806 at the battle of Auerstadt in Germany, while serving under Napoleon Bonaparte. His is one of the 660 military names commemorated on the Arc de Triomphe.

Passerelle Debilly:
View from the left bank to the
right bank, looking upstream.

By 1903 the bridge had become a permanent fixture and the City of Paris took control of it. Three years later it was moved 200 meters (656 feet) farther upstream toward the Pont de l'Alma. The bridge connects the quai Branly and the Musée du quai Branly on the left bank to the Avenue de New York, the Palais de Tokyo, and the Musée d'Art Moderne on the right bank.

The Passerelle Debilly visually resembles a railroad trestle bridge, with a metal frame construction with three spans and its four feet anchored on piles in the river. Along with the Eiffel Tower and the Viaduc d'Austerlitz, it displays the type of metal architecture that was representative of the late nineteenth and early twentieth centuries.

In 1941 the president of the Society of Architects severely criticized its design, calling it an "*accessoire oublié d'une fête*" (forgotten accessory from a past event). Nevertheless, in 1966 it was included in the supplementary registry of historical monuments.

It was restored in 1983–1984 and repainted in 1991. In 1997 the deck was replaced with the same exotic Brazilian hardwood that is found on some of the other passerelles.

Today a good many boats and tour boats are moored at the port de Debilly downstream from the passerelle and at the port de La Bourdonnais upstream.

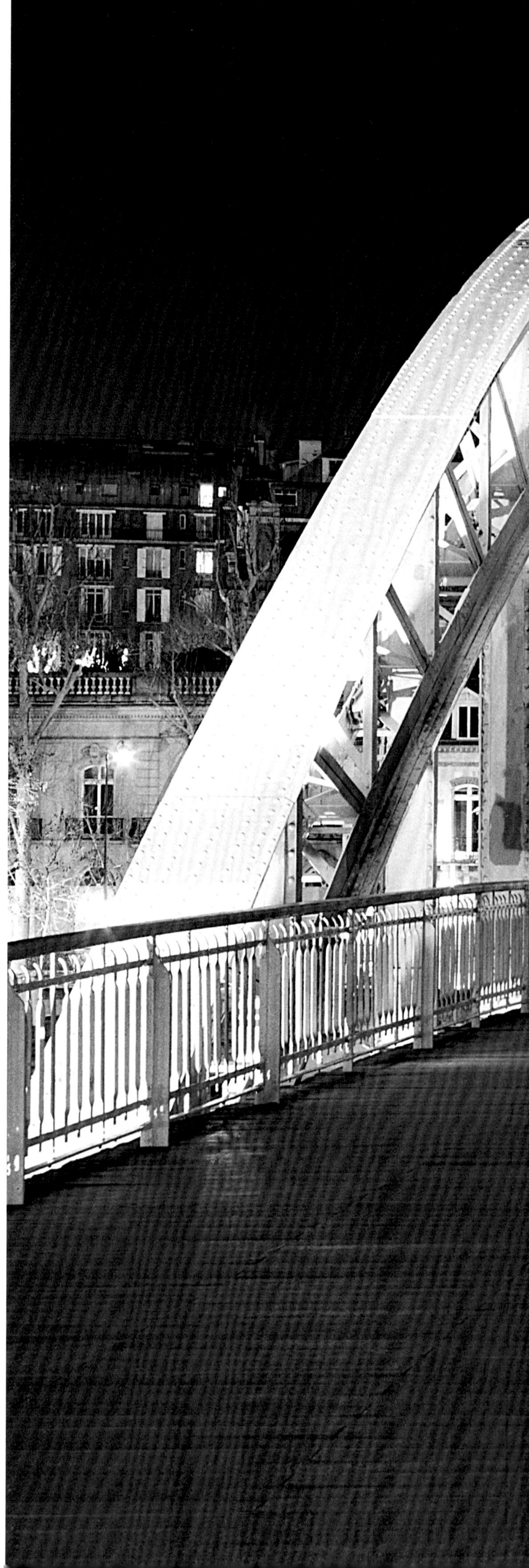

Passerelle Debilly:
The wooden surface
of the passerelle.

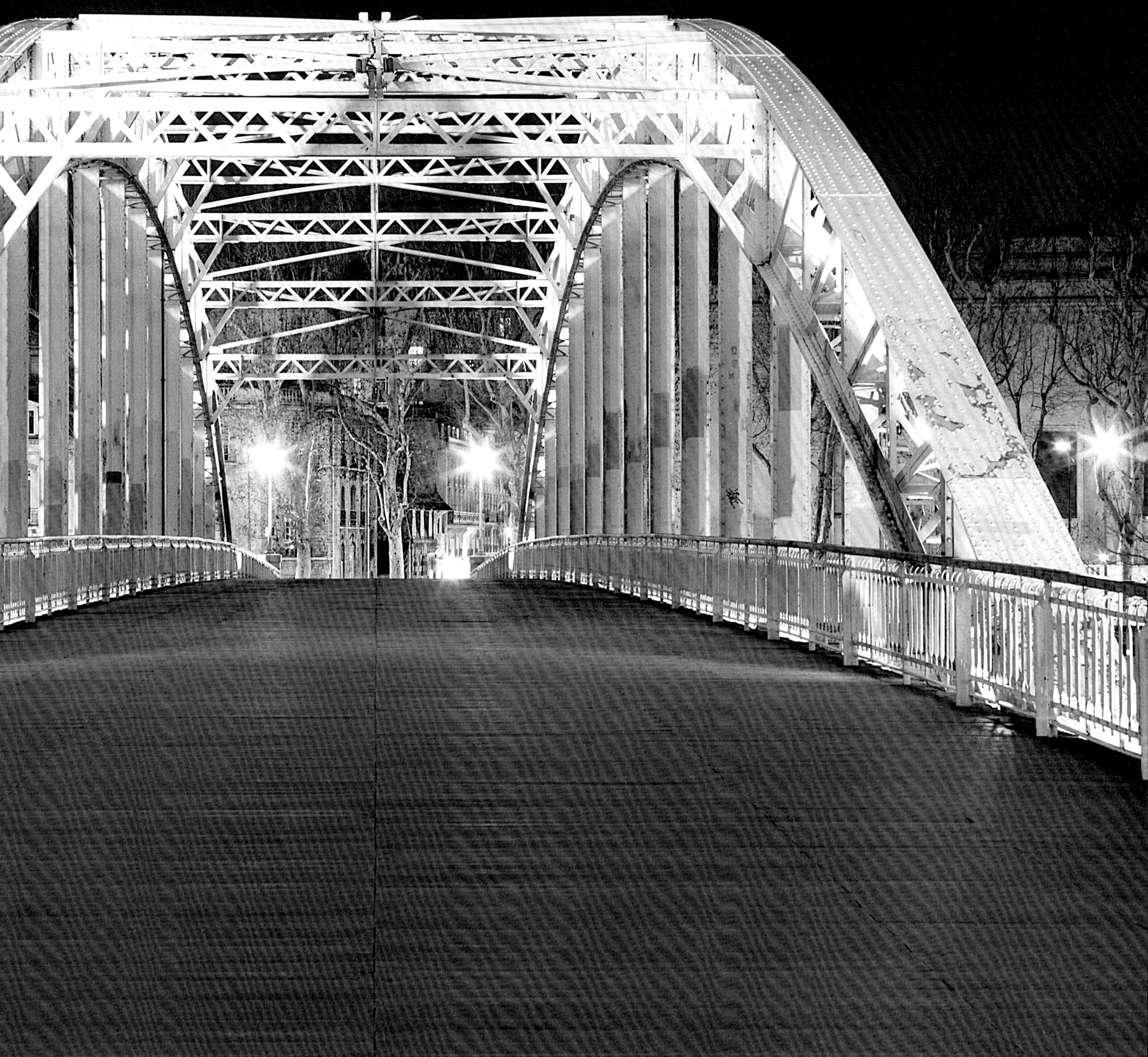

Pont d'Iéna

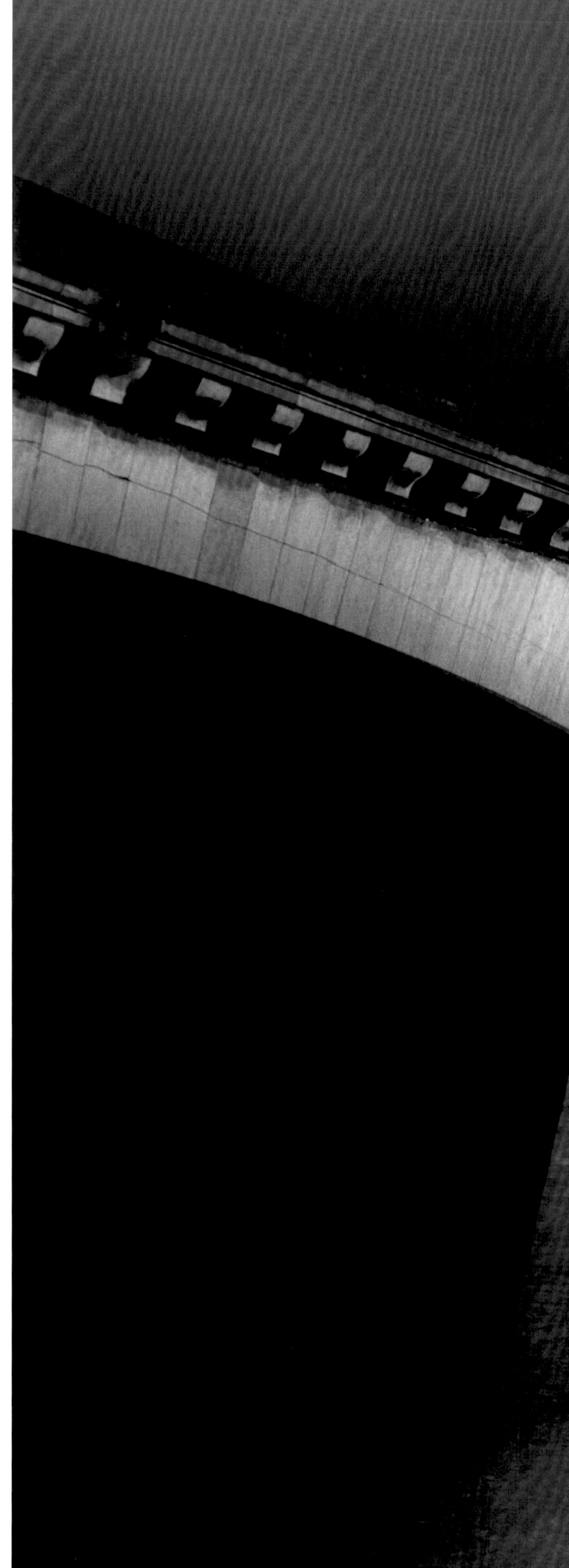

The Pont d'Iéna was originally supposed to be named either Pont du Champ de Mars or Pont de l'École Militaire. Both were logical names because the bridge crossed the river at the Champ de Mars, and the École Militaire was located adjacent to the Champ de Mars. But Napoleon Bonaparte decided to name it Pont d'Iéna to commemorate his victory over the Prussians at the battle of Iéna, a small German town, in October 1806.

Napoleon's army of 150,000 soundly defeated the Prussian army of roughly the same size. His forces suffered 7,500 dead or wounded while the Prussians suffered 38,000 dead, wounded, and captured. One of the commanders of the defeated forces was a certain General Gerhard von Blucher.

In March 1806 Napoleon signed a law authorizing the bridge. Construction began and the bridge went into service in 1813. It is a stone bridge with five equal arches. In 1814 eight large sculpted eagles, representing the empire, were installed at the intersection of each of the arches. Pedestals for statues were built at each of the four corners of the bridge, but no statues were erected at that time.

Pont d'Iéna:
Connecting the Trocadero
with the Eiffel tower.

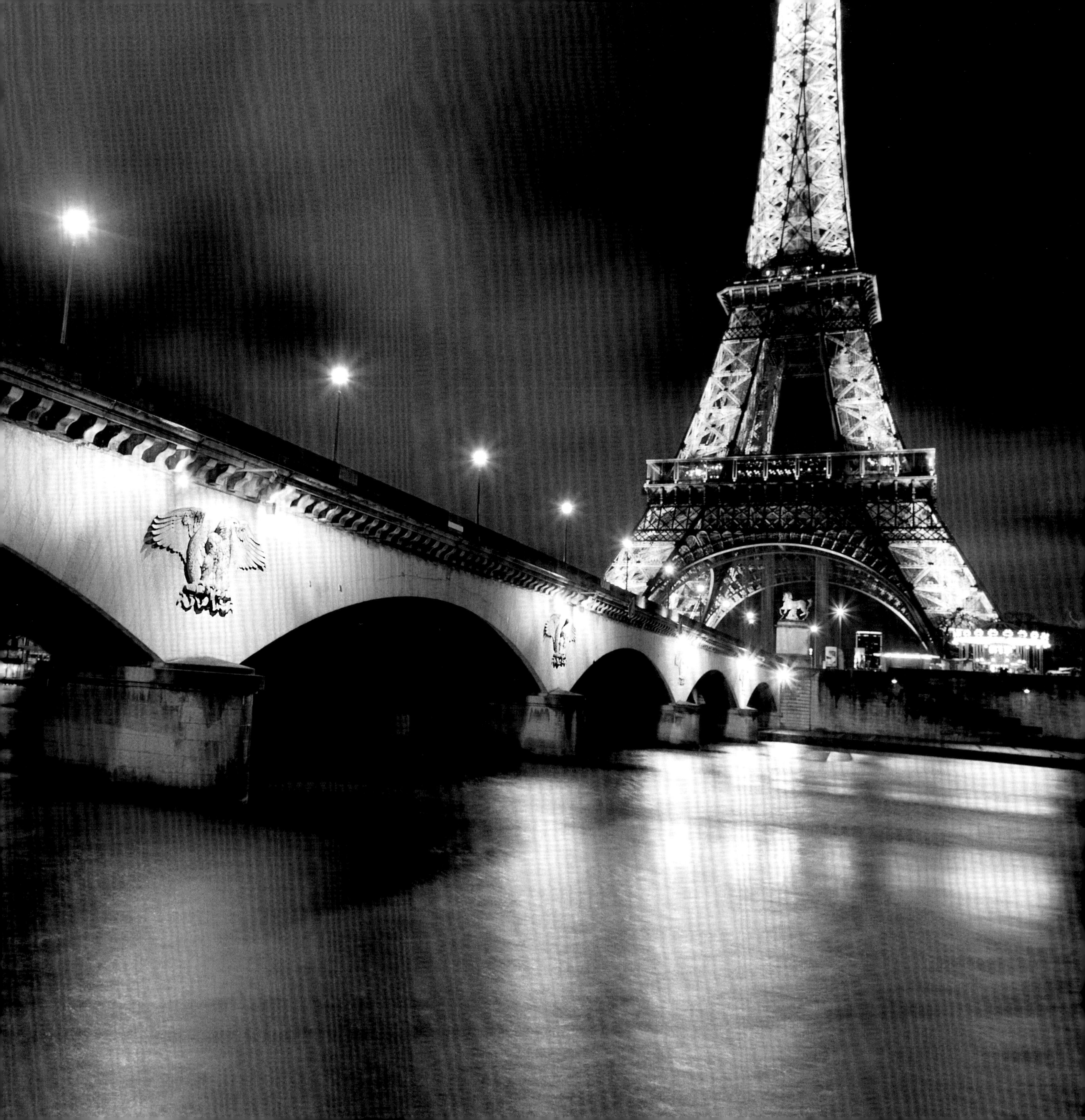

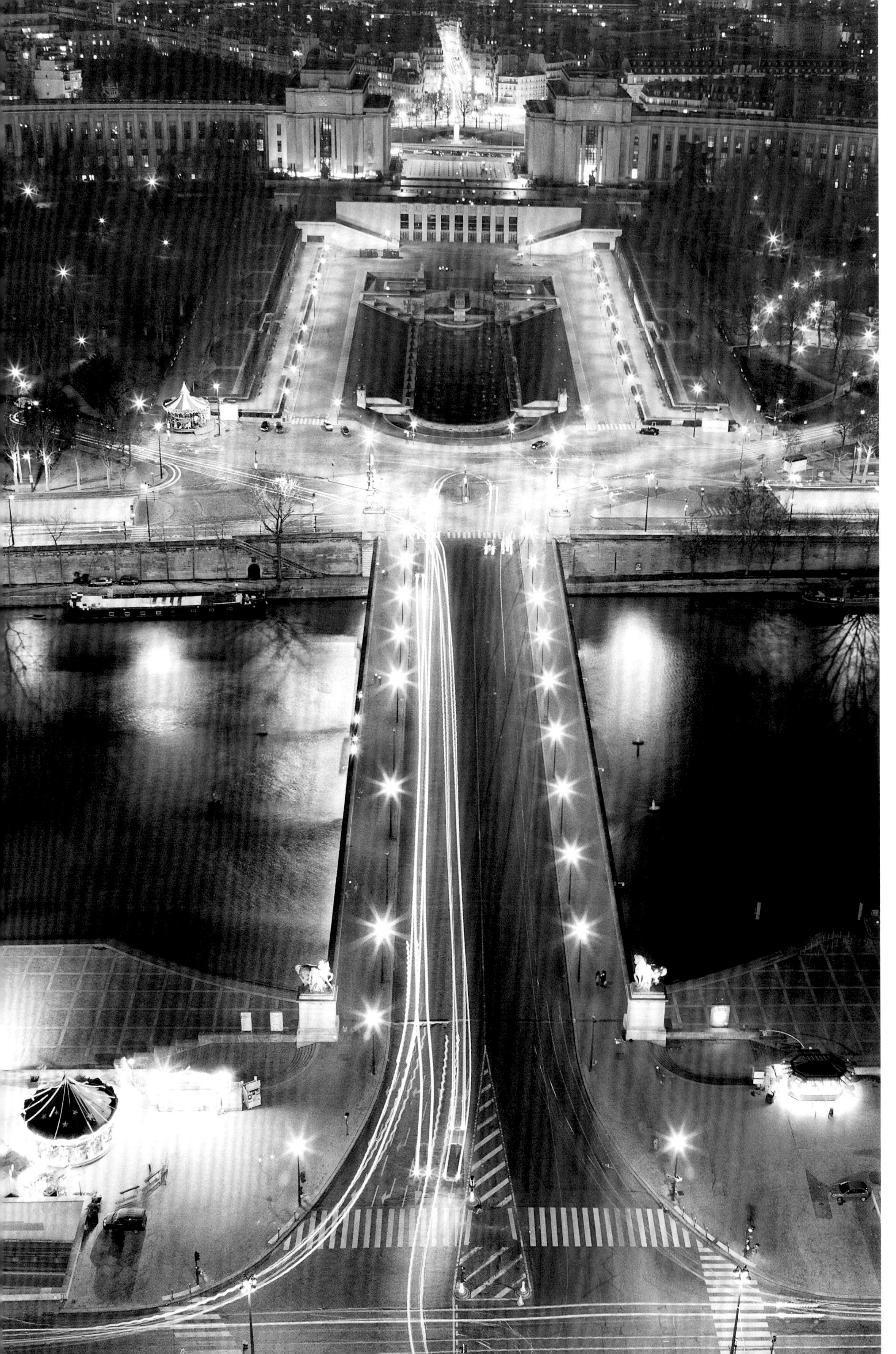

Pont d'Iena:
Aerial view from the Eiffel Tower.

Like most bridges at that time, the Pont d'Iéna was to be a toll bridge. The right to collect the tolls would be given to whomever provided the money to build the bridge. However, nobody was interested in putting up the funds, so the government built the bridge and there was no toll.

In 1814 Napoleon's empire fell and he was exiled to the island of Elba. Having now been promoted to Field Marshal, Gerhard von Blucher led the Prussian troops of the Sixth Coalition into Paris, and Louis XVIII, who had been living in exile in Prussia, was installed as the monarch.

Because of the humiliating 1806 defeat at the Battle of Iéna, Blucher wanted to destroy the symbolic Pont d'Iéna. He instructed his troops to mine the bridge for demolition. Louis XVIII and his minister, Talleyrand, interceded and were able to dissuade Blucher from destroying the bridge. As a concession, the name was changed to Pont de l'École Militaire and the eagles were removed, but the bridge was saved.

Little more than a year later, Napoleon returned from exile to fight the battle of Waterloo. His forces were up against those of the English Duke of Wellington. It was Field Marshall Blucher's Prussian forces that arrived to reinforce the English, leading to Napoleon's final defeat.

The bridge regained its Pont d'Iéna name following the July Revolution of 1830 when Charles X was overthrown and Louis Philippe became monarch. In 1840 Napoleon's ashes were returned to France to rest at Hôtel des Invalides. With the return of his ashes, the idea of restoring the eagles began to take shape. The newly sculpted replacement eagles were finally positioned on the bridge in 1852, when Napoleon III became emperor of the Second Empire.

One year later statues were erected on the four pedestals that had been bare since the bridge was first built. They depict warriors on foot leading their horses by the reins. Each warrior is from a different era of history. On the left bank upstream is a Gallic warrior and downstream a Roman warrior; on the right bank upstream is an Arab warrior and downstream a Greek warrior.

For a long time after it was first built, Pont d'Iéna was the least used of the Paris bridges. However, that began to change when the Palace of the Trocadero was built in 1878 and the Eiffel Tower in 1889. Then, in 1937, the Palace of Chaillot was built for the International Exposition dedicated to Art and Technology in Modern Life, which was held at the Trocadero on the right bank and the Champ de Mars on the left bank. The Pont d'Iéna was the only direct connection between the two locations, and the bridge was substantially widened to accommodate the traffic.

The bridge and its environs have now become one of the most visited tourist destinations in Paris.

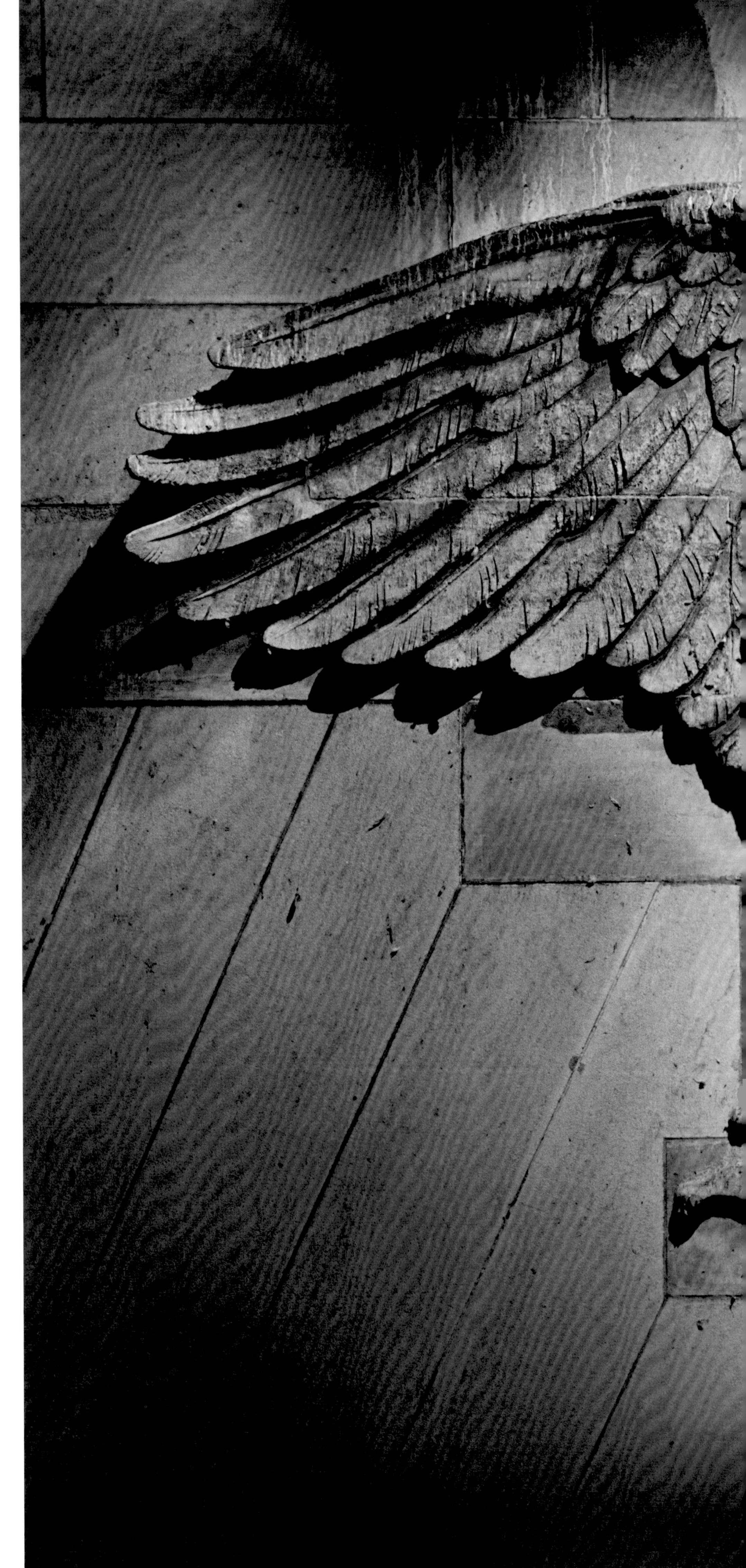

Pont d'Iéna:
The eagle representing the
empire of Napoleon Bonaparte.

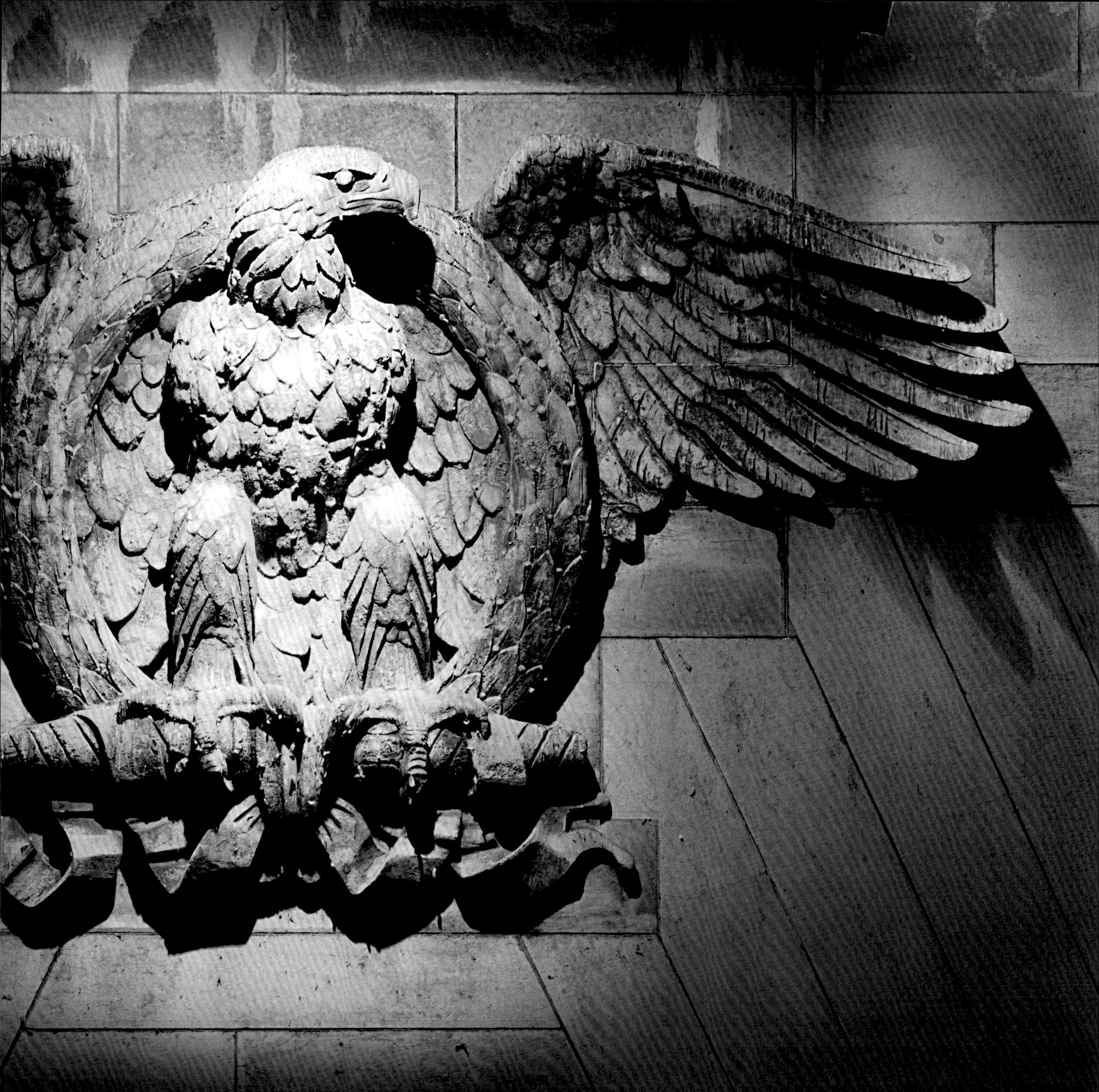

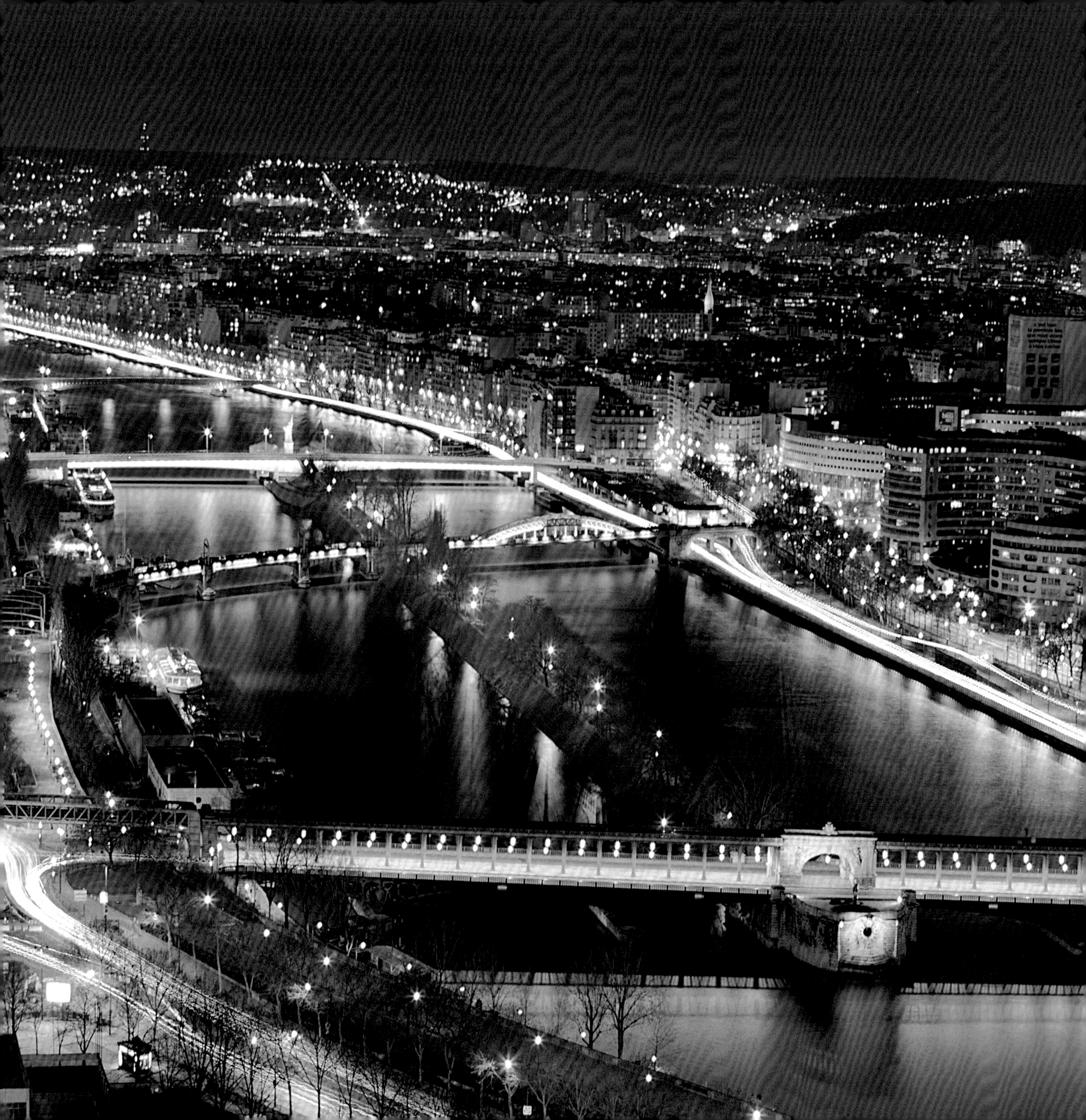

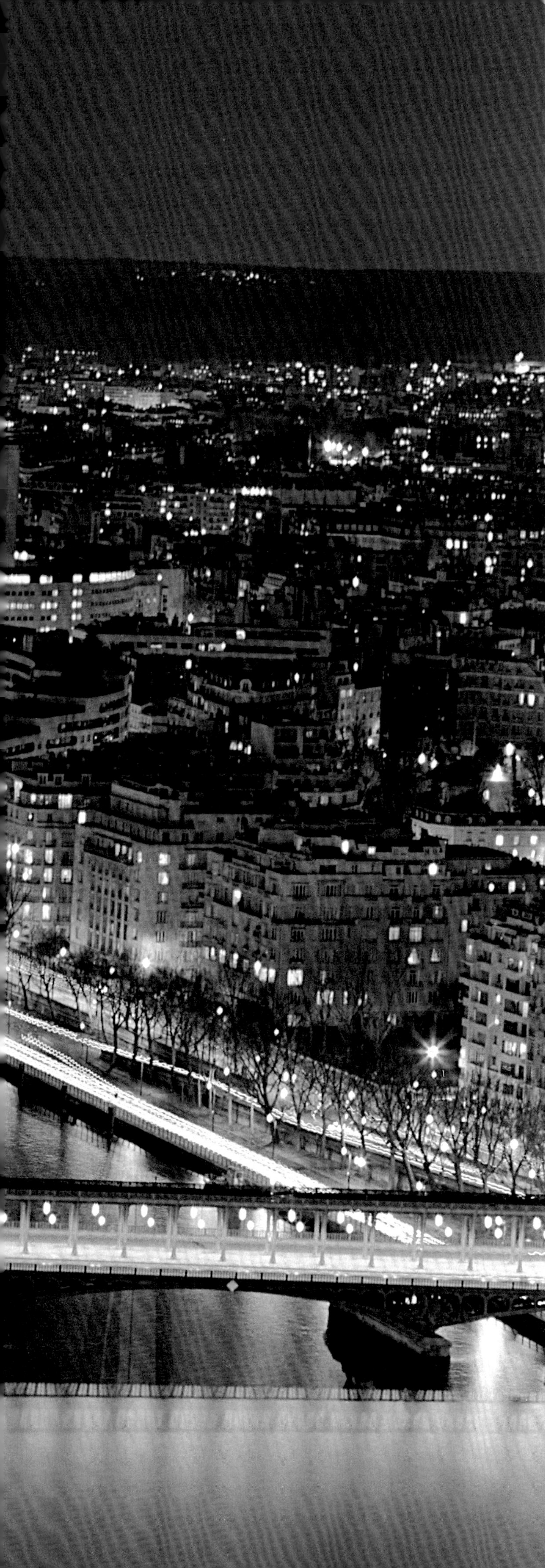

PONT DE BIR-HAKEIM

I t could be said that the Pont de Bir-Hakeim and the Pont de Bercy are sister bridges.

That would be partially correct. Both offer four different methods of crossing: by automobile, by Paris Metro, on a bicycle, or on foot (or in past days, on horseback). But there is a marked difference between them: the Pont de Bercy is a stone and reinforced concrete construction whereas the Pont de Bir-Hakeim is made of metal and cast iron.

The first bridge at this spot was the Passerelle de Passy, a footbridge built for the International Exposition of 1878. That bridge stood until 1905 when it was replaced by the current bridge. Both were metal structures.

The Pont de Bir-Hakeim crosses the river by transiting the Île aux Cygnes (Isle of Swans) at its farthest upstream tip. Created in 1827, the Île aux Cygnes is a man-made island 850 meters (2,789 feet) long and 11 meters (36 feet) across at its widest point.

Three components link to create the Pont de Bir-Hakeim. Two separate metal bridges run from opposite sides of the river to meet in the middle

Pont de Bir-Hakeim:
The Pont de Bir-Hakeim followed
by Pont de Rouelle, Pont de Grenelle,
and Pont Mirabeau.

where they connect with a robust concrete and masonry arch bridge on the Île aux Cygnes.

The bridge has two levels: the lower is for motor vehicles, pedestrians, and bicycles, and the upper is a viaduct for line 6 of the Paris Metro. The corridor for bicycles runs underneath the viaduct, which is supported by massive steel columns with protruding, round rivets.

There is an abundance of sculpture created in cast metal and in bas-relief on the bridge. Works by famous French sculptors include the remarkable *La Science* and *Le Travail* by Jules Coutan; *Les Nautes* and *Les Forgerons-Riveteurs* by Gustave Michel; and *L'Électricité* and *Le Commerce* by Jean-Antoine Injalbert, who also created the four sculptures on the Pont Mirabeau.

One of the most impressive sights at the Pont de Bir-Hakeim is *La France Renaissante*, a statue that sits at the very tip of the Île aux Cygnes. Created by Danish sculptor Holger W. Wederkinch (1886–1959) in 1930, it is a stunning work of art given to the city of Paris by the Danish community in Paris.

The sculpture represents a woman on horseback, facing toward the sky in a battle stance, sword in hand, charging toward the enemy; it exudes great power and an impressive dynamic. The statue was originally intended to be representative of Joan of Arc. However, the city found it to be too warrior-like and too aggressive, contrary to the usual idea of Joan of Arc. Thus it was renamed *La France Renaissante*. The inauguration of the renamed work took place on the bridge in 1958, in the presence of the Ambassador of Denmark.

The Pont de Bir-Hakeim was originally named Viaduc de Passy. In 1948 it was renamed to commemorate the battle of Bir-Hakeim that took place in the North African desert during World War II.

Bir-Hakeim was a remote oasis in the Libyan Desert. The men of the Free French 1st Division, commanded by General Marie Pierre Kœnig, distinguished themselves with uncommon valor. The outpost of Bir-Hakeim was surrounded and outnumbered by the Afrika Korps tank forces of General Erwin Rommel. The Free French 1st Division held out against a sure defeat. First attacked and then surrounded and overwhelmed, they held their position in the midst of intense fighting from May 27, 1942, until June 10. Their resolve required Rommel to commit forces to the battle at Bir-Hakeim that left him fewer resources for the ensuing battle at El Alamein, where the standoff halted the advance of the Axis forces into Egypt.

Later, Rommel himself declared that "nowhere in Africa was I given a stiffer fight."

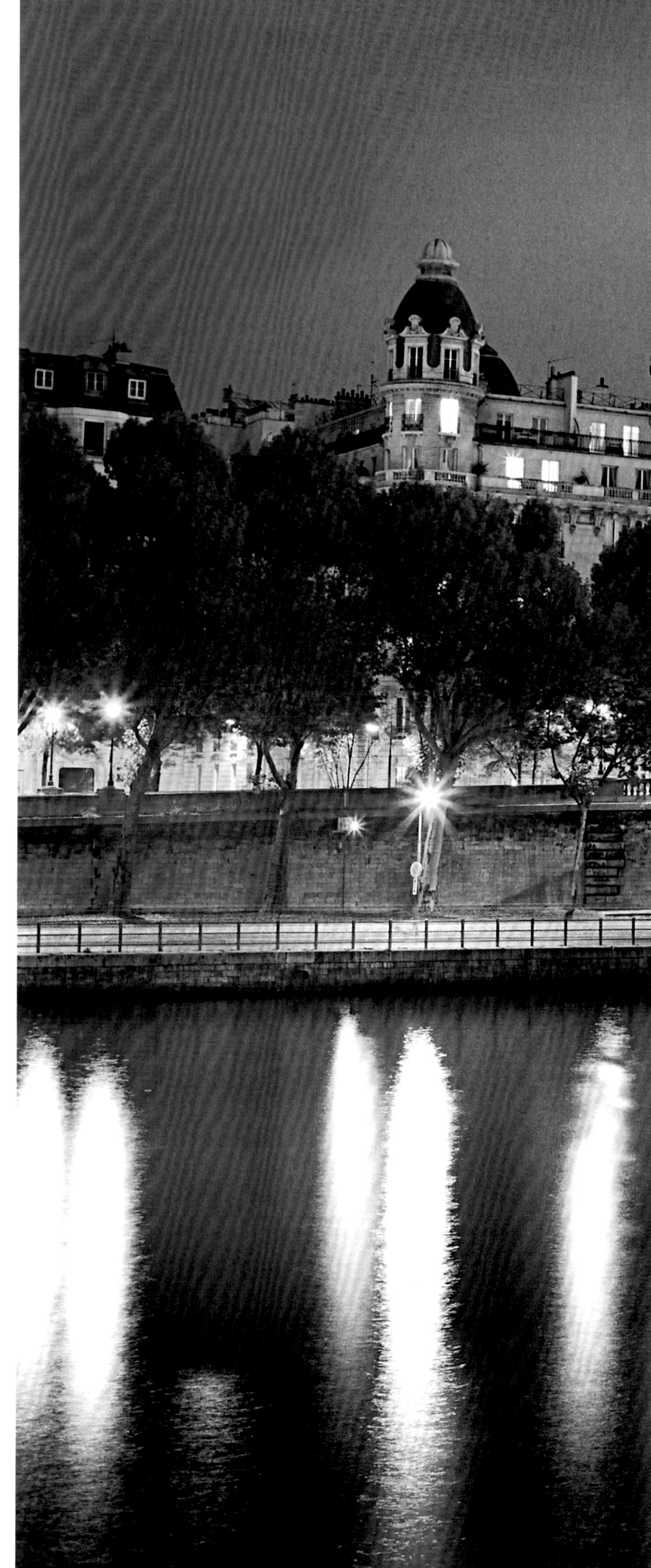

Pont de Bir-Hakeim:
View from Île aux Cygnes with Voie
Georges Pompidou expressway passing
under the bridge on the right bank.

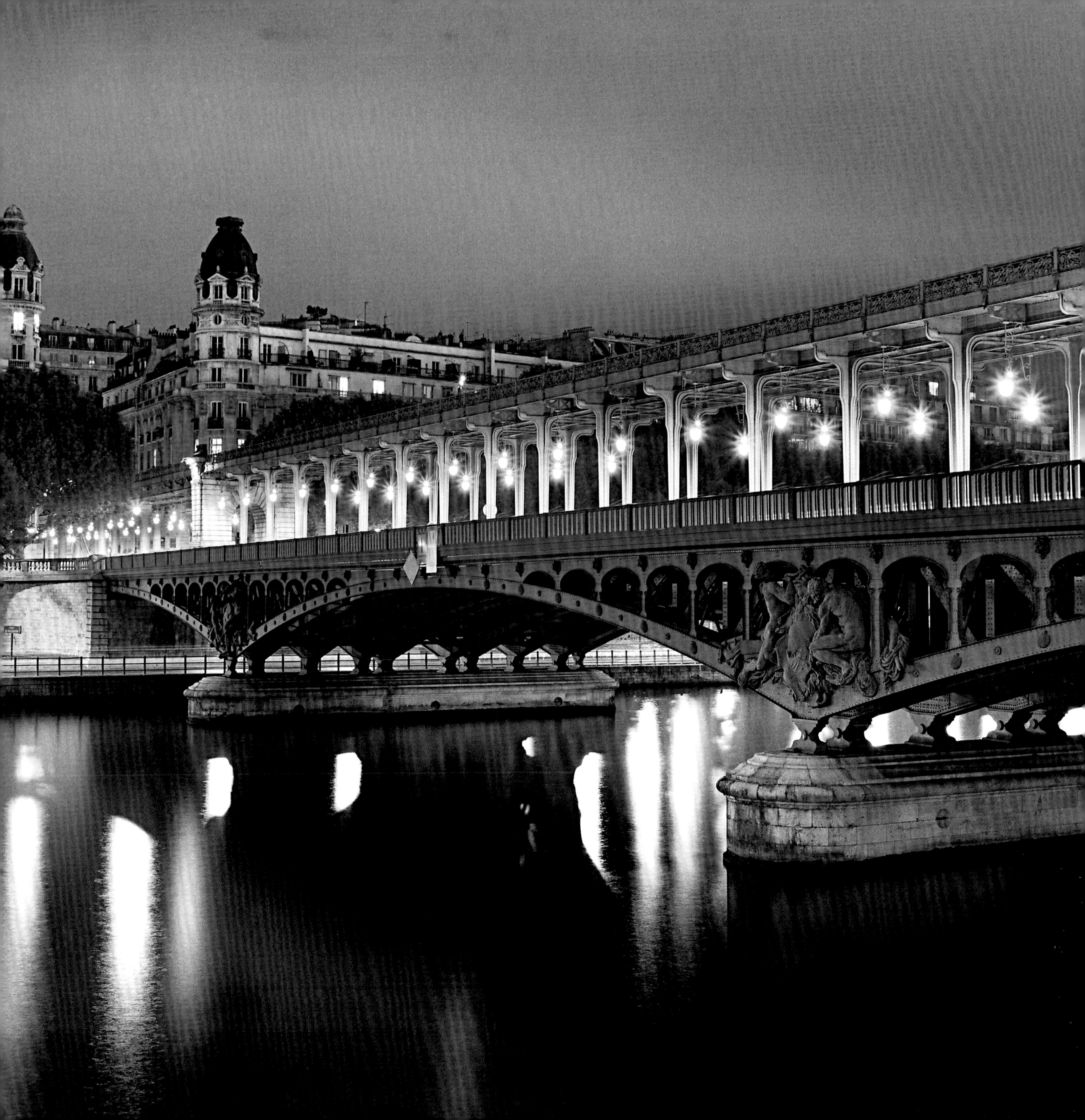

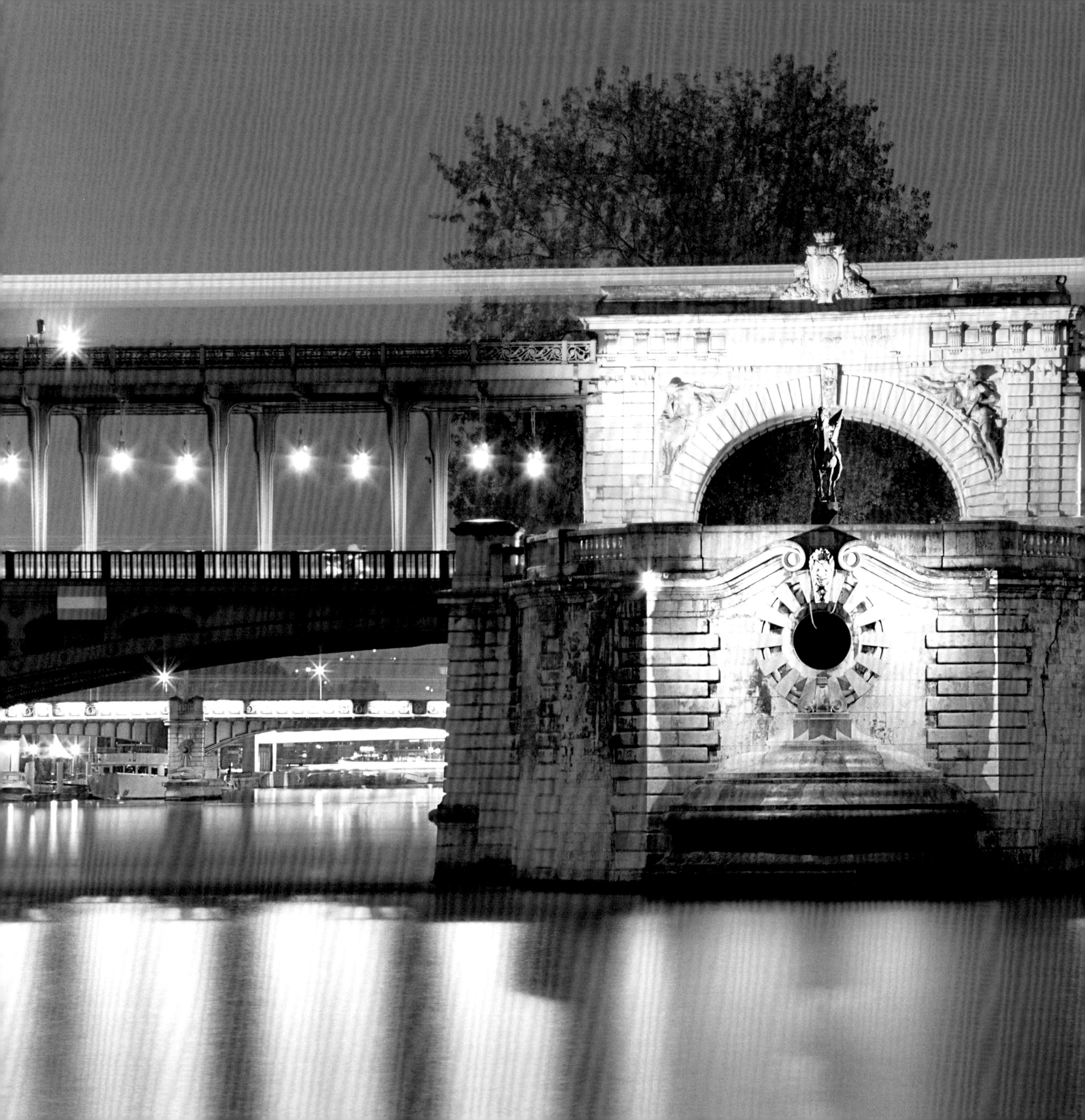

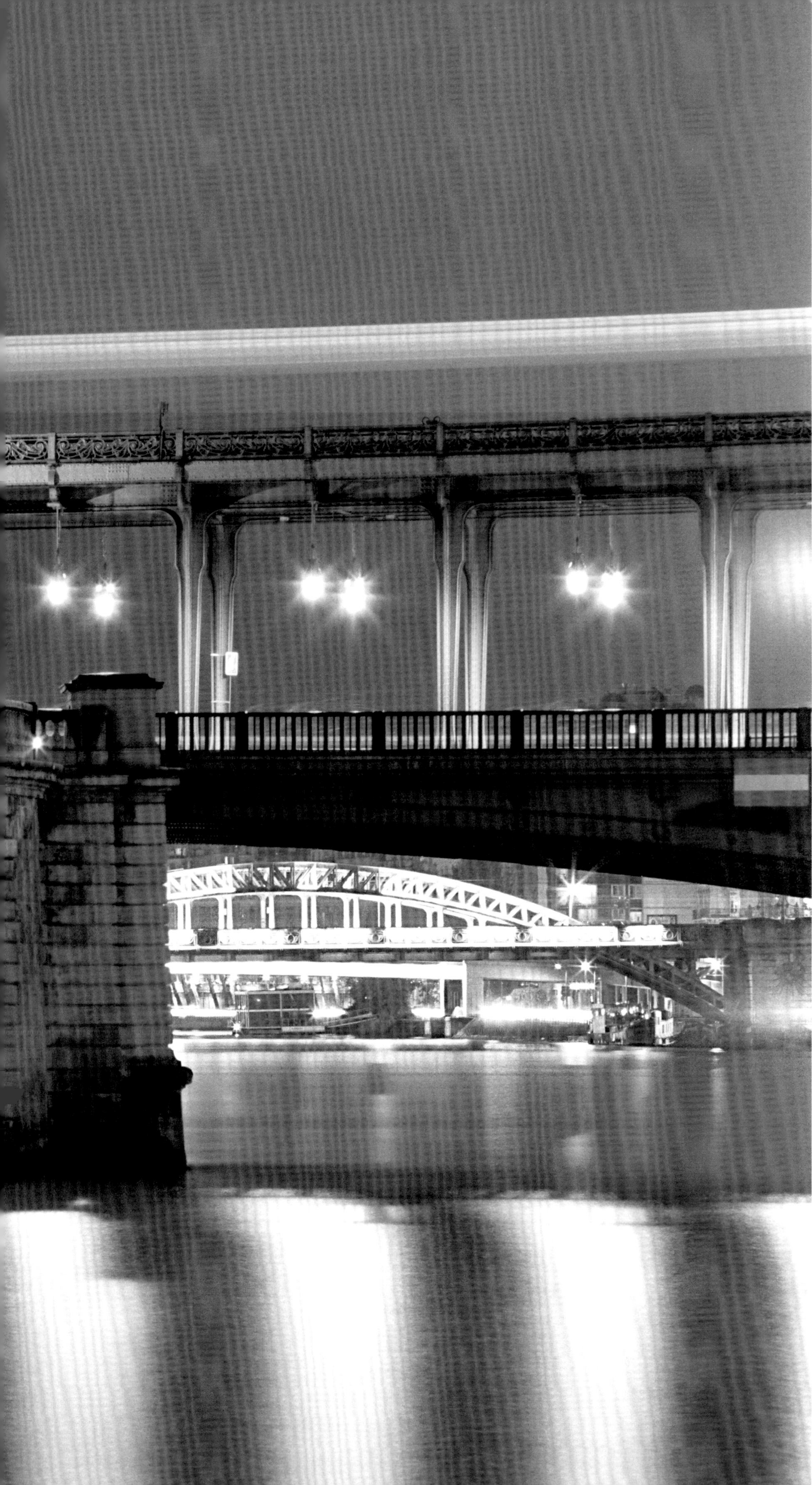

Winston Churchill was more terse: "Holding back for fifteen days Rommel's offensive, the free French of Bir-Hakeim have contributed to save Egypt and the Suez Canal's destinies."

On June 18, 1949, the Viaduc de Passy was re-baptized Pont de Bir-Hakeim in the presence of General Marie Pierre Kœnig and General Charles de Gaulle, who declared the bridge to be renamed in memory of the Battle of Bir-Hakeim.

The bridge has been featured in many memorable movies, including *Zazie Dans le Métro* by Louis Malle in 1960, the well-known *Last Tango in Paris* by Bernardo Bertolucci with Marlon Brando in 1972, and *Frantic* by Roman Polanski in 1988.

The Paris Metro system incorporates a total of 214 kilometers (133 miles), 197 kilometers (122 miles) of which are underground. Obviously visitors do not look inside the Metro system to find the city's greatest sights. However, one of the most stunning views in Paris can be found on Metro line 6. After emerging from underground the line crosses the Seine via the upper level of the Pont de Bir-Hakeim. The view while crossing the river is simply dazzling. ❧

Pont de Bir-Hakeim:
The Metro crossing at the upstream
tip of the Île aux Cygnes.

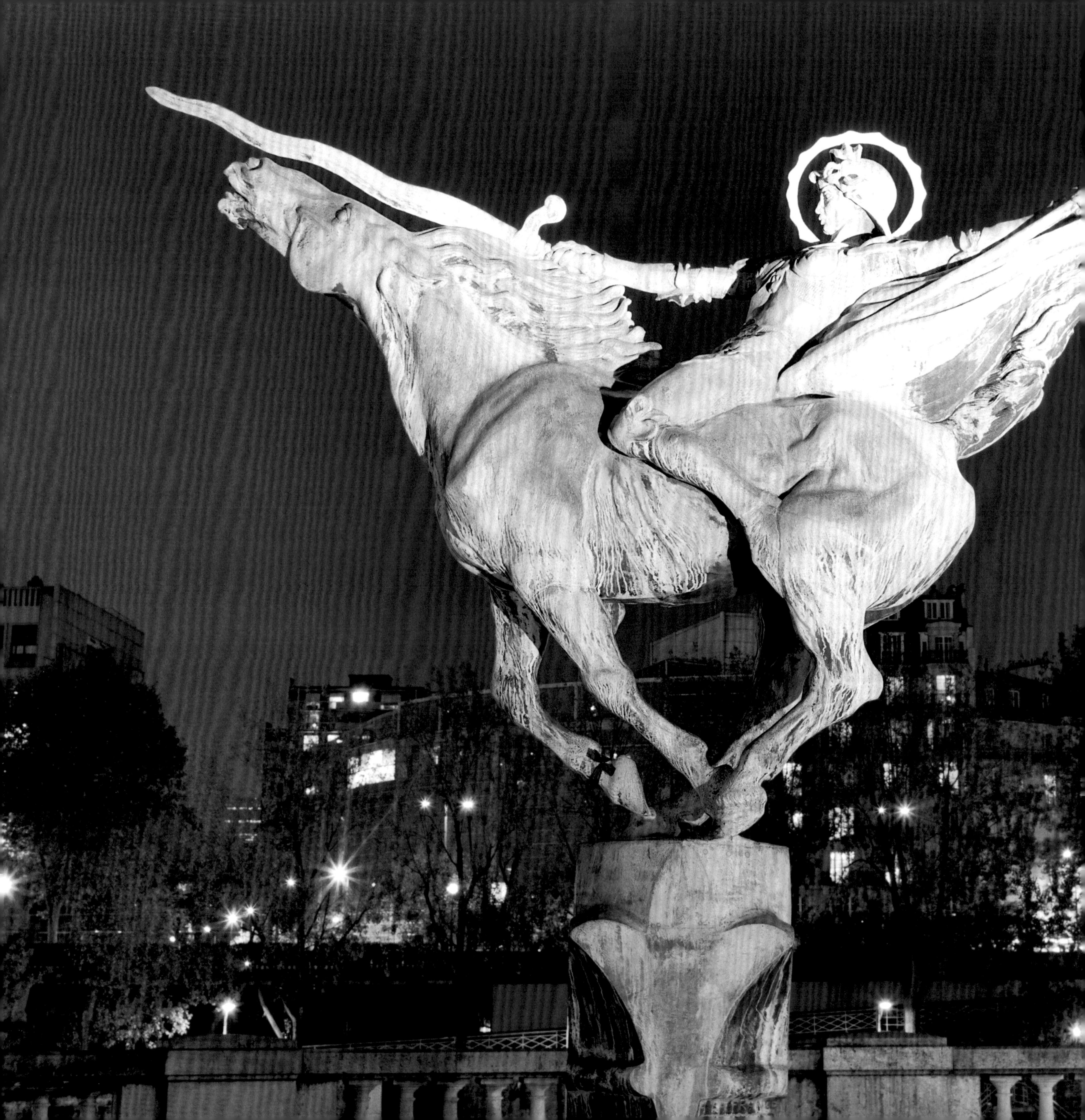

Pont de Bir-Hakeim:
Statue of "La France Renaissante"
by Danish sculptor Holger W.
Wederkinch (1886–1959).

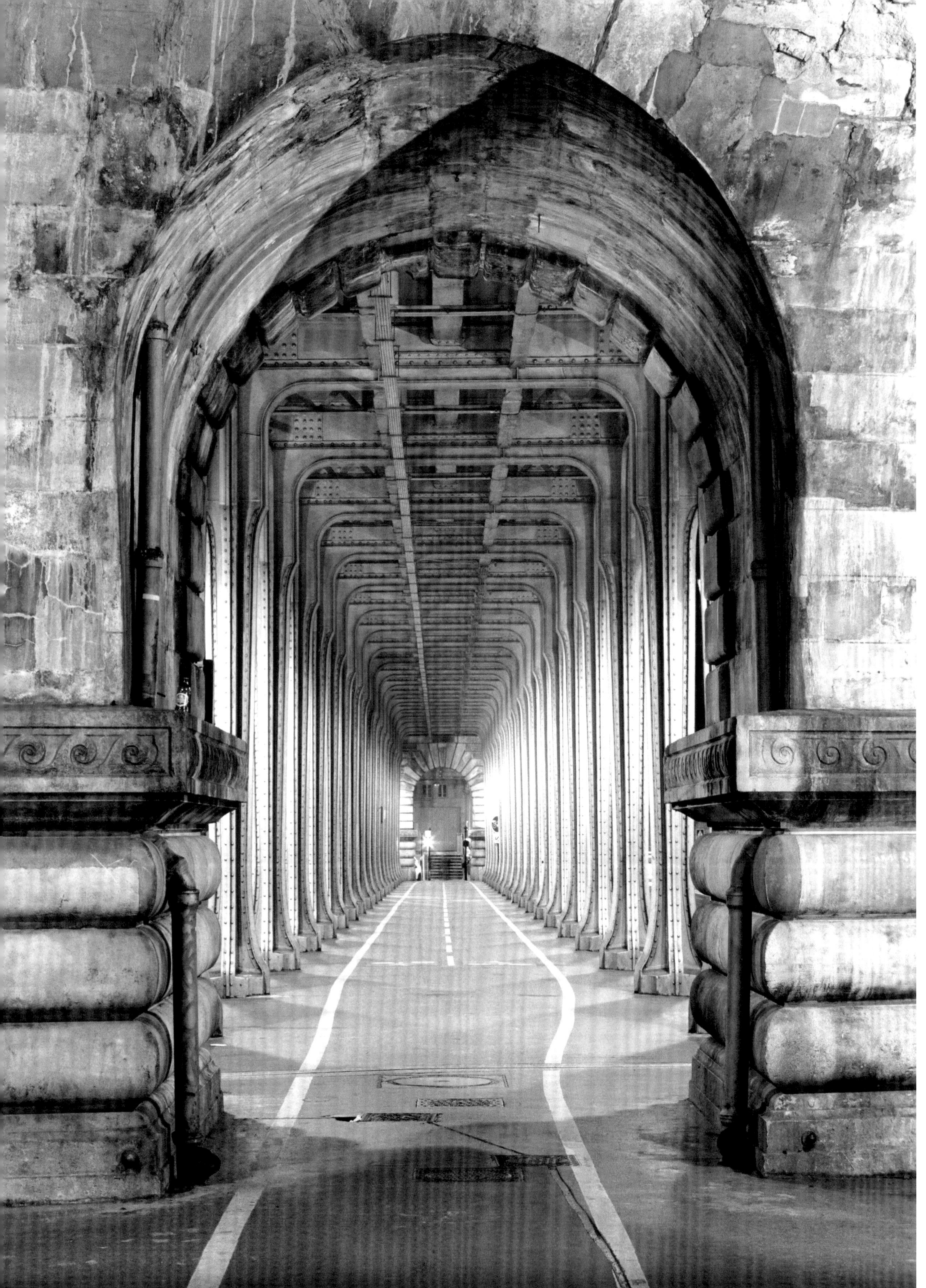

Pont de Bir-Hakeim:
Corridor of the iron structures
supporting the Metro
line 6 above.

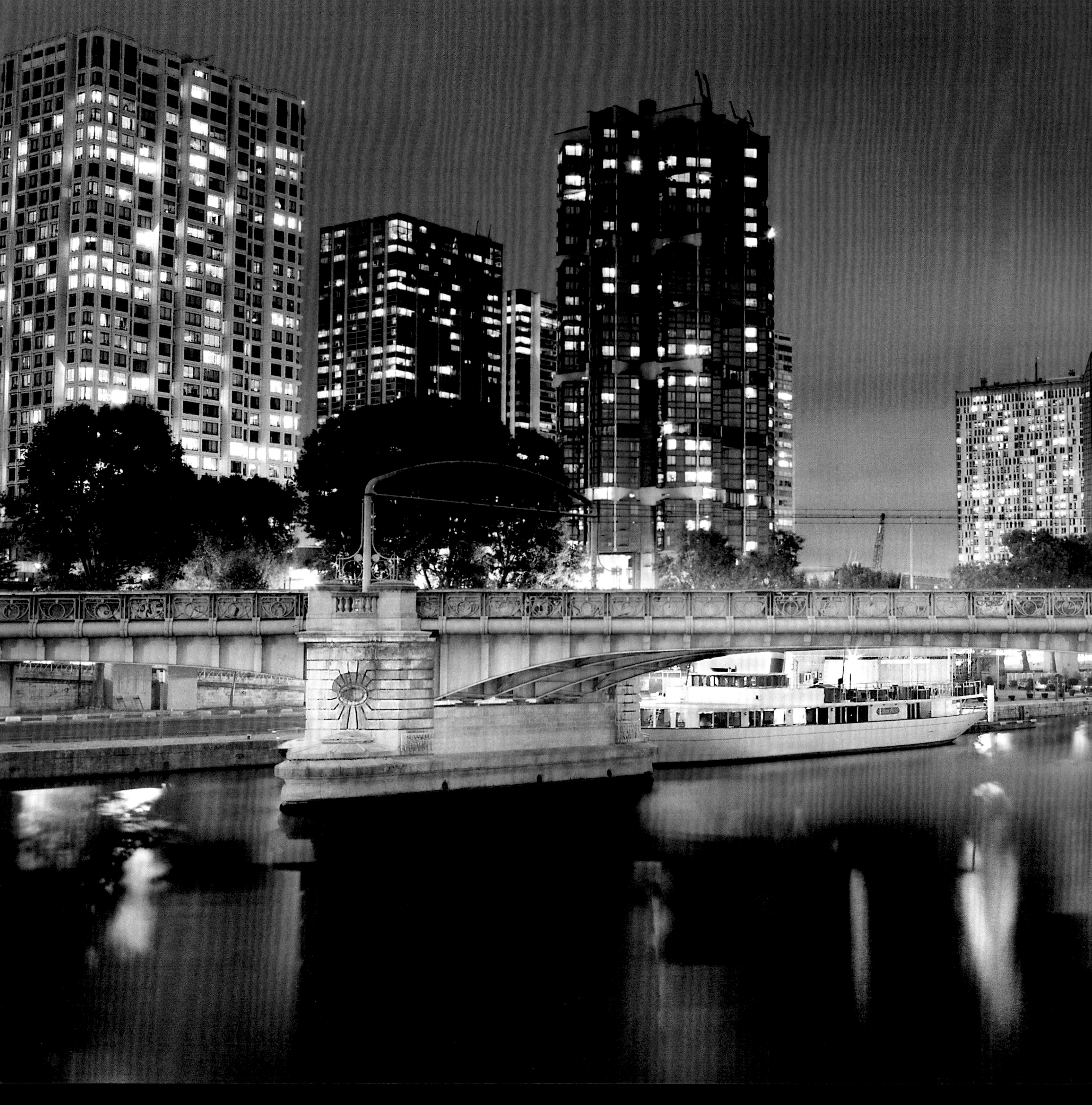

PONT ROUELLE

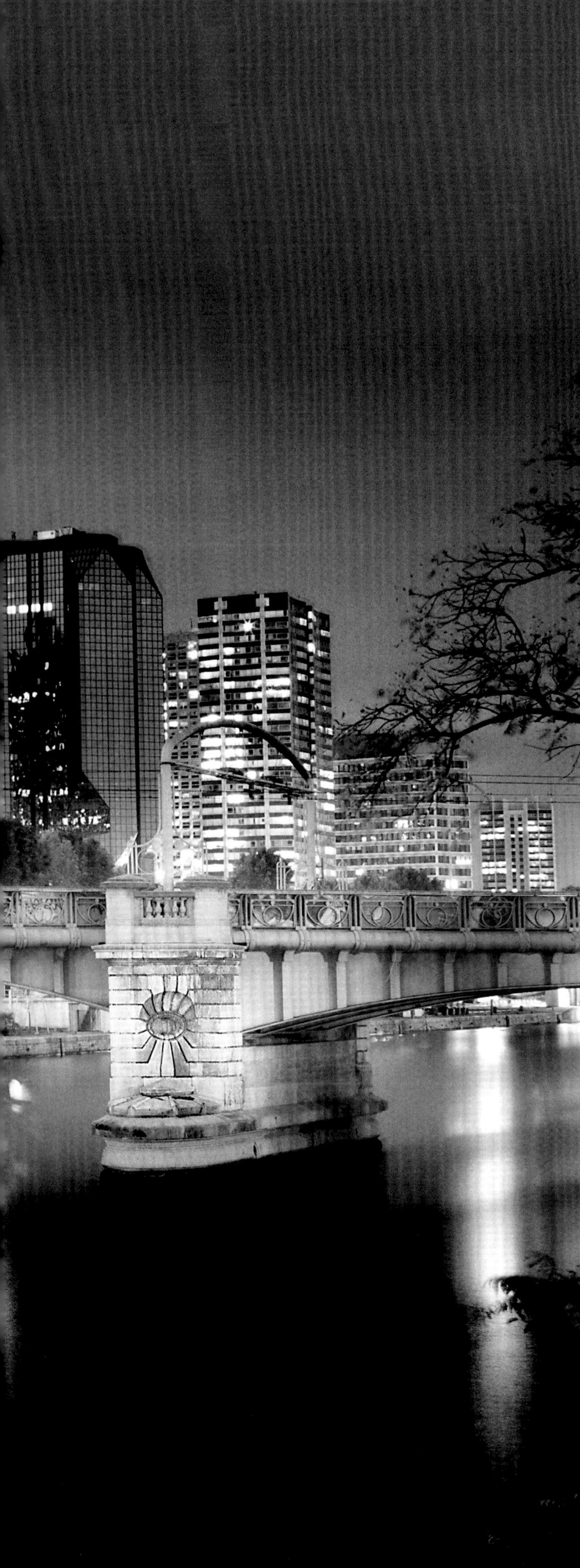

Pont Rouelle:
A modern view not
typical of Paris.

The Pont Rouelle and the Viaduc d'Austerlitz are the only two Paris bridges to serve rail traffic exclusively; they have no automotive or pedestrian traffic. The Viaduc d'Austerlitz has been in continuous use since being built, whereas the Pont Rouelle has had a seesaw history.

The Pont Rouelle was built for the 1900 International Exposition held on the Champ de Mars. The bridge opened on April 12, 1900, two days prior to the opening of the exposition. It was part of the rail line that brought travelers from the north, the east, and the Gare St. Lazare to the station at Champ de Mars. According to the organizers, Pont Rouelle served eight million passengers during the exposition.

When the Paris Metro system first opened in July 1900 it did not include the Pont Rouelle. As the Metro quickly grew, traffic on the Pont Rouelle correspondingly diminished until 1924 when passenger traffic was eliminated. Thereafter, the line carried only freight until 1936 when all operations ceased and the bridge was abandoned.

Paris and its environs grew rapidly from 1950 to 1980, creating more Metro traffic. To meet increasing demand and to connect to the suburbs,

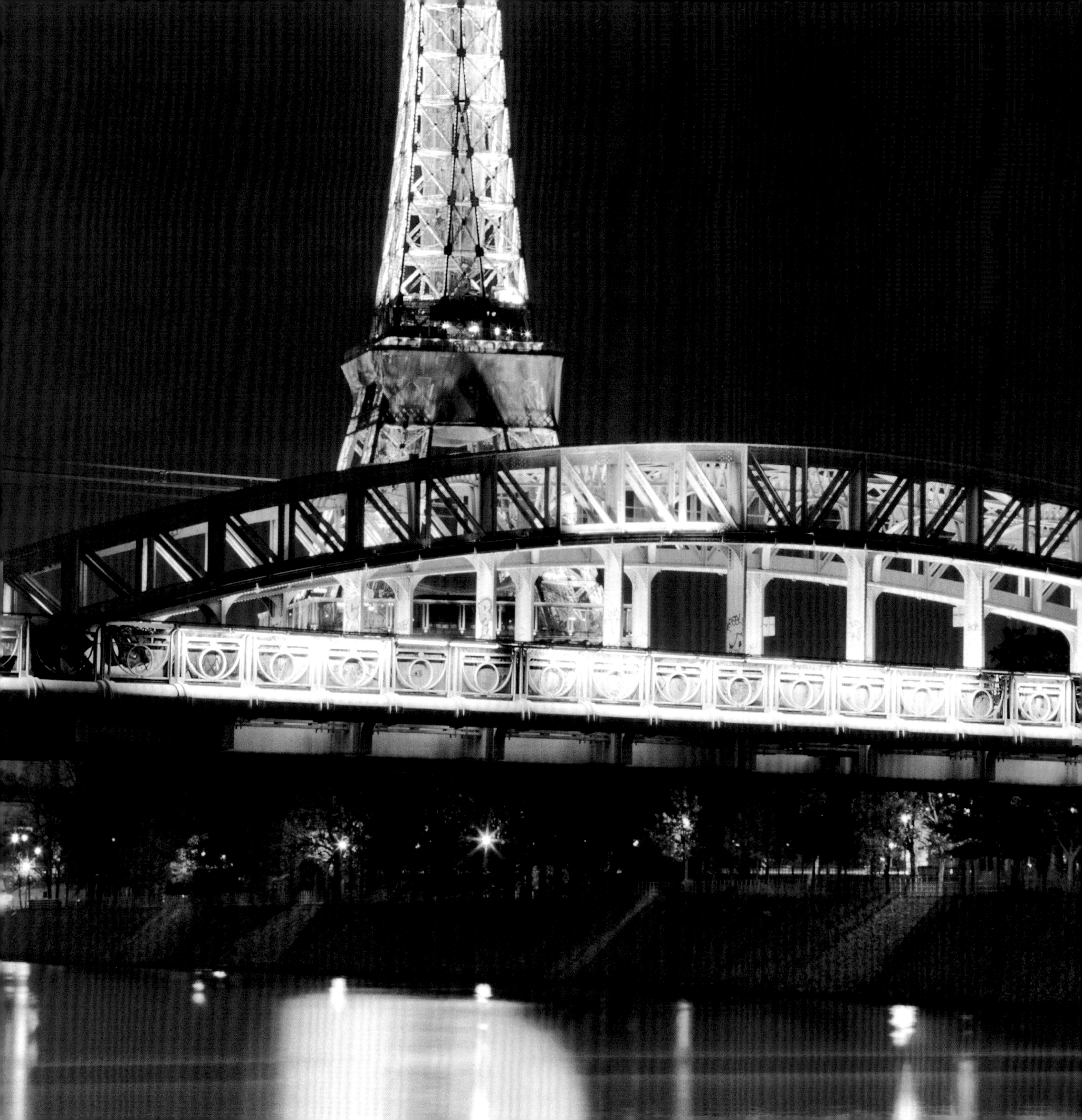

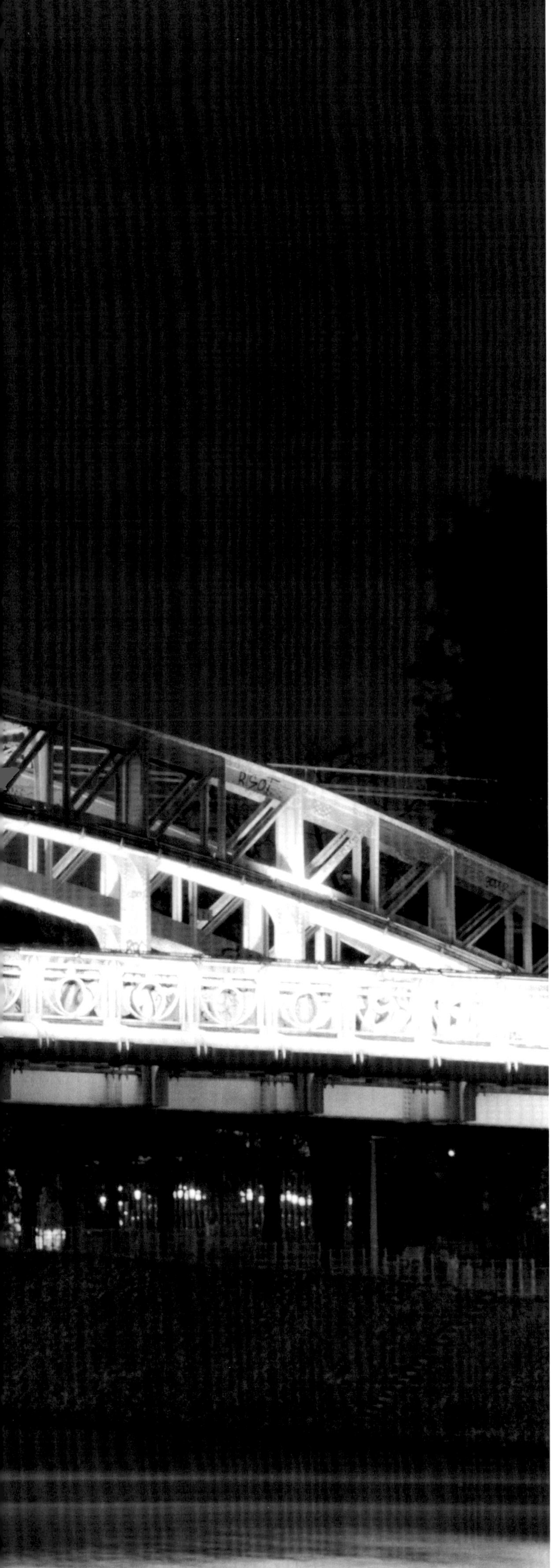

the RER (*réseau express régional* [regional express network]) was created. In 1983 it was decided that the Pont Rouelle would be used as part of the newly planned RER line C. After rehabilitation in 1984 and 1985, the bridge was re-opened in 1988 as part of RER line C. The line runs from Pontoise, a northern suburb, to Versailles, southwest of the city, a distance of roughly 60 kilometers (37 miles).

The bridge has four distinct segments, alternating between masonry and metal structures. On the right bank, before crossing the Seine, a masonry structure passes above the Avenue du President Kennedy and the Georges Pompidou expressway. The first segment crossing the river is a single, wrought iron, arched trestle. On the Île aux Cygnes the masonry construction has an arched passageway that allows strollers, underneath on the island, to pass through. It then connects to the left bank by way of a three-span metal viaduct resting on two masonry piles in the river.

Instead of going straight across the river, the bridge curves from the right bank to a location farther upstream on the left.

The Pont Rouelle is named for the renowned French chemist, Guillaume-François Rouelle (1703–1770), who many consider the father of French chemistry. The rue Rouelle is a nearby street in the 15th arrondissement.

Passing across the middle of the Île aux Cygnes, the Pont Rouelle is located between the Pont de Bir-Hakeim upstream and the Pont de Grenelle downstream, both also on the Île aux Cygnes. The bridge is adjacent to the Front de Seine, a commercial development on the right bank that includes one of the largest concentrations of high-rise buildings in Paris and is a stark departure from typical Paris architecture. A unique view can be seen from the Île aux Cygnes: Looking across the Pont Rouelle, the view resembles a New York skyline with tall buildings of modern design. It is not a view one expects to see in Paris.

Pont Rouelle:
Connecting the right bank with
the Île aux Cygnes.

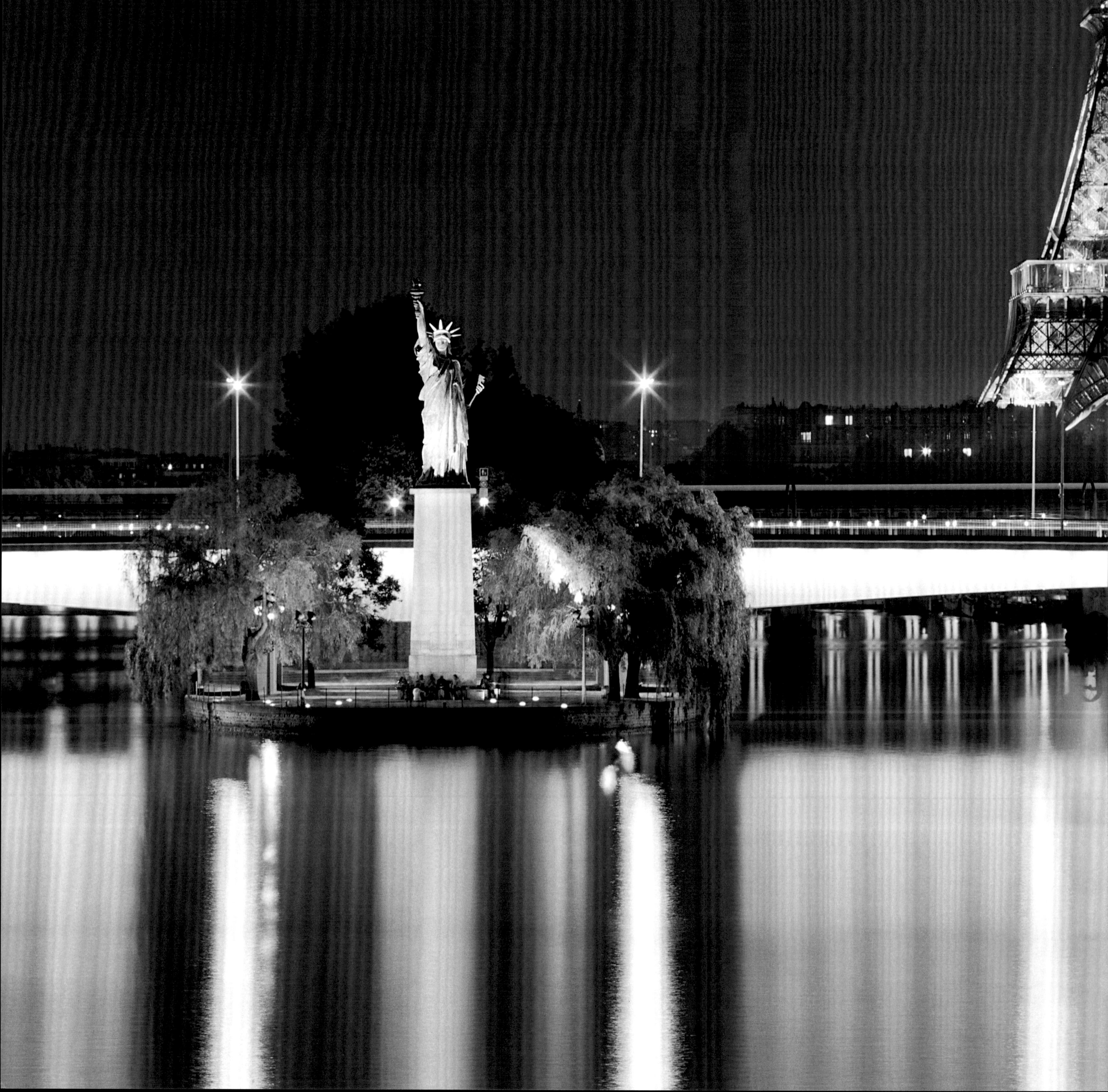

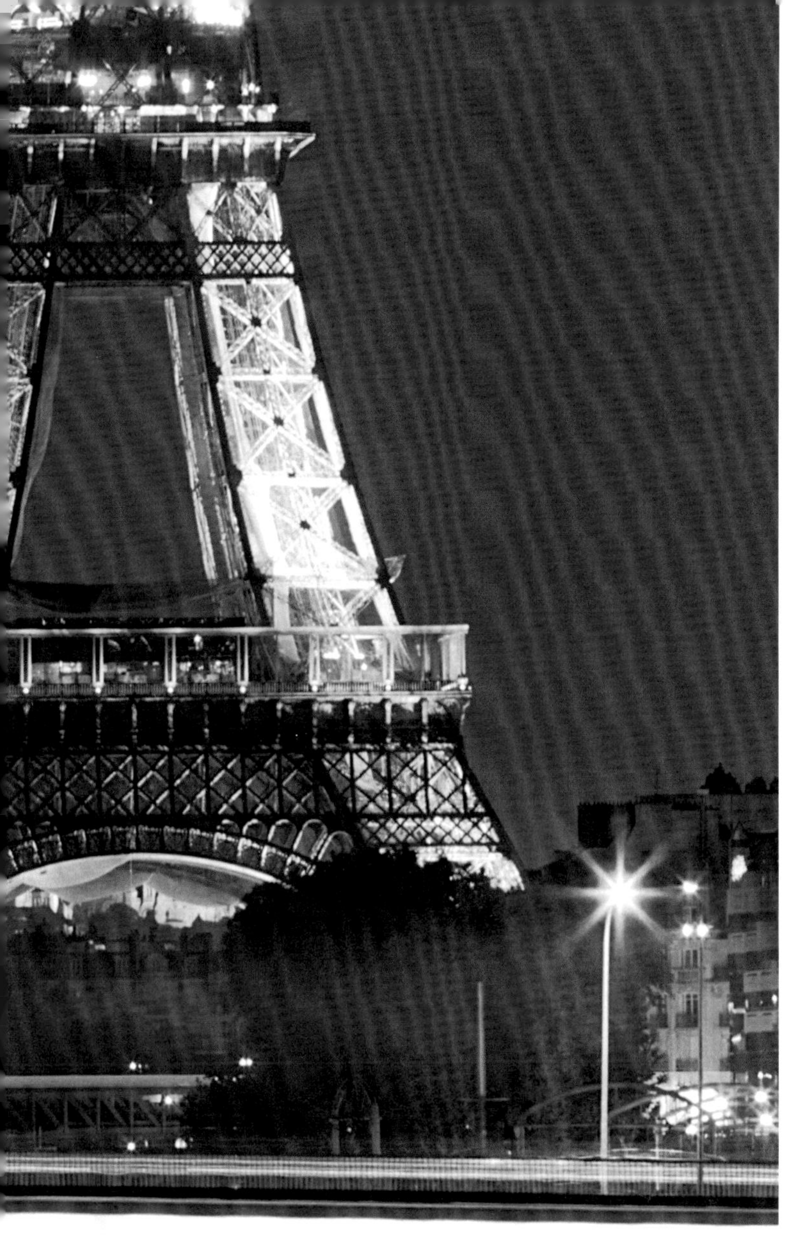

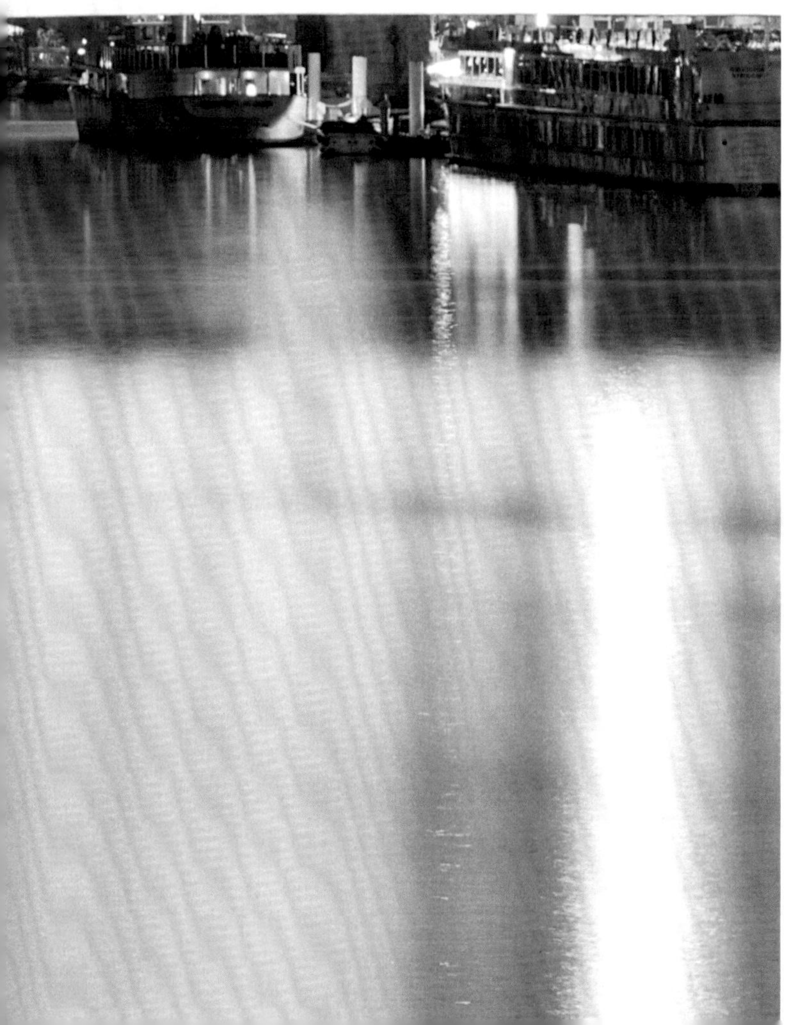

PONT DE GRENELLE

The Pont de Grenelle crosses the Île aux Cygnes at the downstream tip of the island.

The first bridge, opened in 1827, was a toll bridge. The toll was two centimes for a mule, five centimes per person, and twenty-five centimes for a carriage pulled by two horses. It was a wooden bridge with two spans and a center section resting on the Île aux Cygnes. In 1865 the city bought the bridge from the concessionaire but the toll remained in effect until 1874. Between 1849 and 1873 numerous repairs were made to the bridge.

In 1873, during a state visit to France by the Shah of Iran, traffic around the Trocadero was stopped and the surrounding bridges closed. Most of the cross-river traffic was rerouted over the Pont de Grenelle. The increase in traffic caused several of the wooden arches to buckle, making the bridge unsafe. Traffic was initially restricted and the bridge subsequently closed. In 1875 it was replaced by a steel bridge with six arches resting on the piles of the previous bridge.

The replacement was built with a prow toward the tip of the island. The prow was intended for a statue, although none had yet been chosen.

Pont de Grenelle:
Crossing the downstream tip of the Île aux Cygnes with the Statue of Liberty.

Fourteen years later a replica of the Statue of Liberty that had been sent to the United States was erected on the prow. President Carnot inaugurated the statue on July 4, 1889, three years after the inauguration of the original in New York harbor.

The statue, by French sculptor Frédéric Auguste Bartholdi (1834–1904), was a one-fourth scale replica of the statue he had previously created for the United States. It was 11.5 meters (38 feet) tall, whereas the U.S. statue is 46.5 meters (153 feet) tall.

The statues were originally named *La Liberté éclairant le monde* (Freedom illuminating the world); they later became known as the Statues of Liberty. The statue on the Île aux Cygnes holds a tablet bearing the inscription IV Juillet 1776 = XIV Juillet 1789, recognizing American Independence Day and French Bastille Day.

The statue was installed facing east, much to the chagrin of Bartholdi who had wished for it to face west, toward the United States. During the Universal Exhibition of 1937, his wish was posthumously granted when the statue was turned 180 degrees to face west, toward its sibling in the United States.

By the 1950s the Pont de Grenelle had become structurally incapable of meeting the ever-increasing demands of traffic. And on the right bank its abutment was directly in the path of a new expressway; it had to be removed. In 1959 the decision was made to replace the existing bridge. Work began on July 7, 1966, and was finished on July 7, 1968.

The new steel girder bridge connected the commercial center of Beaugrenelle with the Maison de la Radio across the river. The contemporary design of the new bridge was a reflection of the approach to modern architecture exhibited by the Radio France building on the right bank and by the modern buildings and towers of the Front de Seine development on the left bank.

The construction of the new bridge was also an opportunity to reshape the Île aux Cygnes and to create a garden at the downstream tip, including a new pedestal for the statue. She stands there today, proudly holding her tablet and the Flame of Liberty.

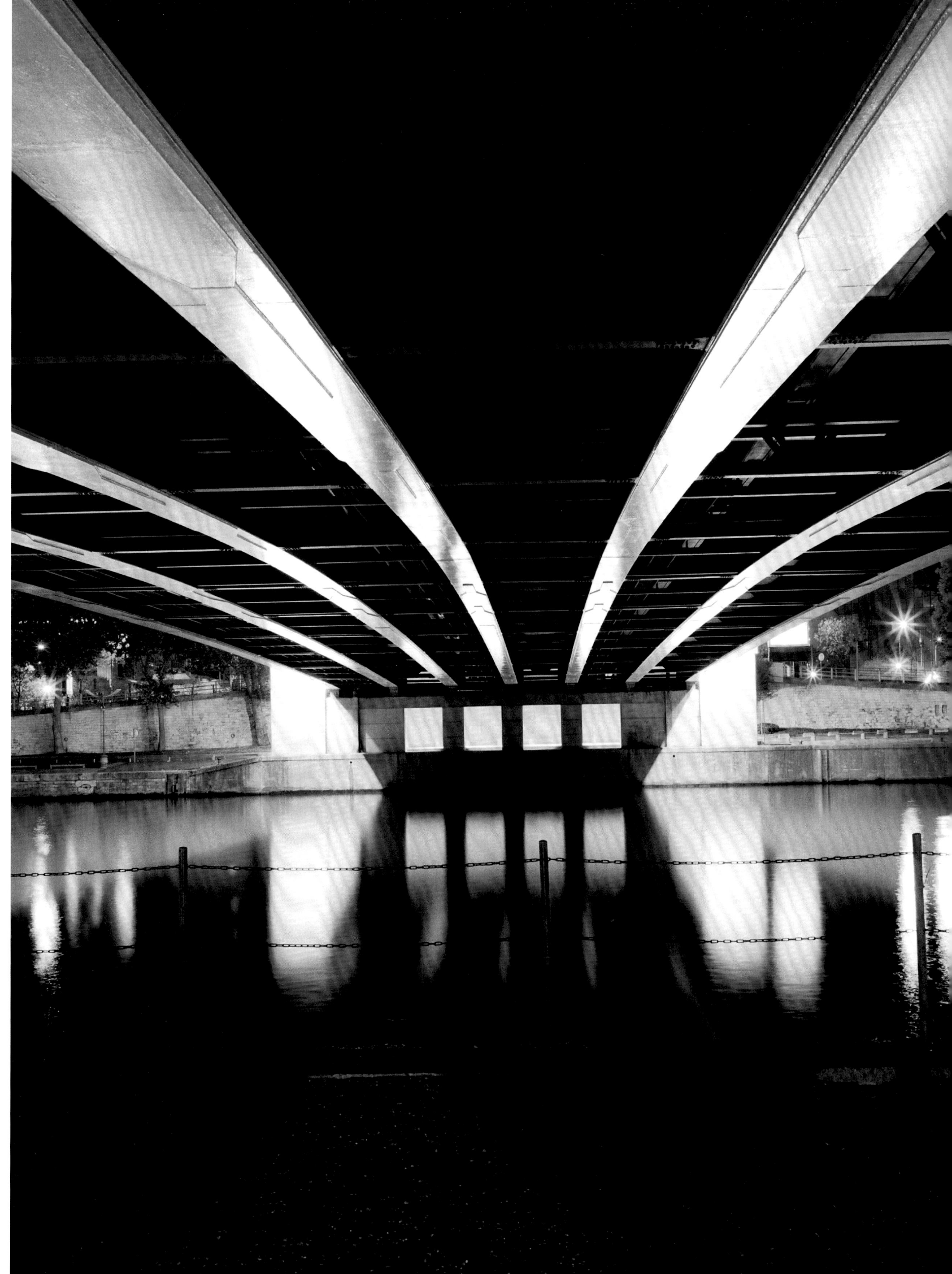

Pont de Grenelle:
Underneath the bridge.

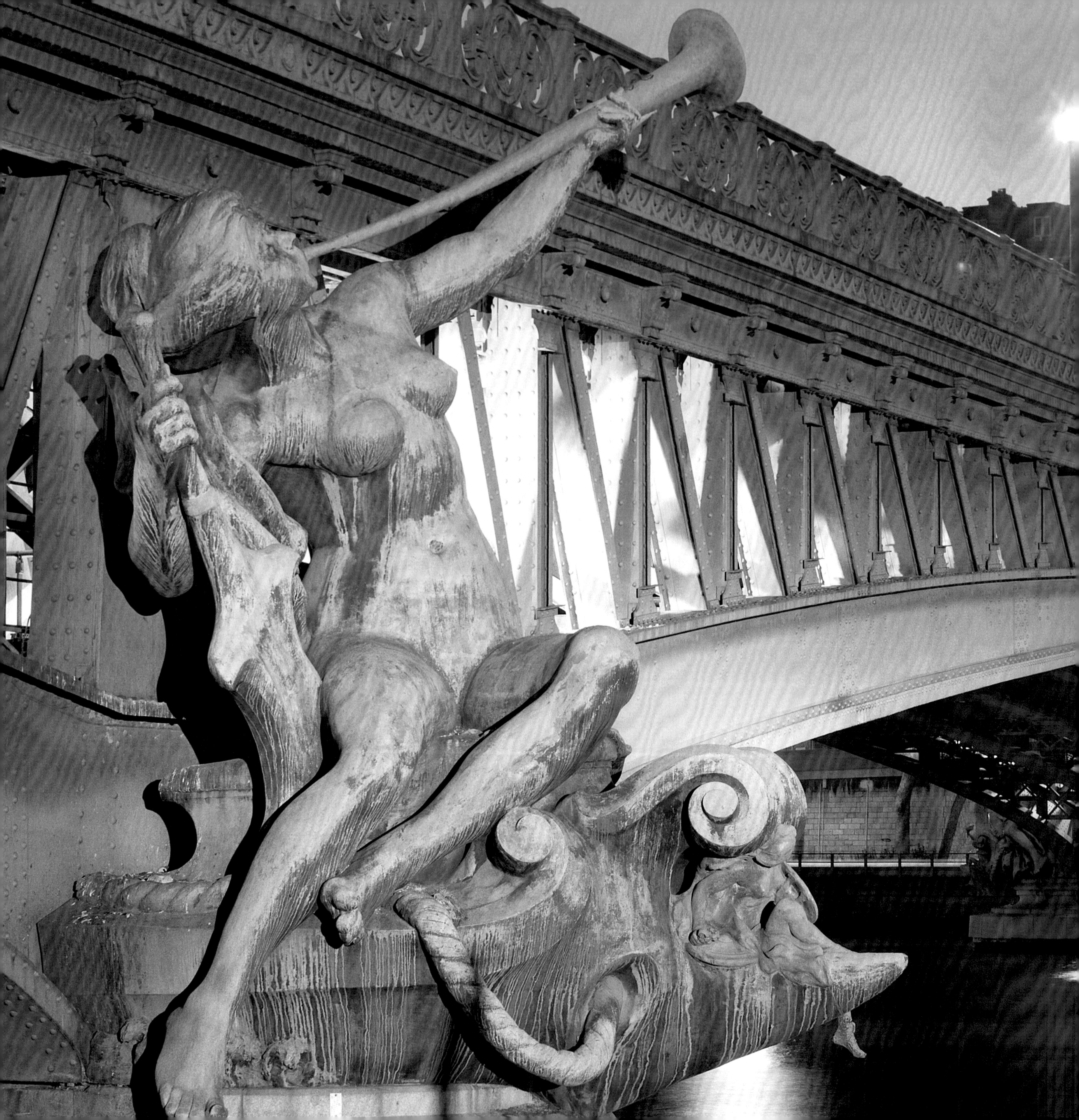

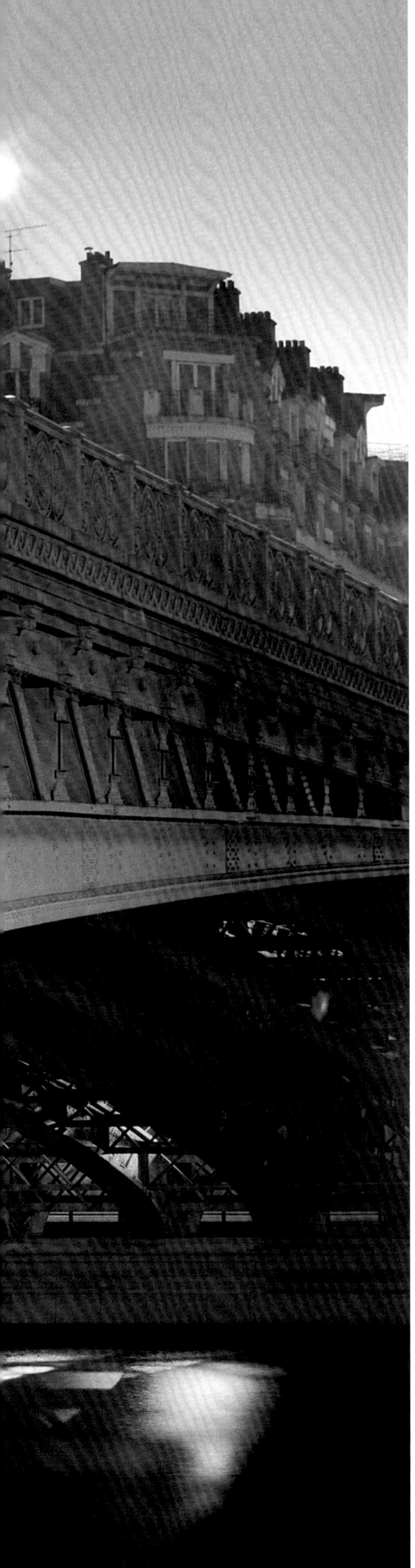

PONT MIRABEAU

Downstream, on the right bank of the Pont Mirabeau, rests a plaque on which is written the first line of a famous poem by Guillaume Apollinaire (1880–1918), one of the foremost French poets of the early twentieth century: "*Sous le pont Mirabeau coule la Seine*" (Under the pont Mirabeau flows the Seine).

He wrote the poem in lament for the rupture of his long-standing, stormy relationship with artist Marie Laurencin. It is a poem of love, sadness, and the passage of time. First published in 1912, the poem is still well known more than one hundred years later.

In 1893, French president Marie François Sadi-Carnot signed a decree authorizing construction of the Pont Mirabeau. He was responding to an appeal by residents of both sides of the river who were asking for a bridge to connect the 15th and the 16th arrondissements.

In December 1895 the new bridge opened to foot traffic and in April 1896 it opened to all traffic. The official inauguration took place in July 1897, presided over by President Felix Faure.

Pont Mirabeau:
Statue of "L'Abondance" Jean-Antonin
Injalbert (1845–1933).

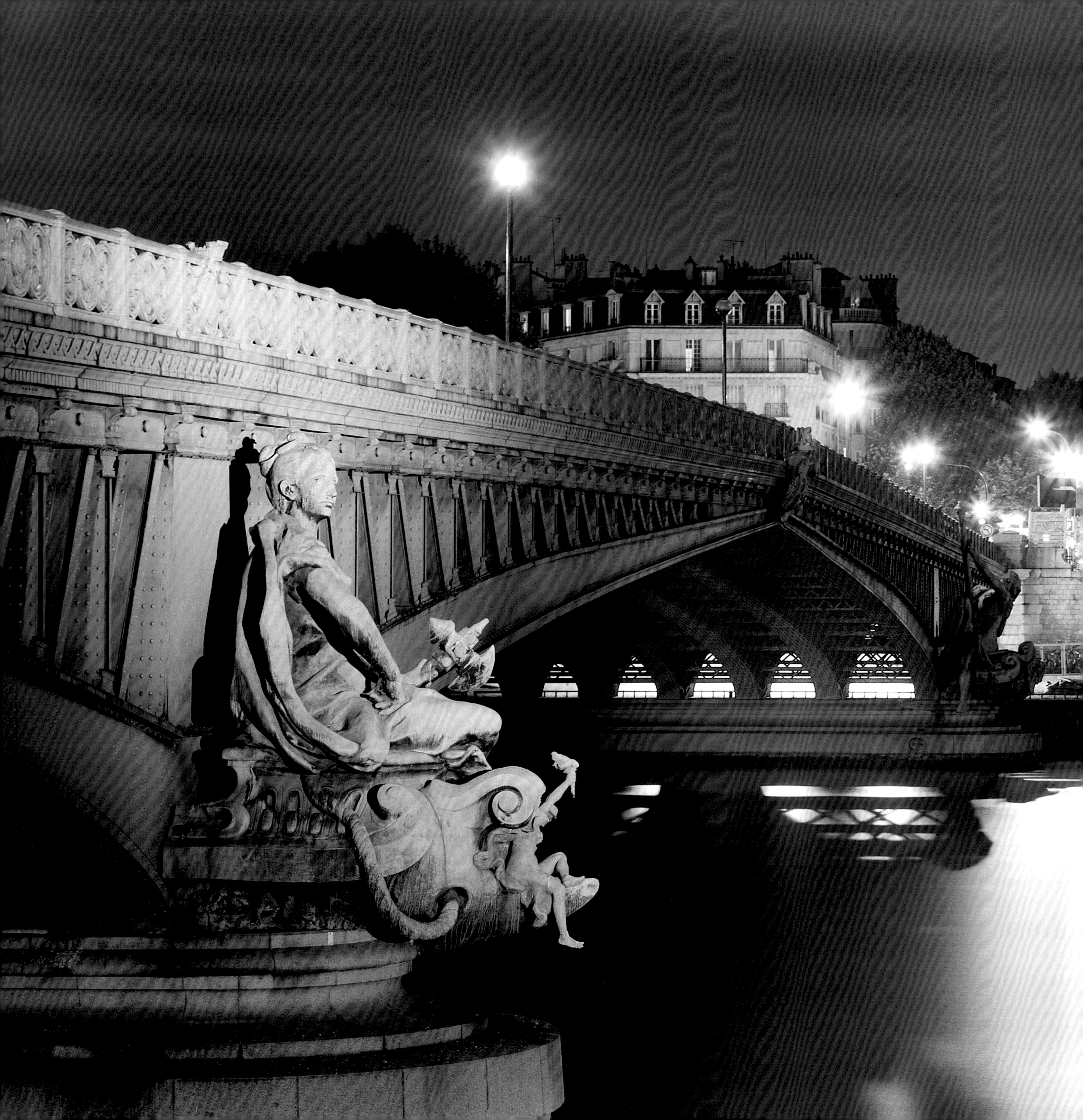

Pont Mirabeau, which gets its name from the nearby rue Mirabeau on the right bank, is located between the Pont de Grenelle upstream and the Pont du Garigliano downstream. A long perimeter road that crosses the south side of Paris provides a direct land-link from Pont Mirabeau to the Pont de Tolbiac, which is located at the farthest upstream environs of the river; Pont Mirabeau is located at the farthest downstream environs. Traveling downstream by river there are thirty bridges between the two. The perimeter road is one road although its name changes four times en route, from rue de la Convention to rue de Vouille, to rue d'Alesia, and finally to rue de Tolbiac.

Jean Resal is regarded as the greatest designer of metal bridges in the late nineteenth century. Assisted by Amédée Alby and Paul Rabcl, Rcsal designed the Pont Mirabeau, which is considered a masterpiece of technique and architectural elegance. He was also instrumental in the design of the Pont Alexandre III, the Passerelle Debilly, the Pont Notre-Dame, and the Pont de Bercy. He was in control of the metal construction of the Grand Palais for the 1900 Universal Exposition for which he was awarded the Légion d'honneur.

The Pont Mirabeau is a metal bridge with a middle arch of 96 meters (315 feet) and a smaller arch of 34 meters (112 feet) on each side. Resal's design and expertise allowed the width of the center arch; the same span-length could not have been achieved with stone and concrete. Although the bridge had a very low profile, it still allowed ample space for the passage of boats.

Famous sculptor Antoine Injalbert, winner of the Prix de Rome for sculpture in 1874 and made an officer of the Légion d'honneur on the day of the inauguration of the Pont Mirabeau, created four colossal figures in bronze that are located on the two piers that support the arches of the bridge.

The piers are designed in the shape of boats, to partially mask the steel skeleton of the bridge. The four allegorical statues are feminine in form. On the right bank downstream sits the bronze titled *la Ville de Paris,* upstream on the same pier *la Navigation,* on the left bank downstream *le Commerce,* and upstream *l'Abondance.* A visually pleasing and intricately designed wrought iron railing is at street level. Its color is light green that trends towards yellow, while the statues have a green patina similar to aged copper. The two colors are quite complementary.

The Pont Mirabeau has been classified as a Monument Historique since 1975.

Like the poem of Apollinaire, the Pont Mirabeau is a masterpiece.

Pont Mirabeau:
Statue of "La Ville de Paris" Jean-Antonin
Injalbert (1845–1933).

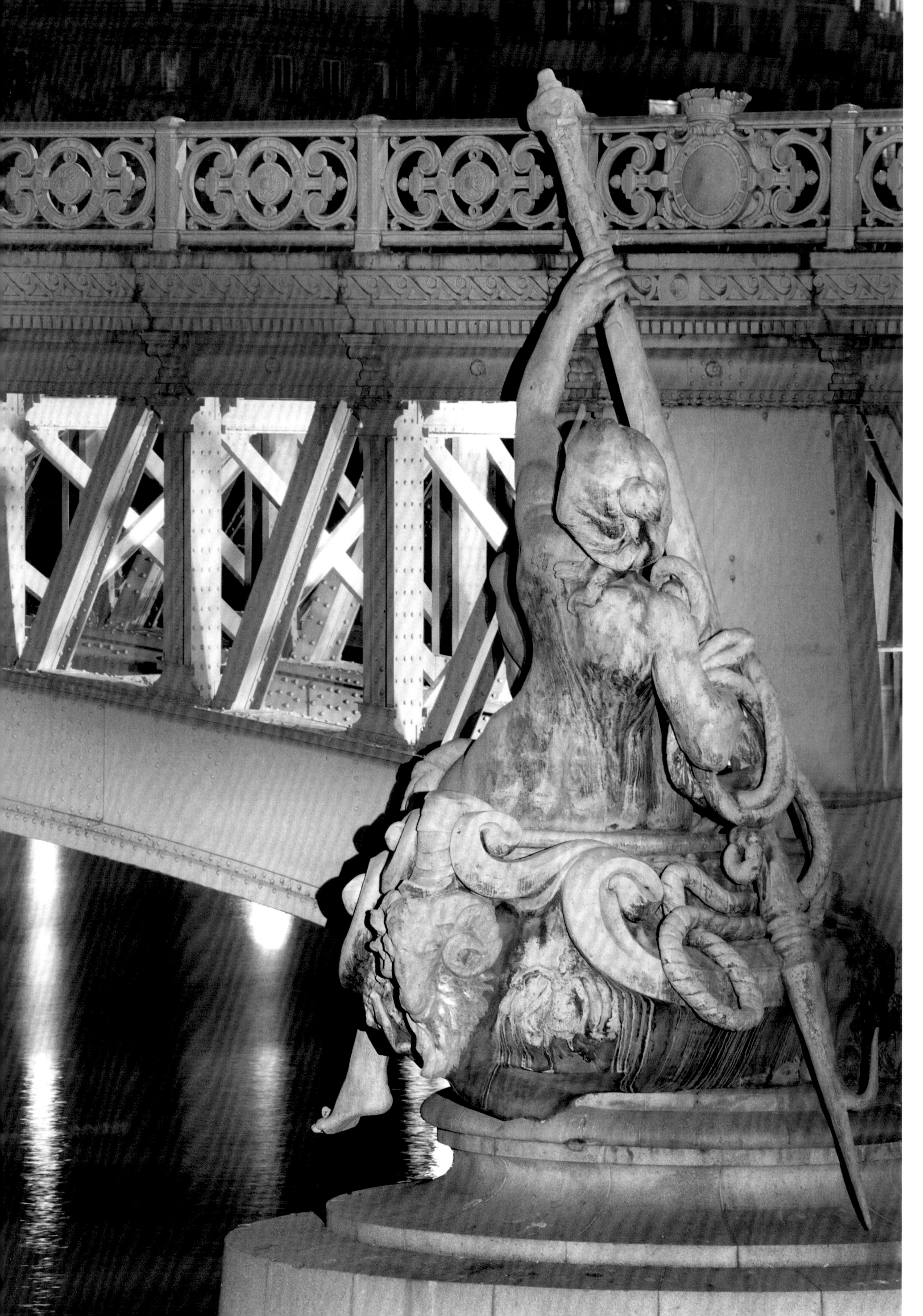

Pont Mirabeau:
Statue of "Le Commerce" Jean-
Antonin Injalbert (1845–1933).

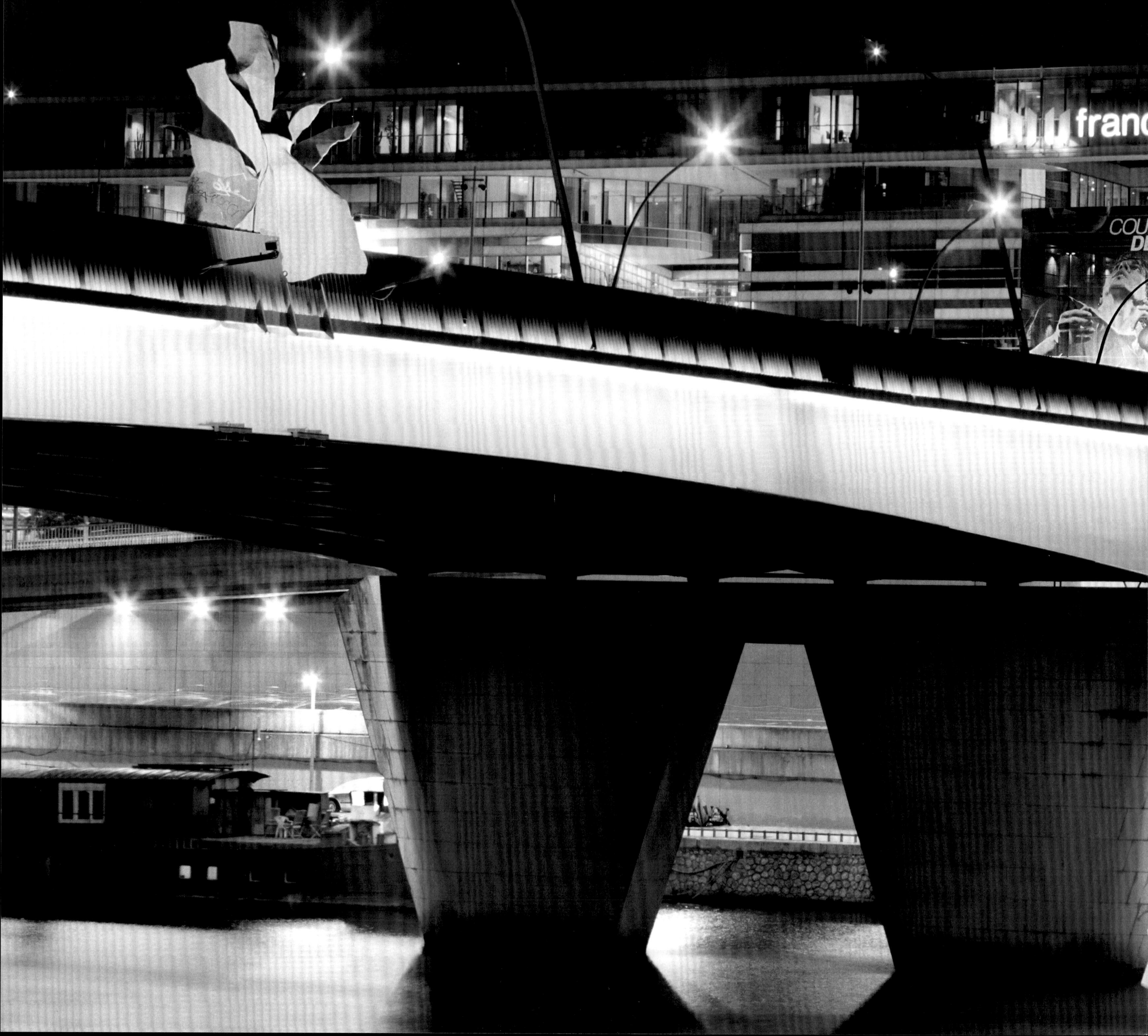

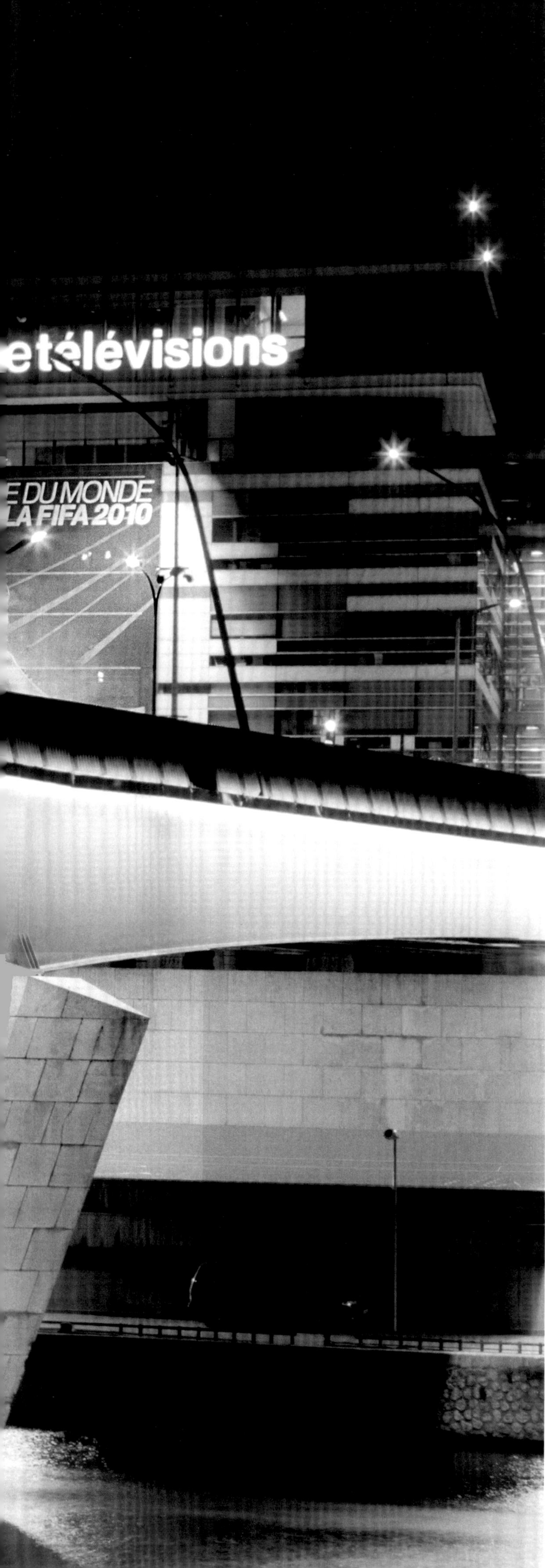

PONT DU GARIGLIANO

The Pont du Garigliano was the first bridge built after World War II. It replaced the Viaduc du Pont du Jour (also called viaduc d'Auteuil), built in 1865 during the Second Empire.

The viaduct was a two-level masonry bridge, similar in appearance to the Pont de Bir-Hakeim in that rail traffic was at the upper level and vehicle traffic and sidewalks were at the lower level. It was built to replace a ferry and to accommodate the railway system that encircled the city (the Petite Ceinture), as well as vehicle and pedestrian traffic. Use of the Petite Ceinture began to diminish when the Paris Metro was built at the beginning of the twentieth century. As a result, passenger traffic on the Petite Ceinture was suspended in 1934 and the line was subsequently closed.

The possibility of the upper level of the viaduct being used for vehicle traffic was discussed in 1954, but discarded because of other problems with the bridge and its low clearance for river traffic.

The bridge suffered war damage on two occasions. The first in 1870 during the siege of Paris, the second in 1943 when it was the only bridge in Paris to be seriously damaged by bombing during World War II.

Pont du Garigliano:
Sculpture of "Le Téléphone" (now removed)
and headquarters of France Télévisions.

The Viaduc du Point du Jour was demolished in 1962 and replaced by the Pont du Garigliano, which was inaugurated on September 1, 1966.

The new bridge was built at an elevation midway between the upper and lower levels of the previous bridge. It is 11 meters (36 feet) above the level of the Seine and is the highest bridge in Paris. It rests on two massive piers of reinforced concrete and spans the river by way of a steel frame covered with a reinforced concrete slab. It also spans a roadway on each side of the river.

The bridge was named in memory of the Battle of Garigliano, which took place during World War II at the Garigliano River in Italy. The French Expeditionary Forces under the command of General Juin won the encounter against German and Italian forces.

The first station of the T3 Tramway, the tramway system that will eventually encircle Paris, is located at the left bank terminus of the Pont du Garigliano, next to the headquarters of Groupe France Télévisions, the French national public television system. The five national channels of the group—France 2, France 3, France 4, France 5, and France Ô—are watched each week by eight out of ten French viewers.

In 2006, an artistic sculpture called *Le Téléphone* was installed in the middle of the bridge on the sidewalk facing downstream. The piece, conceived by artist Sophie Calle and sculpted by architect Frank Gehry, was a telephone booth in the form of a flower. Its only purpose was to receive phone calls from Ms. Calle. It was scheduled to remain until 2012, and has now been removed.

Afterword
Photographer's Notes

The following is a technical explanation of the methods used and the decisions made while photographing the bridges of Paris at night. Many of these decisions are subjective. Everyone needs to determine their own methods and their own comfort zone. I simply hope that, while the following information is not directed towards anyone unfamiliar with photographic methods, it might be helpful to those who want to learn about the methods I employed during this project.

The bridges were photographed on film, using two Mamiya medium format cameras: the Mamiya 645 AFD II (645) and the Mamiya 7 II (M-7).

While I shot only film, the 645 is a dual-use camera that can shoot film or, if configured differently, can shoot digital.

The 645 is a single-lens reflex camera; the M-7 is a rangefinder. Both cameras use 120 medium format film. I have always used Ilford Delta 400 film and find it to be excellent. It is an ISO 400 film that has great latitude and is very adaptable for nighttime shooting.

Before beginning the bridges project, I tested the film for nighttime characteristics, searching for the best way to expose and develop the film to achieve optimum quality negatives. The brightness of nighttime lighting coupled with the darkness of the night presented a challenging high contrast situation. The objective was to obtain a negative with detail in the shadow areas without being "blown out," or overwhelmed by the bright lights. Ansel

Adams addressed this problem in his book *The Negative*. He prescribed overexposure to obtain detail in the shadows, coupled with underdevelopment of the film to prevent full development of the highlights, thereby minimizing blowout.

The Delta 400 film was exposed two stops over the nominal ISO. It was exposed at ISO 100 instead of the nominal ISO of 400. To make sure that I captured the right shot, I also made two longer exposures. That is, after exposing at ISO 100, another exposure was made at ISO 50, and a third exposure made at ISO 64.

That was the "overexposure" portion of the Ansel Adams prescription.

Two exposures were made at each of the three ISO speeds, a total of six exposures for every scene. The reason for duplicate shots was to have a backup if a particular negative was scratched or for some reason became unusable.

Before shooting, I made a daytime scouting visit to the bridge I was planning to shoot. The objective was to look for the best point of view and to ascertain whether there were any potential complications.

Most of the photography was shot during the winter. In Paris, night falls at around 5 PM during the winter, whereas it isn't fully dark in the summer until around 11 PM. The city extinguishes the lighting on the bridges at midnight, which doesn't leave much shooting time during the summer. And, during the winter there are fewer tourists to interfere with shooting.

Because of the long exposure times, all the photographs were taken using a tripod. Almost all of the exposures were made at either f/11 or f/16, depending upon the depth of field required. The scenes were metered with a Sekonic light meter, a digital camera, or both. Exposing with a digital camera at ISO 100 provided a visual preview of what the final photograph would look like, and the histogram helped give an indication of the correct exposure time.

Typically, the indicated exposure times ranged from 1 to 30 seconds, or more. When an exposure was more than one second, the impact of the reciprocity failure of the film had to be taken into consideration. Compensation for reciprocity failure requires an increase in the length of time necessary for a proper exposure. Different films made by different manufacturers have different requirements for reciprocity compensation. With Delta 400 film, an indicated exposure time of 30 seconds becomes a 2-minute 34-second exposure, when properly compensated. Some of the longer exposures on this project ranged from 7 to 9 minutes. Detailed written notes of the exposure times, f-stops, and lenses were made for each photograph.

The exposed film was developed in Kodak Xtol developer, which is a developer I have used with great success. I used a 1:2 dilution of Xtol in a Jobo ATL-1500 rotary processor at 24°C (74°F). The Jobo processor provides consistent, even development with closely controlled time and temperature. That method assured an identical development process for every roll of film.

When testing the Delta 400 film for development in the Jobo, I found that the Normal development time for daylight photography was 6 minutes 45 seconds. This was precisely the time indicated by Kodak in its Xtol Technical Data Information circular. The reduced development time used to compensate for the nighttime work was 4 minutes 45 seconds, 30 percent less than the Normal time suggested for this film. Using this reduced development time allowed the shadows to retain good detail while preserving good separation in the highlights.

That was the "underdevelopment" portion of the Ansel Adams prescription.

Frequently, the contact sheets showed that the best negative was the one that was two and a half stops overexposed.

Prints were made using an Omega/LPL 4550XLG enlarger with a VCCE variable contrast constant exposure head with Nikon enlarging lenses. Images were printed on Ilford Multigrade IV FB glossy fiber-based paper, which is an archival baryta, silver-based paper. The Ilford paper was exposed using a split filter method of printing. The negative was first exposed through the high contrast filter and then developed. When I found a satisfactory high contrast print it was then exposed through the low contrast filter. When I arrived at what I considered to be the best overall print I then made two more prints of increasingly higher contrast value, and two more of increasingly lower contrast value. The final print was made by dodging and burning to incorporate the best aspects from each of the five test prints. The prints were developed in Kodak Dektol developer. The final print was then selenium toned.

Detailed notes and data were kept for every print. When a subsequent print of that photograph is needed, it can be made from the printing notes instead of starting from scratch.

The final print was mounted on conservation quality mat board with a Seal dry mount press.

BIBLIOGRAPHY

Dubly, Henri-Louis. *Ponts de Paris á Travers la Siècles*. La Diffusion Française, 1957.

Whitaker, G. B. *The History of Paris from the Earliest Period to the Present Day, in III Volumes*, Vol. III. Printed for Geo. B. Whittaker, Ave. Maria Lane and A. and W. Galignam, Paris, 1827.

Gaillard, Marc. *The Quays and Bridges of Paris: An Historical Guide*. Martelle Editions, 1994.

Larbodiere, Jean-Marc. *Ponts de Paris, Découverte & Histoire*. Éditions Marie Claire, 2013.

Agnelli, Claude. *37 Bridges of Paris*. Magellan & Cie, 2006.

Vallas, Jean-Louis. *Ponts de Paris*. Éditions Albin Michel, 1951.

Recouvrance, Sébastian. *Les Ponts de Paris*. Éditions Jean-Paul Gisserot, 2007.

Lambert, Guy. *Les Ponts de Paris*. Action Artisique de la Ville de Paris, 1999.

Martym Monique. *Mini-Saga des Ponts de Paris*. Port Autonome de Paris, 1979.

Blume, Mary. "Pont Solferino: Water Under a Troubled Bridge." *The New York Times*, July 29, 2000.

Ganley, Elaine. "WWII liberation anniversary rekindling memories for French" *The Associated Press*, August 23, 2004.

www.lexpress.fr – L'Express magazine website

www.ifsttar.fr – l'Institut français des sciences et technologies des transports, de l'aménagement et des réseaux

www.itnsource.com – Reuters Television 4588/95

www.20minutes.fr

www.leparisien.fr – Le Parisien 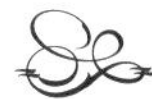

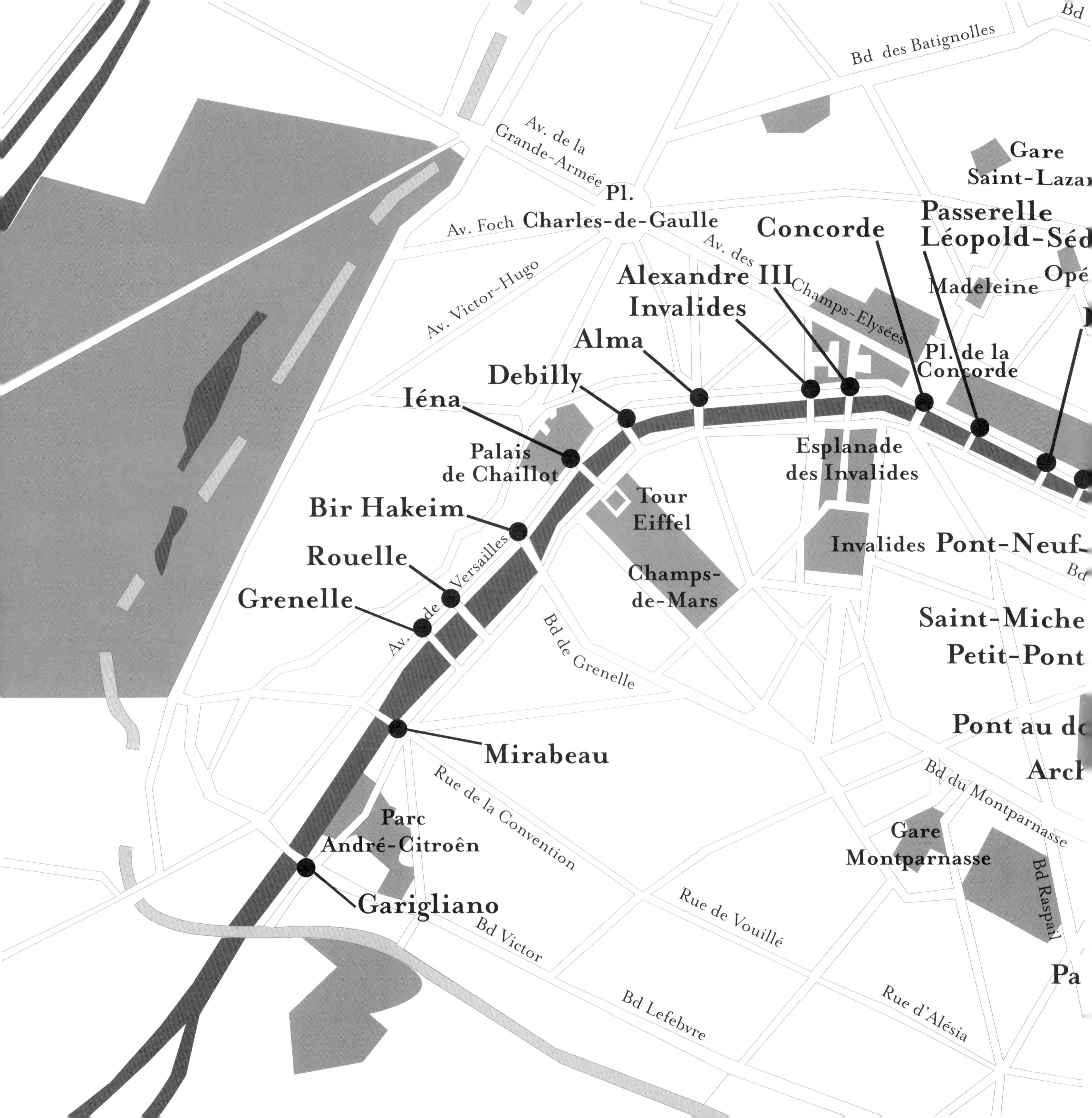

Bd des Batignolles
Av. de la Grande-Armée
Av. Foch
Pl. Charles-de-Gaulle
Av. Victor-Hugo
Av. des Champs-Elysées
Gare Saint-Lazare
Concorde
Passerelle Léopold-Séd
Opé
Madeleine
Alexandre III
Invalides
Pl. de la Concorde
Alma
Debilly
Iéna
Palais de Chaillot
Esplanade des Invalides
Bir Hakeim
Tour Eiffel
Invalides Pont-Neuf-
Av. de Versailles
Rouelle
Champs-de-Mars
Saint-Miche
Petit-Pont
Grenelle
Av. de
Bd de Grenelle
Bd
Mirabeau
Pont au do
Arch
Bd du Montparnasse
Rue de la Convention
Parc André-Citroên
Gare Montparnasse
Bd Raspail
Gariglinano
Bd Victor
Rue de Vouillé
Bd Lefebvre
Rue d'Alésia
Pa